The Construction of English

D1729757

The Construction of English

Culture, Consumerism and Promotion in the ELT Global Coursebook

John Gray
UCL Institute of Education, University College London, UK

First published in hardback 2010
First published in paperback 2015 by
PALGRAVE MACMILLAN

Palgrave Macmillan in the UK is an imprint of Macmillan Publishers Limited, registered in England, company number 785998, of Houndmills, Basingstoke, Hampshire, RG21 6XS.

Palgrave Macmillan in the US is a division of St Martin's Press LLC, 175 Fifth Avenue, New York, NY 10010.

Palgrave is the global academic imprint of the above companies and has companies and representatives throughout the world.

Palgrave® and Macmillan® are registered trademarks in the United States, the United Kingdom, Europe and other countries.

ISBN 978–0–230–22258–8   hardback
ISBN 978–1–137–50724–2   paperback

This book is printed on paper suitable for recycling and made from fully managed and sustained forest sources. Logging, pulping and manufacturing processes are expected to conform to the environmental regulations of the country of origin.

A catalogue record for this book is available from the British Library.

A catalog record for this book is available from the Library of Congress.

Typeset by MPS Limited, Chennai, India.

Contents

List of Figures

List of Tables

Acknowledgements

I would like to take this opportunity to thank those who have stimulated and shaped my thinking over the years with regard to the issues raised by the content of ELT textbooks. Thanks first of all to Catherine Wallace and Euan Reid for a module entitled Language, Culture and Ideology which they taught as part of the Institute of Education MA TESOL in the 1990s and which I was lucky enough to take. Thanks too to David Block who helped shape the research on which this book is based and who has been a constant source of inspiration and encouragement since I have known him. I would also like to thank the teachers and publishers who participated in the research. It is a truism that all books are multiply authored to some extent and this one is no exception. I am indebted to the following who have all been generous with their time and who have commented in detail on earlier drafts: David Block, Deborah Cameron, Marnie Holborow, Constant Leung, Scott Thornbury and Catherine Wallace. Any virtues the book may have are in no small part due to their contributions. I would also like to say thank you to Robert Simpson at the University of East London for helping to keep work at bay, to Priyanka Gibbons at Palgrave Macmillan for having faith in the project from the start and to Melaine Blair for looking after editorial matters. Thanks finally to Sadie for the cover photographs, and to Anne, Paul and Doug for everything else.

1
Introduction

In Lewis Carroll's *Sylvie and Bruno Concluded* a comic character describes a map which was drawn up on the scale of one mile to one mile. Not surprisingly, the map proves to be unusable and has to be abandoned. Although the story is meant to amuse, it also makes a serious point about the nature of representation – that a map, or indeed any other sign, is not a straightforward mirror image of what it represents. In this case the inclusion of too much detail defeats the map's purpose and results in the creation of something which is impractical. At the same time it is clear that scaling down and omitting detail involves a selective view of the terrain to be mapped. In the case of maps there are also implications for the drawing of political boundaries, the terms used to describe geographical entities and decisions about what to represent as central and what to represent as peripheral – all of which combine to make map-making a complex and potentially contested activity. Maps do more than simply describe, they simultaneously seek to construct. The same could also be said about textbooks. They too set out to map a terrain, but like all maps they are the result of decision-making in which the interests, beliefs and values of the map-makers play an all-important role. This is a book about textbooks for the teaching of English and the representational practices they adopt in the mapping of linguistic and cultural terrain. The specific object of investigation is the financially lucrative and widely disseminated UK-produced English language teaching (hereafter ELT) 'global coursebook', a term which refers to that genre of textbook which is produced as part of an incremental English language course designed for the global market. It is the contention of this book that such materials merit our close attention, given the key role they play in many classrooms around the world.

The global coursebook

Early twenty-first-century state-of-the-art assessments of applied linguistics and the specific activity of ELT confirm the enduring impact of what might be called a decisive critical turn (Cook 2005; Kumaravadivelu 2006a). Such a development can be dated to the 1980s and the initial salvos by Robert Phillipson (1986) and Alistair Pennycook (1989) across the bows of an academic discipline which, in the view of the latter, was characterized by an apolitical, ahistorical culture of positivism. Even a cursory look at the bibliographic references in the wave of scholarship which followed these opening shots reveals the pervasive influence of Marxist, feminist, poststructuralist, postmodernist and postcolonial theory. Despite the philosophical differences these positions imply, broadly speaking what unites those engaged in this ongoing recalibration of the field is a rejection of any 'bracketing out' of the social and the ideological from the study of language (Bourdieu 1991: 34), and renewed interest in critical pedagogy as an approach to ELT – an activity which is seen as inherently problematic, value-laden and necessarily political.

While the impact of this turn to varieties of critical social theory has been far-reaching, not all areas of practice and enquiry have been equally affected – indeed, John Kullman (2003: 74) detects signs of 'discourse paralysis' in branches of ELT which have remained impervious to such theoretical perspectives. Nowhere is this more evident than in the literature on ELT materials aimed specifically at practitioners, where textbooks for the teaching of English as an additional, foreign or international language are considered almost exclusively as 'curriculum artefacts' (Apple and Christian-Smith 1991: 4). That is, they are seen as educational tools to be evaluated in terms of 'fitness for purpose', often against normative checklists designed to identify their methodological, task and thematic appropriateness for the contexts in which they are to be used. But apart from some notable exceptions (e.g. Dendrinos 1992), this literature has largely eschewed more detailed *analysis* from any of the aforementioned theoretical positions.

This book is written by way of redress and it is indebted to a growing body of critical work in applied linguistics which, although addressing key issues surrounding ELT materials, has not focused its attention exclusively on materials analysis (Phillipson 1992, 2009; Pennycook 1994; Canagarajah 1999; Holborow 1999; Holliday 2005). Taking my cue from Julian Edge and Jack Richards (1998: 347), who argue that ELT 'sits awkwardly at the intersection of linguistics and education', thereby committing its researchers to inter-disciplinary 'boundary work', and bearing in mind Kullman's charge of 'discourse paralysis', I make the case for a wider perspective on such materials than that normally found in the materials literature. I will argue that, in addition to being 'curriculum artefacts', coursebooks are also cultural artefacts which seek to make English mean in specific and highly selective ways. Elsewhere, Michael Apple and Linda Christian-Smith (1991: 3) have argued along similar lines and they suggest that textbooks, of whatever kind, must also be considered as 'particular constructions of reality' and as commodities to be traded in the market place. As part of my case I will argue for the value of a cultural studies perspective in exploring the 'particular constructions of reality' found in the ELT global coursebook. From this viewpoint, such constructions are seen as *cultural* – where culture is understood to refer to the ways in which meanings are created, and the manner in which they subsequently circulate in society.

What will emerge in the pages which follow is a picture of the global coursebook as a carefully constructed artefact in which discourses of feminism, multiculturalism and globalization are selectively co-opted by ELT publishers as a means of inscribing English with a range of values and associations that include individualism, egalitarianism, cosmopolitanism, mobility and affluence, in which students are increasingly addressed as consumers. However, only some of these meanings will be shown to resonate with those articulated by teachers, for whom such materials are often found to be problematic. As we shall see, broad approval from teachers for the representational practices associated with gender and race does not always extend to other representational practices; nor does it extend to content which is seen as irrelevant to the context of instruction. At the same time, the pervasive 'native speakerism' of these artefacts, as instanced by the privileging of a narrow range of accents in the phonological representation of English, is identified as problematic by those teachers who see themselves as teaching English as an international language. Overall this book questions the continued viability of the global coursebook, an artefact which is predicated on the questionable assumption that 'one size fits all' – regardless of the social, geographical and educational context of use.

I begin with a series of autobiographical snapshots, each of which contributed to my growing sense of the need to problematize the role that coursebooks play in ELT. These snapshots correspond to an earlier stage in my working life – as an English language teacher in Barcelona, as a teacher trainer and as a writer of materials for the Spanish state school system. In adopting this approach I am influenced by the literature on teachers' stories (Abbs 1974; Berk 1980; Woods 1993; Thomas 1995), which have been described as providing the necessary 'high-context knowledge' needed to balance the 'low-context knowledge' of non-practitioner research (Elbaz 1991: 13). It has also been argued that the value of teachers' stories lies in the fact that they are, however subjective, rooted in the chalkface specificities at the heart of so many teachers' concerns, and that their increasing use in educational research (e.g. Johnson and Golombek 2002) marks the incorporation of teachers' voices into a discourse which has been excessively monologic. The use of autobiographical material here is also congruent with my overall aim to incorporate the voices of practising teachers (my own and that of others) into this study of the global coursebook. My approach in the following snapshots is particularly indebted to Claire Kramsch (1993), who draws directly on vignettes and critical incidents from teaching in order to raise theoretical issues which are grounded in classroom realities. The snapshots, related to teaching, training and materials writing, are all anecdotal but I believe they raise issues which invite closer consideration. Each one is followed by a short discussion of the issues which are raised.

Snapshots

Snapshot 1

I am teaching a General English class in a large language school in Barcelona in the early 1990s. The students are a group of young Catalan adults at lower intermediate level – that is, they have completed at least a hundred hours of English language learning. They are typical of many of the students in the school in that they come to evening classes after finishing work or after their university lectures. We are using *The New Cambridge English Course 2* (Swan and Walter 1990a) and working on basic situational/functional language – giving directions, making an appointment, borrowing and so on. As a lead-in to the language, the first exercise asks the students to look at a set of coloured drawings and answer the question 'What is happening in the pictures?' I pre-teach some essential vocabulary and then follow the procedure outlined in the coursebook. After a time I check the activity in open-class format by nominating various students. I ask one of the younger members of the class for an answer to one of the pictures which shows a white man with outstretched hands and a black man taking money from a wallet. I expect him to say 'borrowing' or 'lending'. He does not answer immediately. The student looks at me and after a while says '¿Un atraco?' (a mugging).

Discussion

The student's response can be interpreted in at least two ways – as either a genuine comprehension problem or as one of feigned incomprehension. Beginning with the former, the problem is potentially one of schematic mismatch. Henry Widdowson (1990) points out that two types of knowledge – systemic and schematic – are called into play in the expression and interpretation of meanings. The former refers to knowledge of the language systems while the latter refers to culturally determined knowledge of the world which results from life experience, beliefs, values and education. Guy Cook (1997) argues that such knowledge is important for language teaching as it draws attention to the kind of background information students need for the successful construction of meaning. Martin Hewings (1991: 238), in his study of the interpretation of illustrations in ELT materials, explains how his motivation for the study was triggered by classroom observation, where it became apparent that

> the interpretation of printed illustrations by teachers and [...] students was, not infrequently, rather different. The usual consequence of this was that the students gave the wrong answer or did an exercise incorrectly. While the cause was usually taken by the teacher to be a problem with English, the true cause may in fact have been one of different perceptions of an illustration.

Although Catalonia was neither a culturally nor an ethnically homogenous region in the early 1990s, it had not witnessed the same degree of media debate conducted around issues of multiculturalism which characterized many parts of the English-speaking world from the 1980s onwards. It is just possible that the student may have been less sensitized to issues surrounding the representation of so-called ethnic minorities in various media, including educational textbooks, and drawn instead on his own (negative) schema for the scenario in the illustration. However, as I will show later, British ELT publishers were far from indifferent to such debates and many of the practices associated with them. The image of a white man borrowing money from a black friend, while potentially more representative of British experience, was certainly, I will argue, representative of a position being taken on multiculturalism.

On the other hand, the student's response could be seen as an instance of an oppositional stance being taken over the inclusion of such an image in a coursebook for the teaching of English as a foreign language (EFL). It is possible that the image was read as an example of 'political correctness' – that is, in terms of those linguistic and representational practices which are designed to promote inclusivity and to avoid offending or demeaning women, members of different ethnic groups, lesbians and gays, disabled people and so on – but, in this instance, and in line with critics such as Robert Hughes (1993), negatively understood as indicating an obsessive concern with such matters.

Ultimately, I cannot be sure about the reason for the student's response. However, the incident was significant in that it led to a realization on my part that coursebook content might not be seen in quite the same way by students and teachers, and that my own reading of the coursebook was also filtered through culturally determined schemata. In spite of the problem which arose I also recognized that the inclusivity of the image was something I believed *should* be in a coursebook. As Apple (1992: 10) has argued, it is not only students, but teachers too, who bring their 'classed, raced, and gendered biographies' with them into the classroom. The snapshot serves to raise the broader question of what kind of 'carrier content' (i.e. the characters, situations, texts and artwork used to contextualize the language being taught) teachers and publishers consider appropriate for global coursebooks, and what the purpose of this content is.

Snapshot 2

I am teaching a group of trainee teachers at the same institution. Short pre-service certificate courses are normally delivered by three trainers to a maximum of 15 trainees. Mornings consist of input seminars on ELT methodology and language analysis, and the afternoons are taken up with teaching practice classes, which are followed by guided lesson planning for the following day. Trainees are divided into three groups for teaching practice – each group is the responsibility of one trainer. The material they use in their practice lessons comes from global coursebooks and is allocated to them by the trainers. At the end of the day trainers often meet to discuss the course and how the trainees are progressing.

At the end of a long day I meet a colleague in the school coffee bar to discuss teaching practice. She explains how one of the trainees who has been doing well on the course suddenly became angry during guided lesson planning and refused to teach the material he had been allocated. The material, which was taken from *The Beginner's Choice* (Acklam and Mohammed 1992), consisted of a listening exercise in which students talked about fast food and a reading which reproduced an advertisement for McDonald's. The artwork also featured a half-page photograph showing a multiethnic group of smiling young people in a McDonald's restaurant. The trainee argued that coursebooks should not provide advertising space for companies like McDonald's and that he did not want to promote McDonald's in his teaching.

Discussion

In fact this trainee's unease resonates with growing scholarly concern about the nature of ELT materials. Two areas which have received a degree of attention – and which are central to this volume – are the marketing and the content of textbooks. Phillipson (1992) and Pennycook (1994) have argued that government financing of teaching materials for developing world countries has a hidden economic and ideological dimension, while Suresh Canagarajah (1999: 99) has described the cultural content of North American textbooks being used in Sri Lanka as 'alien and intrusive'. Elsewhere Desmond Thomas (1999) has documented the way in which British ELT publishers were quick to establish themselves in Slovakia and market books which were underselling elsewhere. Beyond the world of ELT, a report produced for *The Economist* magazine (McCallan 1990) following the downfall of the Berlin Wall advocated the supply of ELT textbooks to the newly independent countries of the east as having considerable promotional potential for British trade.

A lesson based around an advertisement for McDonald's may have been seen by the writers of *The Beginner's Choice* as innocuous – the sheer ubiquity of McDonald's in many countries providing them with sufficient justification for its inclusion in a coursebook aimed at the global market. But such a view, it could be argued, ignores the fact that the reading – however recontextualized as a pedagogic text – remains an advertisement for a powerful global company. Its inclusion in a language teaching coursebook where it is treated mainly as a source of language – and not as an object for critical examination – cannot be said to completely negate its original function.

It has been suggested that pedagogic texts come imbued with an authority which makes contestation by teachers and students difficult (Luke *et al.* 1989; Dendrinos 1992). But as Apple (1992) and Canagarajah (1999) show, contestation is not only possible, it also takes place (see also Hutchinson and Torres 1994). However, a small-scale survey I carried out in Barcelona suggests that beginning teachers do not have the confidence to challenge the authority of the coursebook – either by adapting material they dislike or by making it available for critical discussion in the classroom (Gray 2000). The trainee in the snapshot, I would suggest, did not have the experience or the confidence to use the material in a way other than that suggested by the rubric. On a short training course, where his performance in the classroom was constantly being evaluated, he may also have been unaware that alternative ways of using published material were even permissible.

The snapshot raises the issue of ELT's involvement in processes beyond the linguistic and the pedagogic. Clearly I am not suggesting that *The Beginner's Choice* was sponsored by McDonald's – although corporate sponsorship of mainstream educational material is becoming increasingly common in the United States (Klein 2000). Rather, I wish to suggest that teachers may feel that coursebooks can introduce elements into their teaching which do not accord with their views on the scope and aims of ELT. In this particular instance the trainee teacher may have felt that the coursebook presented a controversial global company in a positive and unproblematic light, while at the same time providing it with advertising space. Simply following the rubric may have seemed like teacher endorsement of such a practice.

Snapshot 3

It is the mid-1990s and I have been asked by a British ELT publisher to write the teacher's book for a secondary school coursebook being written to meet the demands of the new Spanish national curriculum. The coursebook has been written by a successful British-based materials writer and is aimed at younger teenagers. The publishers have provided me with translations and summaries of all key Ministry of Education documents to enable me to refer where appropriate to the *temas transversales* – the social themes which inform the curriculum. Although the book was not designed as a global coursebook, the publishers did want to sell the course in other countries if it proved successful in Spain. In fact the course was successful and went on to sell in eastern Europe and South America. For these editions, all specifically Spanish references were excised from the student's book and the teacher's book.

Unit 4 of the coursebook is about River Phoenix, the North American actor who died from a drug overdose. Students are taken through a reading and listening cycle before being asked to write about a famous person of their own choice from history. Questions are provided in the student's book to enable them to structure their answer, for example, When was this person born? Where did she/he go to school? Did she/he get married? Did she/he have a happy life? One of my tasks is to provide additional material in the teacher's book. For this exercise I choose three well-known Spanish artists and writers and provide biographical data on each of them. If students have few ideas of their own then teachers can write the biographical data on the board to help with the writing. One of those I choose is Federico García Lorca. Against the category 'married' I put 'no'. I toy briefly with the notion of adding that Lorca was gay and then decide that there is no point as the editor will probably remove it.

Discussion

Andrew Littlejohn's (1992) research on coursebooks concluded that the relationship between the author and the ELT publisher is essentially that of an agent writing to an agenda determined by the publisher. My own experience confirms this – the editor I had most contact with during the writing went so far as to claim that a number of well-known coursebooks had been so reworked by their editors that it could be said the editors were in fact the real authors. Publishers' demands extend far beyond methodological and language syllabus requirements. The authors of the successful *Headway* series are on record as saying that the degree of 'political correctness' required of them by their publishers was a source of dispute (Soars and Soars 2000a). The publishers' agendas as expressed in their guidelines for authors – an area I will examine in greater detail later – address a number of issues to do with representation, one of which is the non-sexist representation of women and men.

Early surveys of sexism in ELT materials (Hill 1980; Jaworski 1983; Porreca 1984) concluded that women were under-represented, trivialized and stereotyped in a wide selection of coursebooks. Scott Thornbury (1999) points out that many of the iniquities identified by Karen Porreca (1984) have since been redressed, but he adds that the policy of omission she identified with regard to women still applies to lesbians and gay men:

> Gayness is about as omitted as anything can be. The EFL situation mirrors the way Hollywood used to be, where 'gay characters and references to the existence of homosexuality were routinely laundered off the screen for the better part of half a century' [...] And it is not just coursebooks that are de-gayed. Significantly, the issue of heterosexism is glaringly absent from discussions of material bias and cultural content. (Thornbury 1999: 15)

Thornbury goes on to make the case for the unmarked incorporation of lesbian and gay characters into coursebooks aimed at the global market (e.g. through the inclusion of same-sex flatmates). Such an approach, he suggests, 'apart from discreetly acknowledging a significant segment of [the publishers'] clientele' (ibid.: 17), makes it possible for the topic to be explicitly addressed in those contexts where it is appropriate and possible.

Henny Burke (2000) goes much further and claims that the way in which publishers ignore same-sex orientation amounts to a form of discrimination. Excluding lesbians and gay men from coursebooks is, she argues, out of line with European Union legislation – in particular Article 13 of the Amsterdam Treaty which states that discrimination against homosexuals is a violation of equal rights. Writing before its repeal in 2003, Burke attributes lesbian and gay invisibility in British ELT to the climate created by Section 28 of the 1988 Local Government Act which forbade local authorities in Britain to 'promote the teaching in any maintained school of the acceptability of homosexuality as a pretended family relationship' (ibid.). It should be pointed out that coursebooks intended for the global market are also used in private language schools, colleges of further education and university language centres in Britain. Burke proposes that publishers should treat lesbianism and gayness as part of human diversity, and she suggests an approach which would incorporate the texts produced by the lesbian and gay community as a legitimate basis for language work. This would, she argues, have the effect of giving lesbian and gay identities an official seal of approval through their incorporation into pedagogic texts, while simultaneously allowing classrooms to reflect more adequately 'the realities and complexities of society' (ibid.).

I cannot say that I was conscious of Section 28 when I decided to omit the fact of Lorca's sexual orientation from the biographical data I was preparing. Rather it was the conspicuous absence of lesbian and gay characters from the published materials I was familiar with which acted as a powerful reminder that any explicit reference to homosexuality was probably going to be removed. As Deborah Cameron (1995: 34) has stated elsewhere:

> Authors writing for publication not only anticipate that their work will be edited, they participate in editing it even as they write.

As we shall see later, interviews with British ELT publishers confirm that references to homosexuality are generally viewed as inappropriate. One publisher I spoke to lamented the fact that any love interest in storylines aimed at teenage students had to be heterosexual for fear of 'alienating the market' (personal communication, 2000). In terms of this introductory chapter, the significance of the snapshot lies in the way it drew my attention to this issue and to the issue of exclusion in coursebooks more generally.

Snapshot implications: Beyond anecdote

What then are the implications of these snapshots? On one level they can be seen simply as the personal anecdotes of an ELT practitioner. At the same time, it has been suggested that while no teacher's narrative 'can be regarded as typical or representative' of all teachers, there will be within each story 'episodes, experiences and emotions with which teachers can readily identify' (Thomas 1995: xiv). While no doubt unique as events, the possibility that the issues raised by the snapshots might be indicative of concerns shared more generally by teachers was a key factor in determining the shape this volume would take.

All three snapshots raise issues which I believe can most usefully be understood under the broad heading of cultural content. Not everyone would necessarily agree with this view of the scope of the cultural. Take, for example, Vivian Cook's (1983: 229) view that culture is one of several 'real' but optional types of content. In a survey of six coursebooks, Cook found a predominance of what he called 'imaginary' content. He noted a similarity with the content of television soap operas – fictional characters were featured in a variety of imaginary storylines which were designed to entertain students while, he suggested, palliating the pain of language learning. Cook proposed six possible areas of real content to balance this imaginary content: (i) another academic subject, (ii) student-contributed content, (iii) language itself, (iv) literature, (v) culture and (vi) interesting facts. However, as has been pointed out (O'Sullivan *et al.* 1994), culture is a multi-discursive term – its meanings being determined by the discourse within which it is deployed. Cook's view of culture, as one topic among many, derives from the 'background' or 'area' studies tradition in modern foreign languages education – where culture is understood to entail a focus on the eating and drinking habits of target language speakers, their leisure activities, their institutions and their political system.

My own view, which is influenced by the rise of cultural studies as an academic discipline, and in particular by the work of Stuart Hall, is that all representational practices are essentially cultural. This is an expanded view of culture which is concomitant with another key epistemological 'turn' – the so-called cultural turn in the social sciences. From this perspective, Hall (1997a: 222) argues that culture 'is nothing but the sum of the different classificatory and discursive formations, on which language draws in order to give meaning to things'. This is a *productive* and dynamic view of culture which rejects a simplistic base-superstructure model, whereby the realm of the cultural is seen as a mere reflection of a society's material and economic foundations. Hall continues his explication of culture with a definition of discourse, thereby signalling clearly the primacy of the discursive in this view:

> The very term 'discourse' refers to a group of statements in any domain which provides a language for talking about a topic and a way of producing a particular kind of knowledge about that topic. The term refers both to the production of knowledge through language and representation and the way that knowledge is institutionalized, shaping social practices and setting new practices into play. (ibid.: 222)

From this constructionist perspective, it is suggested that culture 'creeps into every nook and crevice of contemporary social life, creating a proliferation of secondary environments, *mediating* everything' (ibid.: 215). This is a deliberate echo of Bronislaw Malinowski (1944), who understood culture as an artificially created secondary environment, in and through which human beings give meaning to their lived experience. It is the nature of the secondary environments constructed in coursebooks – expressly for the mediation of English, which is itself represented in particular ways – which lies at the heart of this volume. These, and other, developments in the concept of culture are discussed more fully in Chapter 2. Suffice it to say here that such an expanded view sees the deliberate inclusion of multiethnic characters in pedagogic texts, the setting of dialogues in branded fast food outlets and the ways in which gender and sexual orientation are consistently represented, as constituting very particular constructions of reality in which English is given a range of specific associations. In fact, the nature of the representational practices deployed in these materials may be said to place culture at the heart of the coursebook.

As a backdrop to my developing interest in the global coursebook as a particular kind of cultural artefact, two areas stand out as being of importance – ongoing debates about the role of culture in ELT and modern foreign languages teaching and the ways in which language (and by extension, ELT) is intimately associated with that complex set of interrelated phenomena known as globalization. In the following two sections, with a view to delineating the broader context for this volume, I provide an initial discussion of both these areas. I begin with globalization.

Globalization and language

Although there is no agreed definition of globalization, a cluster of factors are commonly associated with the term. These include the deregulatory policies of economic neoliberalism, the rise of the so-called new capitalism (Fairclough 2002; Sennett 2006) and the 'new work order' (Gee *et al.* 1996); the challenge to the autonomy of the nation-state ensuing from the ascendancy of powerful transnational corporations; increasing global interconnectedness as a result of technological developments which compress time and space; flows of population, media and ideas; and increasing cultural hybridization (see Block 2006, 2008 for detailed accounts).

Depending on how these phenomena are interpreted, globalization has been viewed in both exclusively dystopian (Berger 1998/99) and utopian terms (Perlmutter 1991), with a range of positions in between (e.g. Tomlinson 1999; Beck 2000; Scholte 2000). Those tending towards the dystopian view (e.g. Hertz 2001; Harvey 2005) have consistently focused on the economic dimension, and indeed the 2008 crisis in the global financial markets and the ongoing fallout from this could be said to confirm the dangers and contradictions presaged by these scholars. For this reason it is useful to recall briefly just what is meant by terms such as neoliberalism, the new capitalism and new work order and the ways in which they are fundamental to globalization.

Neoliberalism may be said to entail the opening up of domestic markets to unrestricted free trade, the privatization of state assets and the marketization of areas such as health and education, along with the scaling down of the welfare state. It also entails, in Pierre Bourdieu's (1998: no pagination) view, the destruction of 'all collective structures that could serve as an obstacle to the logic of the pure market'. Hence, for example, the introduction in many countries of legislation aimed at curtailing the power of unionized labour. The World Bank, itself a powerful neoliberalizing force, spells out clearly in its millennium report on global poverty that neoliberal economic policies are integral to globalization. Such policies have, the report argues, 'spurred and in turn have been reinforced by globalization' (The World Bank 2000: 1). Paradoxically, as pointed out by Noreena Hertz (2001) and George Ritzer (2007), the nation-state, for all its supposed decline, remains a powerful instrument for the introduction and maintenance of such policies. To which – post 2008 – we can now add the financial rescue by governments of institutions whose deregulated activities risk producing (inter)national economic collapse. Norman Fairclough (2002) uses the term 'new capitalism' to describe the current economic system in the age of globalization – that is, an economy which is typified by neoliberal policies on the one hand, and on the other, by technological innovations which instantaneously and profoundly yoke the local and the global together. At the same time, the world of work is held to be radically reconfigured. For Bourdieu (1998) and Richard Sennett (2006), the new work order is typified by constant change and high levels of instability and stress. The latter cites, by way of example, the frequent use of consultants in such an environment to manage change (i.e. to restructure, sack and redeploy) – a process which also fulfils the important ideological function of signalling to a workforce that 'power is being exercised' (ibid.: 57). Those workers who are prepared and able to switch tasks, change jobs, retrain and relocate at short notice are described by Manuel Castells (2000) as 'self-programmable labour' and by Zygmunt Bauman (2007) as having 'zero drag' – the latter a Silicon Valley term for the high degree of flexibility viewed most favourably in the current job market.

At the same time, several commentators have drawn attention to the centrality of language within the new work order, where the ability to talk a certain kind of talk becomes a marketable and highly portable skill (Cameron 2000, 2002; Fairclough 2002). Monica Heller (2002, 2003, 2005) has argued that language is in fact increasingly commodified in the contemporary period – a position similar to that adopted by David Harvey (2005), who argues that neoliberalism entails the commodification of a vast array of diverse phenomena not initially produced as commodities. From this perspective, languages are viewed primarily in terms of the 'added value' they bring to speakers in a highly competitive and flexible job market (see also Tan and Rubdy 2008 for similar positions). However, not all scholars agree with this assessment. Marnie Holborow (2007: 56) argues that 'the notion that language in global capitalism has been transformed into a product like any other overlooks the dependence of the system on *real products* for its profits' (emphasis added). She continues,

> Although language is used and inculcated in people for the purposes of selling, this does not in itself make language a product, nor its speakers collaborating independently or in a way 'external to capital'. Advertising, branding, call centres, styles of selling, and

customer care service are conducted in the service of actually selling something – a product or good. (ibid.: 68)

Holborow's concern is that undue attention to the role of language in the neoliberal economy runs the risk of obscuring the production of 'real products' and, from a Marxist perspective, strays uncomfortably close to philosophical idealism. And of course she is entirely right to assert that language cannot be seen as a product like any other in a capitalist economy. However, when language is viewed as *part of labour-power* rather than the *product of labour* – then it seems to me there is a precedent for viewing language as increasingly commodified. Indeed, it is Karl Marx (1867/1967: 168) who states that '[l]abor-power can appear in the market as a commodity', precisely when 'its possessor, the individual whose labor-power it is, offers it for sale, or sells it, as a commodity'. Language in the new work order (whether in terms of varieties of stylized talk or in terms of specific languages) is in fact, in many instances, very much a part of labour-power – given that it is the ability to produce certain kinds of talk that is being sold.[1]

At the same time, Bourdieu (1991) shows that economic metaphors for language (e.g. as a form of wealth or treasure) not only have a long history stretching back through Ferdinand de Saussure to Auguste Comte, but they can also have considerable explanatory power – at least within his particular reformulation. Bourdieu proposes a view of language as a symbolic product within what he calls the economy of linguistic exchanges. From this perspective, he argues that language can be understood as a form of capital whereby the 'legitimate competence' of the standard variety can be used to obtain what he calls 'a profit of distinction' (ibid.: 55) – that is, the ability to produce a certain kind of socially legitimated talk can lead to various forms of profit (whether symbolic or material) for the language user. Those with limited access to the 'treasure' of the standard variety are thus less able to compete in a market place where linguistic forms are produced and recognized as 'signs of wealth' (ibid.: 66). Bourdieu's case for what might be called an economy of the sign is presented as a challenge to the asocial view of language found in the Saussurean tradition and is a deliberate attempt to locate language-using firmly within the context of a capitalist economy. Although Bourdieu is mainly concerned with the economics of standard and non-standard varieties, such a perspective is illuminating when we consider the role of certain languages within the context of globalized economies. The work of Heller (referred to above) charts a move away from the role of French in Canada as a particular kind of identity marker towards one in which it functions increasingly as a sign of a speaker's economic value. Similar parallels with English are clearly relevant, given its close association with globalization. And it is to the place of English and its association with globalization that I now wish to turn.

As David Block (2006) explains there is no agreement on when globalization may be said to have started, although several commentators see its origins as being more or less coterminous with the birth of the modern European nation-state. Conservative historians such as Niall Ferguson (2003: xxi) see globalization benignly in terms of the growth of the British Empire and the imposition of a system of political governance, 'the rule of law' and the 'imperialism of free trade' on a quarter of the world, along with the religious, cultural, population and linguistic flows which this enterprise set in motion. In fact, Ferguson uses the term 'Anglobalization' to characterize the way in which the empire, English and globalization were linked. He puts the English language at the top of his list of distinctive features disseminated by Angloblization and concludes that it has been 'perhaps the most important single export of the last 300 years' (ibid.: 366). Similar connections, at least between English and empire, are fundamental to the work of Phillipson (1992) and Pennycook (1994, 1998).

In its contemporary form, globalization can also be seen as continuing this close connection with English. For some commentators, such as Claus Gnutzmann and Frauke Intemann (2005: 9), English is '*the* language of globalization'. Elsewhere I have suggested that there are at least three main points of connection (Gray 2002). Firstly, there is the way in which transnational corporations promote the spread of English through its adoption as a lingua franca, not only for communication between geographically dispersed centres of production but also for dealing with local companies in non-English-speaking countries. Secondly, there is the rise of international organizations, particularly in the period following the Second World War, which use English as their working language – not to mention the globally disseminated products of Anglophone popular culture, particularly pop music. Thirdly, there is the rise of the Internet and the use of English (alongside other languages) by a wide variety of virtual communities and special interest groups, including the anti-globalization movement and other dissident groups. All these points of connection may be said to have implications for the increased learning and teaching of English globally. Against this background of profound imbrication in the processes of globalization, I would suggest that it makes sense to view English both as a form of linguistic capital, capable of bringing a profit of distinction to those speakers with the ability to access it (or, more accurately, its socially legitimated varieties), and as an increasingly commodified dimension of labour-power.

However, as Gnutzmann and Intemann (2005: 10) add, 'English is not only the language of globalization, but it is itself deeply affected by it.' They suggest that

> the norms of written and spoken English for international purposes are not necessarily identical with those of British and American standard varieties of English any more. (ibid.)

The statement provides those of us involved in ELT with additional food for thought. In much the same way that the 'Anglobalization' described by Ferguson may be said to have resulted in the rise of new Englishes in the ex-colonies, so too the current phase of globalization may be said to have consequences for English when it is being used for lingua franca purposes by speakers (and writers) for whom it is not a first language and for whom it may be seen primarily as a form of linguistic capital. Certainly the appearance of acronyms such as EIL (English as an international language) and ELF (English as a lingua franca), which reflect new global uses of English, can be seen as indicating a growing awareness of the impact of globalization on ELT. These are issues I will return to again. For the moment my intention has simply been to raise them and to signal their centrality to the concerns of this volume as a whole.

The problem of culture in ELT

In addition to issues related specifically to globalization, the role of culture in modern foreign languages teaching and ELT continues to be thoroughly re-examined. The collocation of terms such as 'transnational' and 'intercultural' with communicative competence (Baumgratz 1987, in Kramsch 1998a; Byram 1990; Council of Europe 1996), along with the concept of the 'intercultural speaker' (Kramsch 1998a), may be said to indicate a reassessment of the aims of language teaching and learning generally. With regard to the role of culture in ELT, Adrian Holliday (1994a: 125–126) has suggested that there are two aspects of importance:

> (a) the question of the teaching of culture along with language, whether or not it should or must be taught, and if so, which culture should be taught, and how it should be taught; and (b) the influence of cultural differences on the learning behaviour of students from different parts of the world.

Much ELT attention has focused on the second of these points, and in particular on the issue of appropriate methodology and educational context (Holliday 1994a, 1994b; Cogan 1996; Ellis 1996; Kramsch and Sullivan 1996). The syllabus changes to the Cambridge ESOL teacher training schemes made during the mid-1990s, aimed at foreground-ing the learner and the learning context, were described to me at the time as 'a shift from good methodology to appropriate methodology' (UCLES, personal communication, 1996). This shift, in line with Holli-day (1994b), purported to encourage teachers to see methodology as a set of culturally determined practices which might require adjustment in diverse cultural settings if teaching were to be effective.

Issues raised by Holliday's (1994a) first point, particularly with regard to the role of textbooks, have received a considerable amount of atten-tion in modern foreign languages research (e.g. Byram 1993, 1994, 1997; Aarup Jensen *et al.* 1995; Sercu 2000), but they remain, despite important contributions (Cortazzi and Jin 1999; McKay 2002, 2003), significantly under-addressed in ELT. Before embarking on this volume, a small-scale survey I conducted among a group of 20 teachers in a Barcelona language school showed that teachers were concerned about a range of issues: stereotypical representations of Britain and other coun-tries in coursebooks, sexist attitudes and the inclusion of irrelevant or incomprehensible cultural information about Britain (Gray 2000). They also revealed a wish not to offend students' own cultural sensibilities through using culturally inappropriate materials. However, as Hitomi Masuhara (1998) has pointed out, very little is actually known about teachers' thinking on coursebooks and their content in general.

As stated earlier, the purpose of this volume is to redress some of the research imbalance in the materials literature by carrying out what can best be described as a cultural study of the ELT global coursebook. My interest therefore is not in the specific teaching of culture *per se* (how-ever that might be understood), but in the ways in which culture, in the cultural studies sense, is used in coursebooks to make English mean in specific ways. At the same time, given my cultural studies orientation in which culture is seen as an endlessly recursive process of mean-ing making *and* meaning taking, it is essential to address the ways in which consumers construe these artefacts. As John Thompson (1990: 153) reminds us:

Individuals do not passively absorb symbolic forms but creatively and actively make sense of them, and thereby produce meaning in the very process of reception.

In the case of ELT coursebooks there are two sets of consumers – teachers and students. Here I have had to be selective and I have deliberately taken the decision not to include students in this particular study. Clearly their thinking on the nature of coursebook content is important and needs to be investigated. Indeed, Snapshot 1 above suggests that the meanings constructed by teachers and students can be very different. But students are secondary consumers of coursebooks, in the sense that although they may pay for them, but they do not select them. Teachers, on the other hand, are primary consumers, in the sense that they often have a decisive say in the institutional selection of materials; and even in those contexts where they are chosen by Ministries of Education, teachers retain considerable power in determining the uses to which they are put in the classroom. It is the current lack of research on teachers' thinking on coursebooks and cultural content in general which ultimately determined the focus of this study.

My overall aim is threefold: firstly, to describe the cultural content in a sample of ELT global coursebooks produced in Britain since the 1970s – when the commercial boom in ELT may be said to have started; secondly, to attempt to explain the form this content takes; and thirdly, to explore what practising teachers – as the primary consumers of such artefacts – think about this content, and by extension, how they construe the relationship between culture and ELT against a background of increasing globalization.

Outline of the volume

The remainder of this volume is structured as follows: Chapter 2 explores the central theme of culture and examines the ways in which the concept has developed historically, paying particular attention to the emergence of a cultural studies perspective. From there I move on to look at the way in which culture has featured in modern foreign languages teaching and ELT and the ways in which this role is currently being reappraised. Chapter 3 explains the design of the cultural study and introduces the theoretical model known as the 'circuit of culture' (Du Gay *et al.* 1997) on which the present study is based. This model provides the means for the multi-dimensional exploration of key moments in the life of any cultural artefact from production through to consumption. The chapter introduces the descriptive framework used in this study and makes a strong case for the use of the tools provided by social semiotics for the analysis of artwork – a much under-theorized and under-researched aspect of one of the most salient elements of ELT materials from the mid-1970s onwards. Chapters 4 and 5 discuss the results of the application of the descriptive framework to the coursebook sample. Chapter 6 attempts to explain the nature of this content and begins by looking at documentary evidence provided by ELT publishers outlining the representational practices which authors are expected to follow in coursebook writing. In addition, the chapter draws on interview data in which ELT publishing managers and commissioning editors discuss issues surrounding the nature of such content. Then, in an attempt to provide a fuller and more socially situated explanation, the chapter opens into a theoretical discussion in which it is argued that the literatures on visual communication (Berger 1972; Schroeder 2002), consumerism (Featherstone 1991; Baudrillard 1998; Bauman 2007), the commodification of social issues (Goldman 1992; Tinic 1997; Benwell and Stokoe 2006) and promotional culture (Wernick 1991) have considerable explanatory power. Chapter 7 completes the circuit and explores teachers' thinking on the topic through interviews with a group of 22 teachers of EFL as they outline their views on cultural content in global materials and on the relationship between culture and ELT more generally. Chapter 8 concludes by exploring the implications of this particular cultural study for teacher education, the teaching of English as an international language and the future of the global coursebook.

2
Culture and English Language Teaching

Evolving meanings in the concept of culture

In his dictionary of social science terminology, the critic Raymond Williams (1976: 87) began his entry for culture on a cautionary note:

> Culture is one of the two or three most complicated words in the English language. This is partly because of its intricate historical development, in several European languages, but mainly because it has now come to be used for important concepts in several distinct intellectual disciplines and in several distinct and incompatible systems of thought.

Given my earlier assertion that a cultural studies perspective places culture at the heart of the coursebook, it is necessary to shed some historical light on this complicated term before looking more closely at what such a perspective entails. Williams points out that in its earliest uses culture was a noun of process referring to crop cultivation. Gradually this meaning was extended to include the metaphoric cultivation of the mind, so that by the eighteenth century it is central to the Enlightenment belief in universal human progress. In this early modern understanding of culture the human spirit is held to liberate itself gradually from the confines of the biological self through a process of spiritual, artistic and scientific education or 'shaping'. Elements of this conception survive today in the notion of 'high culture', which is generally understood as something morally formative and spiritually uplifting, and in the continuing semantic link in some European languages between culture and education or types of 'shaping'. In modern Spanish, for example, 'una persona culta' is the term used to describe an educated person, while in French the term for body-building is 'culturisme'. The study of classical languages such as Greek and Latin has often been seen as integral to this view of culture, as indeed has the study of modern foreign languages, particularly when undertaken to access their literary creations. A second key meaning is identified by Williams (1976) and Thompson (1990) as emerging in the late eighteenth century in the work of the German philosopher Johann von Herder. Unlike many of his contemporaries who regarded Europe as representing the apex of human development and achievement in culture, Herder chose to speak of cultures – that is, in the plural – and he attacked the notion of a straightforward evolutionary process which culminated in the achievements of Europe. By introducing the idea of a less Eurocentric plurality to the concept of culture, Herder may be said to have paved the way for subsequent anthropological formulations in the nineteenth and twentieth centuries in which culture came to be understood as referring to the distinctive way of life of a people – a meaning which is still current today and one which is frequently found in language teaching textbooks. He also contributed to the explicit association of specific cultures with specific languages, arguing that culture and language were symbiotically linked – an association that was to prove enduring in the sense that culture increasingly came to share the same epistemological space as language.

This is particularly evident in twentieth-century anthropological conceptions of culture, the most influential of which is found in the structuralism of Claude Lévi-Strauss – an approach which was to impact significantly on the development of cultural studies. Lévi-Strauss (1963: 68–69) argued that culture and language are both sign systems composed essentially of the same materials – 'logical relations, oppositions, correlations, and the like' and that it was possible to look beneath the surface manifestation of cultural phenomena (e.g. myths, culinary practices and kinship patterns) and identify their invariant elements and the manner in which these were related. What this meant in practice was that key elements of Saussurean linguistics were borrowed and applied to a wide range of cultural phenomena other than language. In much the same way that language-in-use (Saussurean *parole*) is based on abstract rules of grammar (Saussurean *langue*), so too were cultural phenomena said to be based on an equivalent set of rules. The Saussurean model of the sign, composed of a signifier (e.g. the sound /kæt/) and a signified (the concept of the four-legged animal to which it refers), was similarly transposed to cultural analysis. Structuralists such as Lévi-Strauss and Roland Barthes then applied these conceptual tools in their analyses of phenomena as diverse as Amazonian Indian myths and contemporary French photography. Thus Barthes (1972) famously 'read' the photograph on a magazine cover in which a young black soldier was shown saluting the French flag as a complex visual sign and explored the meanings it sought to create in terms of its multiple signifiers and signifieds. Seen in this way, culture is a sign system for the communication of meaning.

At the same time, structuralism held that while human beings create culture from whatever elements are found in their immediate environment, they are also simultaneously created by culture – so much so in fact that Lévi-Strauss (1978: 4) viewed the individual as simply 'a crossroads where things happen. The crossroads is purely passive; something happens there.' This sidelining of the individual reflected the challenge structuralism sought to pose to the concept of the autonomous individual mind (often referred to as the Cartesian subject) as the uniquely agentive source of all human action. Both these elements – that of culture as a sign system for the communication of meaning and that of the human subject as a site rather than an essence – were to determine in part the shape that cultural studies would eventually take, and it is to this that I now turn.

The cultural studies perspective

As an evolving field of inquiry, cultural studies had its origins in postwar Britain. It rejected elitist views of culture and refused to accept the high/low distinction found in some earlier conceptions of the term. Since its beginnings it has been concerned with the analysis of the production, circulation and reception of social meanings. In Hall's (1980a) view, it represents the socialization and democratization of culture – something which is reflected in its particular interest in the material and symbolic products of consumer society, in the explosion of new media, television and advertising and the representational practices deployed in the construction of categories such as class, gender, race and nationality. These concerns can also be seen as a reaction against structuralism's overwhelming concern with the *internal* structures of cultural forms and the Marxist privileging of the economic as the ultimately determining *external* structure within which such forms are produced. In many ways cultural studies, particularly in the work of Hall, can be seen as *post*-Marxist and *post*-structuralist in orientation. At the same time, it also sought to rescue the concept of agency from structuralist neglect and to theorize identity in terms which were congruent with changes in the social sciences more generally.

With regard to the latter, Hall (1992a: 285) takes the view that identity has become fragmented and pluralized in late modernity. This is seen partly as a consequence of the whirligig effects of increasing globalization and rapid technological change and partly the result of what he calls the five great 'de-centrings' ushered in by Marx, Freud, Saussure, Foucault and feminism, that is, those intellectual traditions, all of which see the individual and identity as either partly constrained or wholly constructed by a range of social and psychological forces. From this perspective identities are not seen as essential, but as composite, conflicted, positional and process-based. Hall (1996: 4) outlines his view as follows:

> Though they seem to invoke an origin in a historical past with which they continue to correspond, actually identities are about using the resources of history, language and culture in the process of becoming rather than being: not 'who we are' or 'where we came from', so much as what we might become, how we have been represented and how that bears on how we might represent ourselves. Identities are therefore constituted within, not outside representation.

The question of how we have been represented and how we might represent ourselves raises the concepts of articulation and ideology, both of which were key to the emergence of a cultural studies perspective and both of which, as understood by Hall, appeared to allow greater space for agency than structuralism did. On the subject of articulation, Hall (1986, in Morley and Chen 1996: 141) explains that it carries the double meaning of 'language-ing, of expressing' and that of connection or linkage – similar, he suggests, to the way in which an articulated lorry is composed of separate, but pivotally linked, parts. An articulation has been defined by Paul du Gay (1997: 3) as

> the connection that can make a unity of two or more different or distinct elements, under certain conditions. It is a linkage which is not necessary, determined, or absolute for all time; rather it is a linkage whose conditions of existence or emergence need to be located in the contingences of circumstances.

By way of example, Hall (1997a) shows how the concept of Englishness might be articulated very differently through a linkage with Romantic poetry, or by association with the concept of rugged Victorian entrepreneurialism – that is, through its association with specific discourses. Such articulations, Hall (1986) explains, can also be culturally transformative, as in the case of Rastafarianism, whereby a sector of Jamaican society literally reinvented itself through a specific reading of black history and a highly particularized interpretation of the Bible. Thus articulations not only draw on existing discourses but, under certain conditions, can also generate new discursive formations – in this case a powerful myth of national origin.

Articulation in turn raises the issue of ideology, given that certain representations and meanings may be produced to serve particular social ends. In Hall's view ideology is not seen as some kind of false consciousness (i.e. a misunderstanding of the true nature of reality) – rather he suggests it has to do with

> the winning of a universal validity and legitimacy for accounts of the world which are partial and particular, and [...] the grounding of these particular constructions in the taken-for-grantedness of 'the real'. (Hall 1982 in Gurevitch *et al.* 1982: 65)

Thus ideology has to do with the construction of versions of reality which favour the interests of particular groups and the ways in which these versions are accepted – what Thompson (1990: 7) refers to as 'meaning in the service of power'. At the same time, ideology is also held to be present in the 'frameworks of interpretation and understanding' (Hall 1983, no pagination) which we, as readers, viewers and consumers, deploy in making sense of such constructions and in understanding 'what is going on around us, what our position is, and what we are likely to do' (ibid.). Such frameworks, he argues, are ultimately always partial and particular, and referring to the readings of media messages which readers construct, he suggests that there is no place outside ideology:

> I think we are all in that sense inside ideology. There is no space outside – totally outside – of ideology where we have no stake in the analyses of the media that we are offering. (ibid.)

At the same time, although ideology is seen as being pervasive, Hall argues that human beings are also capable of reflexivity and that we can take up a variety of positions, which, although also partial, enable us to identify the 'selectivity' of whatever representation we are confronted with and to identify where its 'absences and the silences are' (ibid.). This view of readership (broadly understood to incorporate reception of all representational practices) suggests that consumers of culture are far from passive, as was frequently suggested in mass-communication studies from the 1930s and 1940s. In his paper 'Encoding/decoding' Hall (1980b: 131) makes the point that mass-media research was dogged by 'a lingering behaviourism' in which the reader/viewer/consumer was construed as a more or less passive dope. He posited a more active role in which three positions were held to be available – a dominant-hegemonic position in which the receiver understood the preferred meaning of whatever message was received in exactly the same terms in which it was sent; a negotiated position in which the receiver did not accept completely the preferred meaning of the sender; and finally an oppositional position in which the preferred meaning was rejected and the message was understood in terms altogether different to those of the sender. On this view, culture can also be seen as 'a sort of battlefield' (Hall 1981, in Storey 2006: 482) in which the meanings which are articulated are not guaranteed or in any way held to be stable, but are seen as contingent, interested and potentially contested.

It is this view of culture which lies at the heart of this study and it is one which I hope to show will bear fruit in terms of the kind of analysis it can produce. It is a view of culture which allows us to view the ELT coursebook as a set of representational practices in which English is articulated with particular discourses which seek to construct it in specific ways. It is a view of culture which allows us to explore the selectivity of these representations and to identify their absences and their silences. It is also a view of culture which holds that the meanings which are constructed on the pages of the coursebook are not unproblematically transferred to the mind of the reader. Rather the reader is understood as agentive and capable of reading against the text and constructing alternative meanings. In this study the focus is on teachers – although clearly reading against the text can also apply to students. I now turn my attention in the following sections of this chapter to the ways in which culture has figured, and continues to figure, in language teaching and ELT. As we shall see, despite some points of contact, the perspective there has been somewhat different.

Language and worldview

As pointed out above, culture and language have been closely associated from the early modern period onwards. One of the most persistent elements in this association is that provided by Wilhelm von Humboldt (1836/1971) who argued that language was uniquely expressive of the worldview of its speakers. There is a direct link between this view and what came to be known in the twentieth century as the Sapir-Whorf hypothesis – what George Steiner (1975) suggests should more accurately be referred to as the Humboldt-Sapir-Whorf hypothesis. Two key statements by Sapir and Benjamin Lee Whorf are worth quoting in full, given the controversy which interpretations of their views have engendered. First Sapir (1949/1985: 162), who claimed,

> The fact of the matter is that the 'real world' is to a large extent unconsciously built up on the language habits of the group. No two languages are ever sufficiently similar to be considered as representing the same social reality. The worlds in which different societies live are distinct worlds, not merely the same world with different labels attached.

His pupil Whorf (1956: 221) stated his view, of what he called the linguistic relativity principle, as follows:

> [U]sers of markedly different grammars are pointed by the grammars toward different types of observations and different evaluations of extremely similar acts of observation, and hence are not equivalent as observers but must arrive at somewhat different views of the world.

Interpretations of their work have led to strong and weak versions of the hypothesis. Strong versions of the hypothesis are noticeable, for example, in certain strands of twentieth-century feminist thinking, which accorded language a major role in the creation and reproduction of patriarchy (e.g. Spender 1980). Interestingly Humboldt may also be said to have anticipated certain feminist concerns. Writing about the power of language to constrain, he stated,

> Albeit language is wholly inward, it nevertheless possesses at the same time an autonomous, external identity and being which does violence to man himself [*sic*]. (in Steiner 1975: 82)

Many feminists have described such a sense of violence in their experience of alienation from language which they feel is not wholly theirs (in Cameron 1985). In its strongest form the hypothesis suggests that language literally determines what an individual can think and implies the near impossibility of translation from one language to another. This interpretation has been attacked for its overly deterministic view (Pinker 1994). However, as many (Cameron 1985; Gumperz and Levinson

1991; O'Halloran 1997) have argued, Whorf in particular has been misrepresented by detractors and oversimplified by followers. The kind of linguistic relativity Sapir and Whorf subscribed to is based on an altogether more subtle understanding of the relationship between language, thought and worldview than critics like Steven Pinker (1994) have given them credit for. Being 'pointed' by grammar towards an interpretation of events is altogether different from being mentally imprisoned by grammar. Even Dale Spender (1980), who may be said to have subscribed to a strong version of the hypothesis, argues that women *can* remake language and transform society along more equitable lines. Indeed, as we shall see later, what became known as feminist language reform was to impact significantly on language as it as used in ELT coursebooks from the 1980s onwards. Clearly Whorf, as suggested in the quotation above, believed that language predisposed speakers to interpret events in a certain way, but he also believed that it was possible to transcend these limitations and that learning other languages was one way of doing this:

> It was to me almost as enlightening to see English from the entirely new angle necessitated in order to translate it into Hopi as it was to discover the meanings of the Hopi forms themselves. (Whorf 1956: 112)

It is this aspect of their work, in line with the Humboldtian view of the inseparability of language and culture, which has animated much current thinking on the role of culture in language teaching. On this view language learning is uniquely suited to enable students to relativize their worldview. In the following sections I will show how certain strands of current thinking posit a key role for a particular view of culture in language teaching by emphasizing the educational value of such a relativizing approach.

Culture and language teaching

Humboldt was instrumental in placing historical and comparative language studies at the centre of nineteenth-century German university education. This was based on the view that such studies were a means to better self-understanding. Similarly the teaching of modern foreign languages also owed much to Humboldt, and their introduction to the school curriculum in the mid-nineteenth century assumed the same educationally formative objective previously reserved for the classical languages (Hüllen 2000). However, the Reform Movement with its focus on the production of spoken language represented a major change of direction for the teaching of modern foreign languages. Hans Heinrich Stern (1983: 263) points out that Henry Sweet's (1899) *Practical Study* included no reference to the distinctive way of life view of culture. The rise of commercial language schools (e.g. Berlitz) may be said to have moved modern foreign languages teaching away from the Humboldtian model more firmly. Gerhard Stieglitz (1955: 301), in his assessment of the first 75 years of Berlitz teaching, makes it clear that the method 'is concerned primarily with the linguistic, and *not the cultural*, aspects of foreign language teaching' (emphasis added). It is, he argues (with no apparent irony), a method which is thoroughly American and freed from all 'the staid traditions of Old World formalism' (ibid.: 300). That said, culture was held to be present in the person of the 'native speaker' teacher required to deliver the method and it was assumed that some information about the target culture would automatically be conveyed to students.[1] Although the Reform Movement was to set the tone for developments in language teaching in the twentieth century, the Humboldtian view did not disappear.

In the post-war period the work of scholars such as Robert Lado (1957, 1964) and Wilga Rivers (1981) made the case for a return to a more Humboldtian perspective on language teaching. In some countries, particularly in the state school sector, language teaching did include a more general introduction to the target culture, for example, *civilization* in the case of France, *civiltà* in Italy and *background studies* in Britain. However, the teaching of modern foreign languages and English – particularly to adults – in much of western Europe and North America in the twentieth century was concerned mainly with language as a purely formal system. The rise of Communicative Language Teaching (CLT) and the adoption of Dell Hymes' (1972) concept of communicative competence as the goal of language learning was seen by Stern (1983) as something of a welcome change of direction. Despite this he argued that language teaching continued to lack 'a well-defined sociocultural emphasis' (ibid.: 246). One attempt to provide this is found in the work of Jan van Ek and John Trim (1991: 102) who define 'sociocultural competence' in terms of familiarity with the distinctive way of life view of culture. Their definition includes knowledge of the 'every day life', 'living conditions' and 'interpersonal relations' (ibid.: 103) of 'native speakers' of the language being learnt. However, as we shall see in the following section, some of those making the case for an explicit role for culture in language teaching have taken this a step further.

Culture and language teaching – an alternative approach

Since the 1980s Michael Byram and Claire Kramsch have been influential in making the case for a more Humboldtian approach to language teaching and learning. Both take the view that it has a specific kind of educational value. Learning a foreign language, Byram argues, affords 'the opportunity for emancipation from the confines of learners' native habitat and culture, with the development of new perceptions and insights into foreign and native cultures alike' (1988: 15), and at the same time provides 'the opportunity to reflect upon oneself and one's own culture from the archimedian standpoint of another language and culture, and the acquisition of new insight into self and native surrounds which are fundamental to the notion of education' (ibid.). For Kramsch (1993), the fact that meanings are not universal and that languages do not neatly translate into each other means that students are continually being tripped up by culture. Thus, she argues, language learning has the potential to afford students a unique vantage point on their own culture and that embodied in the foreign language.

The considerable body of work which both have produced may be seen as an attack on language teaching as it has been conducted in much of western Europe and North America in the post-war period, and the simultaneous outline of a very different alternative. Byram (1988, 1989, 1997) has argued consistently that the dominant paradigm in language teaching is based on a narrow interpretation of communication as a way of bridging information gaps and transferring messages. Such a view, he holds, is both impoverished and conservative. It is impoverished because communication not only involves the bridging of such gaps but also includes the projection of social and cultural identities, and it is conservative because it fails to accommodate the emancipatory potential and reflexivity that language learning can entail. Similarly Kramsch (1993) argues that the dominant paradigm in language teaching regards culture, understood as 'the very way we order, classify, and organize the world around us through language' (Kramsch 1998a: 12), as 'an expendable fifth skill' (Kramsch 1993: 1).

As the Council of Europe began to articulate the need for a sociocultural dimension in language teaching (e.g. Van Ek and Trim 1991), Byram's perspective on what this might mean came to assume increasing importance. This is evidenced by the official endorsement by the Council of Europe (1996) of the Byram-Zarate (1994) model of intercultural communicative competence as a European educational goal for language teaching and learning (similar developments in the US are described in Kumaravadivelu 2008). The model consists of 'savoirs' or competencies which break down as follows: 'savoirs' – declarative knowledge of both one's own and one's interlocutor's culture; 'savoir être' – a mental attitude towards one's interlocutor's culture which is ethnographic in orientation; 'savoir comprendre' – the ability to interpret documents and/or events from another culture and relate them to one's own; 'savoir apprendre/faire' – the ability to acquire and put into practice knowledge learnt under the pressure of real-time communication; and finally, 'savoir s'engager' – the ability to critically evaluate aspects of one's own and others' culture (Byram 1997). Intercultural communicative competence is associated with the concept of the 'intercultural speaker' (Byram and Zarate 1994: 11) who is both ethnographically sensitive (and thus equipped to learn) and culturally self-aware.

Such a redefinition of the goal of language teaching and learning is necessary, Byram (1997) argues, because Hymes' (1972) idea of communicative competence (for so long the goal of language teaching and learning) has been misapplied to second language learning. Hymes' original idea did not refer to cross-cultural communication – the context which Byram views as most relevant to language learners. This misapplication, he suggests, condemns language learners to failure, as teachers try to turn them into ersatz 'native speakers'. More recently Constant Leung (2005: 128) has stated that the 'native speaker' remains 'part of the bedrock of transnationalized ELT'. He argues that the appropriation and transfer of Hymes' concept of communicative competence from an initial ethnographic research context to a pedagogic one has resulted in the use of 'abstracted contexts and idealized social rules of use based on (English language) native-speakerness' (Leung 2005: 119). In this recontextualization, he suggests, key concepts such as appropriateness can be misleadingly recast as a set of prescriptions for language learning.

Like Byram, Kramsch also aims to redraw the boundaries of language teaching so that culture is foregrounded. However, where Byram concentrates mainly on the identification of the competencies which comprise intercultural communicative competence, and how these might be tested, Kramsch focuses largely on the experience of the student as an 'intercultural speaker' and the ways in which intercultural communicative competence might be developed. In much the same way that Raja Rao (1938: vii) claimed colonial writers who wrote in English faced the problem of trying to 'convey in a language that is not one's own the spirit that is one's own', Kramsch argues that language learners struggle to find a voice in the foreign language that can carry the weight of their own cultural experience. She sees this as a struggle for an emerging 'third place' (Kramsch 1993: 236) or cultural space of a 'third kind' (ibid.: 235) in which students are able to develop a new more hybrid identity.

To achieve this she proposes a pedagogy of conflict (understood as opposition to the dominant paradigm) in which the goal of language teaching and learning is redefined as the identification and exploration of linguistic and cultural boundaries and the simultaneous exploration of the self in the process (Kramsch 1993). Ideally the ideological inflections in the student's own voice become apparent in the learning process and are made available for questioning. For Kramsch (1995) language teaching is not about maintaining the status quo – rather her view is one in which the teacher becomes an agent of social change. Such a pedagogy is based on a kind of 'conscientização' (or conscientization) – a term used by Paulo Freire (1970/1996) to refer to the way in which learners become subjects rather than objects or recipients in the educational process. Following Freire, Kramsch (1993: 28) advocates a dialogic pedagogy in which boundaries are explored in the classroom, so that learners 'can start using the foreign language not merely as imperfect native speakers, but as speakers in their own right'. Such an approach involves what might be termed 'the right to behave and to sound foreign' and a move away from the 'native speaker' as the model for learners to approximate. Following Byram and Geneviève Zarate (1994), Kramsch (1998b) endorses the concept of the intercultural speaker – understood as a speaker who is aware of the cultural implications of language choices and who can adapt (should she choose) her language to meet contextual demands – as the desirable outcome of successful language teaching. The knowledge required for such a speaker can be developed in the classroom – recast as 'the privileged site of cross-cultural fieldwork, in which the participants are both informants and ethnographers' (Kramsch 1993: 29).

Kramsch (1993) acknowledges, in passing, the importance of other critical educators (e.g. Giroux and Pennycook) for her view of what language teaching should entail. In this she makes a distinction between education and instruction. In Kramsch's view the dominant paradigm in language teaching is instructional and monologic – that is, it is prescriptive and typified by a one-way flow of information from teacher to student in which student output is evaluated solely in terms of 'native speaker' norms. Education, on the other hand, is held to be dialogic and is typified by an acceptance of experimentation with language, a refusal to ignore cultural difference and the recognition of the possibility of cultural incommensurability.

It will be clear from this summary that Byram and Kramsch have much in common. Their view of language teaching and learning as having a specific kind of educational value links them to a European tradition which has its origins in the early modern period, particularly in the work of Humboldt. As such, their work may be said to represent a critique of the role of culture within the dominant paradigm in the teaching of modern languages teaching and ELT. Their critique of the dominant paradigm in foreign language teaching and their proposed alternatives are summarized in Table 2.1.

At the same time it will also be clear that this view of culture is very different from that found in cultural studies. The latter is concerned principally with representation and particularly the politics of representation whereas the Byram/Kramsch perspective is concerned primarily with the interface of intercultural contact. It could also be argued that there is a lingering essentialism in this Humboldtian position, if essentialism is understood to imply 'that groups can be clearly delimited' and 'that group members are more or less alike' (Bucholtz 2003: 400). For example, Byram and Michael Fleming (1998: 2) suggest that learning a foreign language entails 'learning the shared meanings, values and

Table 2.1 Summary of the Byram/Kramsch view of foreign language teaching and learning

Dominant paradigm in foreign language teaching	Proposed educational alternative
Language teaching seen narrowly as skill training	Language teaching seen broadly as education
Impoverished and conservative	Rich and critical
Instructional and monologic	Educational and dialogic
Culture occupies the background	Culture occupies the foreground
Communicative competence as the aim of language learning	Intercultural communicative competence as the aim of language learning
'Native speaker' model	Intercultural speaker model
Aim to enable learners to survive as tourists/consumers	Aim to create learners who are internationally socially aware
Learners construed as skills acquirers	Learners construed as apprentice ethnographers
Textbook as carrier of superficial view of target culture	Textbook as carrier of realistic view of target culture

practices of that group as they are embodied in the language' – a position which does not appear to recognize that meanings are frequently not shared and may be actively contested by speakers of the same language. It is only in the Kramschian subscription to the concept of the 'third space' that the possibility for non-essentialism and hybridity opens up. This is certainly the view taken by Manuela Guilherme (2000: 298) who argues that the concept of the intercultural speaker, understood as someone who 'mediates between two or more cultural identifications', is in fact congruent with the more dynamic and non-essentialist understandings of identity found in cultural studies.

That said, what these views might mean for British ELT remains to be seen. Although largely a commercial enterprise, British ELT does not exist in a vacuum, and as Thornbury (2000a) has suggested elsewhere, it is responsive to debates in mainstream education and political issues more generally. Despite Byram's (1990) suggestion that textbooks need to represent target cultures more realistically, he and Michael Fleming (1998: 8) have acknowledged that the increasing use of English as a lingua franca means that the question of which 'cultures' language learners should be exposed to in ELT settings is problematic, as indeed is the question of 'which, if any, standard form of English should be the reference for learners throughout the world'. While suggesting that such questions must be answered locally, it is clear that they see intercultural communicative competence as an appropriate goal for ELT.

The problem of culture in ELT

As I have suggested, language teaching in many parts of the world during the twentieth century was concerned with language as a purely formal system. Where culture was addressed – particularly in teaching in the state school sector – it often took the form of a general introduction to the life of 'native speakers' of a particular nation-state such as the UK or the US. ELT, as an emerging set of practices with a knowledge base in applied linguistics, has produced little in the way of a clearly articulated approach to the role of culture in language teaching. However, one attempt by Kheira Adaskou *et al.* (1990) to define what culture might mean for English language teachers and what this might imply specifically with regard to content in ELT materials has been viewed favourably in some of the literature (Lessard-Clouston 1996; Hedge 2000). Their framework for materials production divides culture into four senses – the aesthetic (information about the arts), the sociological (information about the everyday life of 'native speakers'), the semantic (how words and concepts relate to a particular way of life) and the pragmatic (norms of politeness, rhetorical conventions in writing, etc.). However, as Sandra McKay (2002) points out, such a framework is inherently problematic, raising as many questions as the solutions it attempts to provide. Which 'native speakers' are to be represented in the materials? Which norms of politeness? Which particular ways of life?

One of the features of English is the extent to which it is spoken around the world and the variety of roles which it fulfils for different kinds of speaker. An early attempt to represent some of this complexity was made by Braj Kachru (1985) who divided the world into three concentric circles – an inner circle, where English is spoken as a first language; an outer circle, where it is spoken as a second language (and where nativized varieties may exist); and an expanding circle, where it is used as a lingua franca. Clearly English takes a number of different forms, has a variety of standards and is used to encode a wide range of cultural meanings. It is for this reason that Kanavillil Rajagopalan (2004) asks whether inner circle countries should continue to serve as a linguistic model for the rest of the world, given the way in which speakers from these countries currently constitute a minority of English speakers globally. Widdowson (1994) too has argued that the global spread of English means that it has ceased to be the cultural property of any particular group of speakers. Increasingly it is taught to students who will use it mainly to interact with other speakers of English as a second language rather than with 'native speakers'. For teachers this raises issues of which variety to teach, what kind of cultural content to include and how explicitly it is to be addressed. It also presents a problem to commercial ELT which seeks to market standardized pedagogic materials to an increasingly plural world.

At the same time it is important to mention that the current interest in culture within the field is partly the consequence of the explosion of ELT globally. Towards the end of the twentieth century as more and more teachers from Anglophone countries found themselves teaching English abroad in contexts very different from those in which they had been trained, essentialist ideas about culture gained considerable currency. A good example of this kind of material can be found in Peta Gray and Sue Leather's (1999) resource book of activities for teachers working with Japanese students. The book is premised on the essentialist assumption that the Japanese are culturally hardwired very differently from western students and that, unless teachers take these cultural differences into account, teaching and learning may be frustrating experiences. The book aims to 'help the non-Japanese teacher to decode the behaviour of their students in the classroom' (ibid.: 7) and makes a number of sweeping statements about the Japanese. These include the information that 'many Japanese people have an excellent visual memory' (ibid.: 12); that 'the Japanese educational system trains students to expect binary oppositions; doubt and uncertainty are not valued very highly' (ibid.: 19); and that 'one of the features of discursive speaking within the western tradition is the ability to say why one holds a certain opinion or believes a certain thing' (ibid.: 25), but that 'this can be quite difficult for Japanese people' (ibid.: 25). This kind of cultural profiling is indebted to Geert Hofstede's (1980) work in the field of international business management training, and it is perhaps not surprising that it should have resonated with many in commercial ELT. However, such an approach has been criticized by Holliday (1999) and Kumaravadivelu (2008) as 'culturist' – by which they refer to the process whereby the student is reduced to a set of cultural stereotypes and all behaviour is then explained in terms of perceived cultural differences. My point in raising this issue here is to suggest that, while Stern (1983: 246) may be largely right in concluding that language teaching in the twentieth century lacked a 'well-defined sociocultural emphasis', the view that students might be perceived as 'culturally' different (and problematic) came to assume greater importance towards the end of the century – thus helping to foreground the question of the role of culture in ELT more generally.

In Chapter 3, I turn to the matter of designing a framework for coursebook analysis which is philosophically and methodologically congruent with the cultural studies perspective outlined above.

3
Describing and Analyzing ELT Coursebooks

Introduction

How then to design and carry out a research project which is congruent with a cultural studies perspective? Du Gay *et al.* (1997: 3) have provided a theoretical model known as the 'circuit of culture' for the study of how culture operates in contemporary society. By way of illustration they subjected the Sony Walkman, as a commonplace contemporary cultural artefact of the 1990s, to an analysis which took the form of a biographical case study. The 'circuit of culture' explores five key moments (also referred to as dimensions or processes) in the life of cultural artefacts: representation – how meaning is inscribed in the way artefacts are represented, either visually and/or verbally; identity – which social identities and lifestyles are associated with the artefact; production – how the artefact is designed, produced and marketed; regulation – how political, economic or other factors regulate the circulation of meanings; and consumption – how the artefact is consumed, and how consumers can identify themselves as members of a group, or make identity statements about themselves through their consumption practices. The various moments are held to co-exist in an articulated relationship whereby all elements are equally constitutive of meaning. Du Gay *et al.* suggest that the model is applicable to any cultural object and in fact it has been used productively by Bethan Benwell (2005) to carry out a study of men's magazines.

Given my contention in Chapter 1 that the ELT coursebook is a highly wrought cultural artefact, the 'circuit of culture' may be said to offer a sound theoretical basis for its exploration. Du Gay *et al.* (1997) point out that there is a considerable degree of overlap between the various

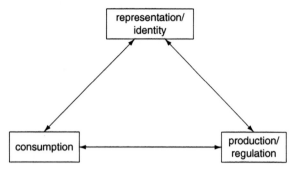

Figure 3.1   Modified circuit of culture

dimensions. Thus, for example, they explain that it is difficult to talk about representation without also talking about the identities which are represented. Similarly, it is difficult to disambiguate the processes of production from those of regulation. For this reason I have modified the model, in Figure 3.1 above, by linking those moments where overlap most clearly occurs in the case of coursebooks. In this way the modified circuit also aligns more closely with my previously stated aims. Thus, my aim to describe the cultural content in a sample of ELT global coursebooks produced in Britain since the 1970s is clearly concerned with identifying the nature of the representations made in coursebooks, and with the identities which are associated with English. My aim to attempt to explain the form this content takes raises issues to do with the ways in which coursebooks are produced and the ways in which their content is regulated. And finally, my aim to explore what practising teachers think about this content, and by extension, how they construe the relationship between culture and ELT more generally, raises issues to do with the ways in which the primary consumers make sense of such artefacts.

I now turn to an account of the issues taken into consideration in the design of a descriptive framework focused on the moments of representation and identity. Issues to do with the exploration of the other moments in the circuit of culture are reserved for later chapters.

Materials analysis and evaluation

As I suggested earlier, the materials literature aimed at teachers has tended to concern itself almost exclusively with the entirely legitimate activity of evaluation and has largely avoided analysis. Evaluation, as

Ian McGrath (2002: 22) explains, aims to 'discover whether *what one is looking for* is there', and traditionally the most common way for teachers to do this has been to examine the coursebook against one of the many pre-determined checklists of characteristics deemed essential (e.g. Cunningsworth 1984; Sheldon 1988; Skierso 1991; Harmer 2001; McDonough and Shaw 2003). Such checklists are clearly normative and reflect the beliefs of their writers about the nature and scope of language teaching and learning. On the other hand, Andrew Littlejohn (1992) points out that analysis is about discovering what is there – an altogether very different activity and one which McGrath (2002: 25) suggests is aimed at reaching a 'general understanding of the philosophy underlying the materials'. As we shall see, frameworks for analysis can also be designed to facilitate subsequent evaluation.

How then does materials analysis proceed? Clearly there has to be an initial description, the product of which will then be analyzed and interpreted. Some of the most systematic and detailed studies of language teaching materials have approached description through the specific methodology of content analysis. Two classic definitions of content analysis have been provided by Bernard Berelson (1952/1971) and Ole Holsti (1969), and while subsequent definitions have sought to elaborate on these, the basic elements they mention remain constant. For Berelson (1952/1971: 18) content analysis is 'a research technique for the objective, systematic, and quantitative description of the manifest content of communication', while for Holsti (1969: 14) it is 'any technique for making inferences by objectively and systematically identifying specified characteristics of messages'. By way of example, Porreca (1984) was able to establish through the quantification of various elements of content (e.g. ratio of women to men, order of mention of women and men, generic uses of masculine pronouns and occupational roles) that sexism was prevalent in all the ELT materials she surveyed. Similarly, Littlejohn (1992) and Lies Sercu (2000) both produced detailed analyses of sets of textbooks for the teaching of English and German respectively through a combination of content analysis and more qualitative approaches. The latter's study is of particular interest here, given that she was concerned exclusively with cultural content – although her view of culture and her aims were altogether different from my own.

Sercu's analytic framework, reproduced in Figure 3.2 below, which she applied to a set of coursebooks for the teaching of German as a foreign language to Belgian school children, was designed to produce a description of cultural content which would enable her to evaluate the materials in terms of their capacity to develop intercultural

```
I   Location
    1.1  Title of book
    1.2  Page
    1.3  Unit
    1.4  Subsection
    1.5  Number assigned on the page

II  Characters
    1.1  Age of characters
    1.2  Gender of characters
    1.3  Situation of interaction

III Cultural dimensions represented
```

Culture(s) addressed/ Dimensions of culture addressed	micro level	macro level	international and intercultural issues
Own culture	x	x	x
Foreign culture	x	x	x

```
IV  Countries represented

V   Intercultural contacts
    5.1  Type of intercultural contact
    5.2  Type of background for intercultural contact
    5.3  Type of intercultural situation

VI  Didactic approach
    6.1  Point of view of authors
         6.1.1  Multiperspectivity – monoperspectivity
         6.1.2  Qualitative direction of point of view
    6.2  Text-types used
         6.2.1  Text-types
         6.2.2  Visuals
    6.3  Task types
         6.3.1  Educational potential of tasks
         6.3.2  Main objective of tasks
         6.3.3  Level of co-operation required
         6.3.4  Other task characteristics
                –  address pupils' prior knowledge about the foreign culture
                –  address pupils' attitude to the foreign culture
                –  address pupils' own cultural frame of reference

VII Space
```

Figure 3.2   Sercu's framework for cultural content

communicative competence. In introducing her framework, Sercu asserted that

> a textbook's potential for promoting culture learning can [...] be said to be dependent on the *amount of culture* it presents, as well as on the *emphasis* that culture gets through repetition or visual accentuation (italics in the original). (ibid.: 255)

This immediately raises the question of what counts as culture in her framework. Sercu's approach was to follow Holsti (1969), who suggested that 'theme' was the most useful unit of analysis. She therefore introduced 33 'themes' derived from a 'minimum content' list of cultural topics which were proposed by Byram (1993: 34–35) to facilitate both the design and the evaluation of materials (see Appendix 1). In Sercu's case, these comprised the following: leisure, culture, geography, transportation, personal identity, commerce/economy, education, occupation/profession, history, food and drinks, media/communication, body culture/fashion, society/social life, life cycle, house/home, environment, foreign language, law, national symbols, feasts and ceremonies, politics/war and peace, mentality, family, language, (im)migration, international relations, science, animal, norms and values, religion, third world, stereotypes and multiculturalism. All other content which could not be categorized under these themes was ignored in the analysis.

Beginning with these themes she then recorded the information she found on each one in the seven sections of her framework (referred to as 'fields'). In terms of design, the framework is also indebted to that produced by Karen Risager (1991) (see Appendix 2). She then calculated the emphasis (or 'weight' in content analysis terminology) accorded to each theme by counting the number of lines devoted to it, or, in the case of artwork, the number of square centimetres it occupied on the page. This information was entered in Field 7 of the framework.

The resulting data eventually allowed her to make quantitative statements of the following type:

> [A]ll investigated series, notwithstanding their own particularities, show very similar patterns in their address of cultural topics over volumes, with leisure (16.99%), geography (10.52%), personal identity (10.44%), culture (9.55%) and transportation (7.43%) being most frequently addressed. (Sercu 2000: 276)

Clearly there are problems with such an approach from a cultural studies perspective. While quantification of aspects of content *can* be useful, as instanced by the Porreca study, the main problem with Sercu's approach is that it essentializes culture through the *a priori* establishment of 33 themes. Interestingly Joan Kelly Hall (2002: 19), who argues that culture is 'a dynamic, vital, and emergent *process*' (emphasis added), also devises a framework based on pre-stated thematic categories for the analysis of cultural content in ELT materials. Her list has 15 separate themes, each of which, with the exception of 'other', can also be linked to Byram's

(1993) minimum content list (see Appendix 3). However, her framework (which is not used as the basis for an actual study) does not seek to quantify 'weight' in terms of numbers of lines or square centimetres. Rather, she describes it as lending itself to a form of discourse analysis in which key words and phrases related to her 15 themes are recorded, and the gender, race, age and location of characters are also noted (and quantified where appropriate). Such an approach, whatever the reservations about the use of 15 themes, would certainly allow for a very different type of description to that provided by Sercu. In the following section I describe how I was able to combine certain elements of content analysis with the concept of a 'representational repertoire' taken from cultural studies in the design of the descriptive framework used in this study.

A representational repertoire

Du Gay *et al.* (1997) began their study by suggesting that the Sony Walkman had no intrinsic meaning – rather, they argued, its meaning was constructed through the representational practices employed in advertising campaigns and through texts, both corporate and journalistic, in which the product was given a specific history and was repeatedly talked about in specific ways. They concluded that the visual and linguistic choices made in the production of promotional material for the Walkman and associated texts constituted what they referred to as a 'representational repertoire' (ibid.: 39) which

> where it is not trading on the 'idea' and credibility-rating of the name of Sony Walkman itself and its technological sophistication and high quality, is relentlessly and overwhelmingly clustered around [...] meanings of mobility, sport, activity, leisure, and youth, youth, youth. (ibid.: 39)

A representational repertoire might thus be described as the stock of ideas, images and ways of talking which are repeatedly deployed in the creation of a set of meanings. The idea of a framework based on such a concept is clearly more philosophically appropriate in terms of this study than one based on the pre-specification of a fixed number of themes deemed cultural. A key feature in the identification of the representational repertoires deployed in the Sony Walkman study was the analysis of the artwork. This is also important here, given that the representational repertoires deployed in coursebooks are constructed not only through language, but also through the use of photographs, line drawings and charts – although font size and font colour are also potential carriers of meaning.

Anthony Howatt (1984) states that the visual dimension in language teaching textbooks has been regarded as important, at least since the time of Comenius – an observation also made by Stephen Pit Corder (1966), who suggests that Comenius was the first to realize the importance of the senses in language teaching, particularly with regard to the teaching of meaning. In his account of the role of the visual dimension in language teaching, Corder (1966: 2) makes a number of points that are worth quoting at length:

> One of the teacher's main duties is to help and guide the learner in forming the correct concepts, and in doing so economically and quickly. The teacher may do this in two ways: by putting the learner in the way of receiving sensory experience in a manner and sequence which will enable him to form correct concepts for himself most quickly, or by judicious giving of information.

And he continues,

> although information is normally mediated by language, it need not always be so. Much ready-conceptualised information is brought to the learner by other means: for example, in diagrams, maps, charts, graphs or models. It can happen that these visual means of conveying information are more effective than language. (ibid.: 3)

That said, the role of artwork in the ELT materials literature has been under-theorized (*pace* Kullman 2003), despite the great changes in the nature and the quantity of visual imagery in coursebooks produced since the 1970s.

Analyzing artwork

In deciding on which approach to follow I was heavily influenced by the literature on social semiotics (Hodge and Kress 1988; Kress and van Leeuwen 1996; Van Leeuwen and Jewitt 2001) and multimodality (Kress and van Leeuwen 2001; Burn and Parker 2003). This approach to text (sign) analysis views the process of representation as *interested* – in the sense that representations, involving the choice and deployment of a range of semiotic resources (e.g. words, images, colour, sound, etc.), may be said to serve the interests of those who create and disseminate them. By way of illustration, Gunther Kress *et al.* (2001) give the example of a science student who, having made a three-dimensional model of a plant cell using a bath sponge to represent the nucleus, decides to dye the sponge red. From the social semiotic/multimodal perspective, the selection of a specific material (in interview the student said she saw the nucleus as having an absorbent brain-like nature) and the use of colour to draw the viewer's attention to the importance of the nucleus are seen as motivated, meaningful choices on the part of the sign maker.

Kress and Theo van Leeuwen (1996), and those working within this paradigm, propose that Michael Halliday's (1978) notion of metafunctions of language – namely, the ideational, the interpersonal and the textual – is applicable to semiotic modes other than the linguistic. These terms have been somewhat recast within social semiotics and multimodal theory – as the 'representational', the 'interactive' and the 'compositional' (Kress and van Leeuwen 1996; Jewitt and Oyama 2001), and as the 'representational', the 'orientational' and the 'organizational' (Burn and Parker 2003) – however, the basic meanings remain the same.

Table 3.1 Social semiotic and multimodal equivalencies for Hallidayean metafunctions of language

Hallidayean metafunctions of language	Social semiotic term	Multimodal term
Ideational (concerned with the representational function of language)	Representational	Representational
Interpersonal (concerned with writer/reader and speaker/hearer interaction)	Interactive	Orientational
Textual (concerned with bringing the ideational and the interpersonal together to from a genre/communicative event)	Compositional	Organizational

Kress and van Leeuwen (1996: 46) point out that 'there are two kinds of participant involved in every semiotic act, the *interactive participants* and the *represented participants*.' The former are those involved in the act of communication (e.g. writer/reader) and the latter are those actually represented in the artwork. In the case of photographs and line drawings a descriptive framework can identify *who* is depicted (e.g.

whether represented participants are real or fictional, their sex, age, ethnicity and job), *where* they are depicted, *how* they are depicted and *what* they are shown doing. Social semiotics also suggests that representational meaning may have a narrative structure (where participants are shown interacting in some way – for example, a photograph of a service encounter) or a conceptual structure (as in the case of a line drawing of the human body with all parts labelled). Such choices are also said to be meaningful. Kress and van Leeuwen (1996) illustrate this with an example from an Australian social studies textbook. They show how the juxtaposition of artwork of Aboriginal tools and weapons (a conceptual structure in which an axe, a basket and a wooden sword are used to represent indigenous peoples) and artwork of government troops actively engaged in military activity against Aboriginals (a dynamic narrative structure) combine to differentiate the two groups in ways which they suggest are ideologically motivated.

Interactive meaning has three aspects (Jewitt and Oyama 2001) – contact, distance and point of view – each of which has to do with establishing a relationship with the viewer. Related to this is the concept of modality, which has to do with the way in which the speaker/writer's stance vis-à-vis the truth/credibility claims of the 'text' is signalled. I will deal with each of these in turn. With regard to contact, represented participants may be shown interacting with each other or they may be shown looking out of the photograph to meet the gaze of an imagined viewer. Again using terminology borrowed from Halliday (1985), the first type of interaction, in which the represented participants are made available for the viewer's contemplation/scrutiny, is referred to as an 'offer' (in the sense that information of some kind or other is being offered to the viewer), and the second type, in which the viewer may be said to enter into a kind of imaginary contact with the represented participant, is referred to as a 'demand'. Kress and van Leeuwen (1996: 122–123) explain this second type as follows:

> the participant's gaze (and gesture, if present) demands something from the viewer, demands that the viewer enter into some kind of imaginary relation with him or her. Exactly what kind of relation is then signified by other means [...] They may smile, in which case the viewer is asked to enter into a relation of social affinity with them; they may stare at the viewer with cold disdain, in which case the viewer is asked to relate to them, perhaps, as an inferior relates to a superior; they may seductively pout at the viewer, in which case the viewer is asked to desire them.

The second aspect of interactive meaning is distance, which draws on proxemics, and refers to the meaning potential of the space implied between the viewer and the represented participants. Film terminology is often used here to categorize distances on a cline from a close-up, showing the head and face only, to types of long shot showing the whole body and surrounding space. The various distances can be used to establish different types of relationship. For example, Carey Jewitt and Rumiko Oyama (2001) suggest that a close-up can be used to suggest intimacy, a medium shot to suggest a social relationship and a long shot to imply a more impersonal relationship. The third aspect of interactive meaning is point of view. This refers to the way in which represented participants can be depicted above, at or below eye-level. It also refers to the choice of whether they are seen from the front, the side or the back. Such perspectives position the viewer quite literally and are part of an image's meaning potential. In the words of Kress and van Leeuwen (1996: 135):

> In the case of the vertical angle this relation will be one of symbolic power. If you look down on something, you will look at it from a position of symbolic power. If you look up at something, that something has some kind of symbolic power over you. At eye-level there is a relation of symbolic equality. In the case of the horizontal angle, the relation will be one of involvement with, or detachment from, what is represented. Frontality allows the creation of maximum involvement. The viewer is directly confronted with what is in the picture. If something is depicted from the side, the viewer literally and figuratively remains on the sidelines.

As mentioned above, a related aspect of interactive meaning is modality which also has its origins in linguistics. As Fairclough (2003: 165 ff.) points out, the scope for the realization of linguistic modality is wide – encompassing the use of modal verbs (e.g. may, might, etc.), modal adverbs (e.g. possibly, certainly, etc.), participial adjectives (e.g. permitted, required, etc.), ways of representing mental process (e.g. I think, we assume, etc.), modal adjectives (e.g. possible, certain), ways of representing appearance (e.g. it seems, it appears) and hedges (e.g. sort of, kind of, etc.). But the concept of modality can also be applied to other semiotic modes such as intonation, gesture and visual images. With regard to the latter, modality refers to the ways in which visual representations are used to make truth/credibility claims within culturally and contextually determined conventions. Drawing on work by Basil Bernstein

(1981), Kress and van Leeuwen (1996) suggest four coding orientations for visual modality – the naturalistic, the sensory, the abstract and the technological. The first of these, in which the convention of 35 mm photography is accepted as 'an adequate stand-in for what is seen by the human eye' (Kuhn 1985: 27), is described by Kress and van Leeuwen (1996) as the current dominant coding orientation; the second, in which colour and image sharpness are manipulated to induce pleasure or elicit some kind of emotional response from the viewer, is often found in advertising texts; the third is found in those contexts (e.g. scientific or academic) in which a phenomenon or a process is shorn of superficial details with a view to representing its essential nature diagrammatically; finally, the fourth is found in those visual representations, such as architectural plans, which function as blueprints. It should also be pointed out that there are degrees of modality within these orientations. Take for example a colour photograph of a street scene. If colour and definition are drained from the image the modality is said to decrease. Similarly, modality decreases if the colour is super-saturated and the definition heightened so that the image begins to assume a surreal quality. With regard to line drawings, the amount of detail, the degree of physiological distortion and the use of colour will combine to determine the modality of the representation.

The elements of compositional meaning are information value, framing and salience. The first of these refers to the placement of elements within a composition. For those using the Roman alphabet the direction in which a written text is read is from left to right and from top to bottom. Within social semiotics and multimodal theory such directionality is also held to be important in texts which draw on other semiotic modes. Kress and van Leeuwen (1996) suggest that the left/right directionality creates a 'given-new' structure and that top/bottom directionality creates an 'ideal-real' structure. An example of what such an approach might mean in practice is provided by their analysis of an advertisement for soap which consists of a photograph of a woman in a bath. This image occupies the top half of the advertisement. Written information about the product is contained in the lower half of the advertisement. This, they suggest, refers to what is real – the product which exits and can be bought, whereas the image of the woman using the product and luxuriating in the bath points to what might be if the viewer were to buy the product.

The second aspect of compositional meaning is framing. This refers to the way in which elements are separated from or linked to each other on the page by the use of lines, arrows, colour or spacing. Framing can be used to suggest connections between various elements and to mark off elements as somehow differentiated. Finally, salience refers to the way in which degrees of significance can be allocated to elements within a composition through the use of colour, relative size and positioning.

That said, it is important to state that social semiotics does not claim to provide a means for the mechanical reading off of textual meaning – rather it provides a set of tools whereby visual resources can be interpreted within the social, cultural and historical context of their deployment. As Robert Ferguson (2004) points out, the Union Jack can function as a signifier of the swinging sixties *and* the political right. Thus social semiotics does not regard meanings as inherent and fixed but as contingent and contextual. It was hoped that by incorporating such a perspective into the descriptive framework advanced below, it would be possible to analyze the artwork and its contribution to the construction of the representational repertoires deployed in the coursebooks.

A descriptive framework

It is worth underlining at this stage that while the 'circuit of culture', on which this study rests, was initially used in a study of a commonplace cultural commodity, the ELT coursebook is an altogether more complex phenomenon than the Sony Walkman. The coursebook can be seen as a commodity in a uniquely double sense – firstly, as a product which is designed to be sold in the market place alongside other products of a similar type, and secondly, as a vehicle for English, which as I suggested in Chapter 1 is itself increasingly commodified in the current phase of globalization. So although the coursebook can be seen as an example of a 'secondary environment' expressly created for the mediation of English, it needs to be remembered that the language itself is represented and served up for consumption in particular ways by coursebooks. Hence the need for any descriptive framework to incorporate this aspect of content as well. Given that cultural content cannot be specified in advance, I therefore took the decision to adopt an inductive approach and to explore the materials in terms of those elements of content which are more or less common to all coursebooks – namely, what is known in ELT as the language systems (i.e. grammar, lexis and phonology) and the texts for developing the language skills (i.e. reading, listening, speaking and writing) – because it is around these that the representational repertoires are constructed.

My starting point was the representation of the language systems – an aspect of content not considered by Byram (1993) or Sercu (2000), but one which, as we shall see in subsequent chapters, is of importance to ELT publishers and to English language teachers. Van Ek (1975) recommended that the standard dialect should form the basis of teaching, and more recently Gnutzman (2004: 358) has argued the ongoing need for '*some kind* of Anglo-American lexical and grammatical standard' (emphasis added). Certainly in much of Europe, as has been pointed out, 'the teaching of English is still largely based on Standard British English and Received Pronunciation' (Preisler 1999: 239). Although definitions of 'standard English' abound, several commentators have argued that the concept is difficult to characterize (e.g. Seidlhofer 2005; Jenkins 2006). However, many definitions include the points made by Peter Trudgill (1999: 125), who describes it in relation to other varieties of English as 'a social dialect which is distinguished [...] by its *grammatical* forms'. Furthermore, he states that

> it is the variety of English normally used in writing, especially printing; it is the variety associated with the education system in all the English-speaking countries of the world, and is therefore the variety spoken by those who are often referred to as 'educated people'; and it is the variety taught to non-native learners. (ibid.)

Similar definitions have been offered by Peter Strevens (1983) and by Jack Richards *et al.* (1985). But as James and Lesley Milroy (1999: 19) suggest, a standard language is best understood as 'an idea in the mind rather than a reality – a set of abstract norms to which actual usage may conform to a greater or lesser extent'. The term 'standard *British* English' recognizes the role of lexis and a model of pronunciation in giving the standard its particular localized form. Thus, for example, we recognize 'faucet' as a lexeme in 'standard American English' and 'tap' as belonging to 'standard British English'. However, as we saw in Chapter 2, Byram and Fleming (1998) have suggested that the increasing use of English as a lingua franca raises the question of what kind of English students should be exposed to in language teaching materials. Against the background of increasing lingua franca use, it is therefore legitimate in analyzing a coursebook, to not only ask which varieties of English are drawn on, but also ask if the spoken and written English of L2 (i.e. second language) users is also represented – and if so, how? Learning English, it could be argued, can be seen as not simply being about the acquisition of a particular variety of the code, but also about developing the skills required to 'decode' the varieties and forms deployed by one's interlocutors.

It is also important to ask to what extent the grammar of spoken English is represented, given that this tends to be more 'culturally' marked than many forms of written grammar (see Prodromou 1997; Carter 1998; Cook 1998). Similarly, the framework needs to consider the kind of lexis which is taught and the issues this raises of variety ('tap' vs 'faucet'), register ('to consult' vs 'to look up'), idiomaticity ('pound' vs 'quid') and so on. And finally, it needs to identify which accents are used in the phonological representation of English, which accents students are encouraged to use as models and in particular the role ascribed to received pronunciation (RP) – generally understood as a non-regional British accent with strong social class associations (Leith 1997; Holborow 1999).

At the same time – as with the texts surrounding the Walkman – the 'secondary environments' created in coursebooks have to be peopled, themed and located if the artefact is to acquire an identity. In this respect the frameworks designed by Risager (1991), Sercu (2000) and Hall (2002) are useful as they all provide for the identification of the characters who people the coursebook and the locations in which they interact. In addition, given the prevalence of so-called authentic texts in ELT, the sources of those texts which are reproduced in coursebooks need to be identified if possible and, again following Risager (1991), their point of view established. Given that student responses to all texts are mediated almost exclusively through comprehension and follow-up activities, it is important to look at these and the kind of responses they seek to elicit, as these may be said to construct or position students in particular ways – permitting certain responses and foreclosing others. Furthermore, the descriptive framework needs to be sensitive, not only to those aspects of identity which comprehension activities seek to draw on, but also to those identities which students are asked to assume in terms of the role plays and practice activities. The language classroom may be said to provide rehearsal opportunities for particular kinds of language use, where the scripts are provided by the material. But, we are entitled to ask, scripts for which roles and for which identities? Following McKay (2002), we can also ask what pragmatic (e.g. norms of politeness) and rhetorical conventions (e.g. formal and informal writing styles) are taught, given that these too are 'culturally' marked. Byram (1997), as we saw in Chapter 2, argued that the dominant paradigm aims to produce an ersatz 'native speaker'. Thus, the descriptive framework presented in Table 3.2 below needs to be capable of establishing the accuracy of this claim.

Table 3.2 Descriptive framework

Elements of content	Representational repertoire
Language systems	
Grammar	Which varieties of English are represented? (British, North American, etc.) Are there any representations of L2 varieties of English? How are they represented? Is the grammar of spoken English distinguished from written grammar? Is there a functional strand to the syllabus? What purposes/contexts of use does this presuppose?
Lexis	Which lexical fields are taught? What purpose does the lexis serve?
Phonology	Is there a model of pronunciation? Which aspects of pronunciation are addressed (e.g. segmental/suprasegmental features)? Is phonological variation represented?
	What role does the accompanying artwork play with regard to the above?
	General comments
Skills content	
Texts to develop reading/ listening/speaking/writing	What topics are addressed? Who are the characters? (real/fictional, sex, age, ethnicity, job, etc.) What locations are used? Which text types are used? What is the source of texts? What is the point of view? What types of exercise are included?
	What topics do students talk about? What types of activities are used to practise speaking (e.g. role play)? Which aspects of pragmatics are addressed?
	Which genres are practised (e.g. letter of complaint)? Are formal/informal registers addressed?
	What role does the accompanying artwork play with regard to the above?
	General comments

Details of the representational practices associated with each of these elements of content were recorded unit by unit for each coursebook in a database for subsequent analysis. The database can be seen as a kind of detailed description, whereby all the topics addressed were recorded, along with the characters and locations featured, the type of text, the point of view, the task types and the accents featured on the accompanying tapes. In addition, I also entered information on the type of artwork featured in each unit. Such an approach allowed for both quantitative and qualitative analysis of the descriptive data.

With regard to the categorization of accents, it is important to clarify how this was done. One of the things I wanted the framework to do was to allow for the identification of the accents drawn on in the creation of a representational repertoire of English at the phonological level. With regard to RP, David Crystal (1995) and Jennifer Jenkins (2000) have pointed out that this accent exists in a state of constant evolution, with many educated speakers having developed a form of speaking known as 'modified RP' (ibid.: 14) in which some regional features may be present. Therefore, the term 'advanced RP' was used for any old-fashioned forms of the accent which occurred and all remaining British accents in which there were no *predominant* regional features were categorized under the blanket term 'RP/modified RP'. Those UK accents which were clearly localized were categorized as 'regional UK'. Kachru's (1985) idea of circles of English provided a useful way of addressing the remainder – thus the accents of inner circle countries other than the UK were classified as 'international inner circle', and all remaining accents as 'outer/expanding circle'. My decision to conflate the outer and the expanding circle was made for a number of reasons. Firstly, my approach was essentially a broad-brush rather than a fine-grained one. Secondly, as Jenkins (2003) points out in her discussion of the limitations of Kachru's model, it is not always possible to identify accurately which circle voices belong in. And thirdly, actors' voices are generally used and in many cases they are pretending to be from countries outside the inner circle – thus compounding the second problem. Despite these problems, the approach I adopted did serve to underline the geographically localized nature of the phonological repertoires constructed in coursebooks.[1]

Coursebook sample

The sample of coursebooks was based on a small selection of historical bestsellers. The reason for adopting a historical approach is that it allowed for speculation about changes which have taken place over time in the nature of cultural content. That said, accurate figures for sales are difficult to obtain but it is widely recognized within the ELT industry that a number of courses have been extremely successful over a great many years – among these are the *Strategies, Streamline, Cambridge English* and *Headway* courses. Thus all the coursebooks analyzed came from these courses and all were confirmed by the UK bookseller's Waterstones as being or having been major bestsellers (personal communication, 2004). All have gone though several editions and/or printings, and one of them was authorized by the Spanish Ministry of Education and Science for use throughout the sizeable state school sector. At the time of writing, three of them are still in print.

Table 3.3 Coursebooks analyzed

Coursebook	Authors	Year of publication/ publisher	Other details
Streamline English Connections	Hartley, B. and P. Viney	1979 OUP	Still in print and currently on its seventy-seventh printing.
Building Strategies (2nd edition)	Abbs, B. and I. Freebairn	1984 Longman	First published in 1979. Authorized by Spanish Ministry of Education and Science for use in state school sector. Currently out of print.
The New Cambridge English Course 2	Swan, M. and C. Walter	1990 CUP	Still in print and currently on ninth printing.
The New Edition New Headway Intermediate	Soars, J. and L. Soars	2003 OUP	First published in 1986; second edition in 1996; third edition 2003; fourth edition 2009.

ELT coursebooks are particularly formulaic, with individual publishing houses keeping a close eye on each other's successful publications with a view to attempted replication. Thus generations of coursebooks tend to resemble each other, not only in terms of format and methodology, but also in terms of content. A similar point has been made by Robert Ariew (1989) about educational textbooks in general. With this in mind I chose for analysis one student's book from each of the above-mentioned courses at intermediate level. The reason for choosing the intermediate level was twofold – most sales for all courses tend to be at the intermediate level (OUP, personal communication, 2000) and in some cases the intermediate coursebook was published first, and provided the model for all subsequent books in the series (e.g. the *Headway* series). I did not include the workbooks for analysis on the grounds that it is the student's book which sets the tone for the whole course. Unlike Littlejohn (1992), who analyzed between 12 per cent and 15 per cent of five coursebooks, I initially decided to apply the framework to all units with the exception of revision units. However, the revision units in *Connections* also introduce new language and those in *Building Strategies* continue the storyline which runs through the coursebook. These units were therefore included as they were considered integral to the material. So although the sample was small, a detailed picture of each coursebook emerged from the application of the framework. This, I would suggest, is valid, given the overwhelmingly conservative nature of ELT publishing and the way in which individual components of a course exemplify the representational practices of the course overall. In chapters 4 and 5, I address each coursebook separately as a discrete historical entity in an attempt to map clearly the kind of changes in representational practices that have taken place over the period.

4
Representational Repertoires 1: *Streamline Connections* and *Building Strategies*

Introduction

From the 1970s onwards the titles of books for the teaching of English to speakers of other languages began to change. The trend was for shorter, snappier titles such as *Mainline* (Alexander 1973), *Strategies* (Abbs *et al.* 1975), *Headway* (Soars and Soars 1986) and *Cutting Edge* (Cunningham and Moor 1998) – in contrast with earlier twentieth-century titles such as *Essential English for Foreign Students* (Eckersley 1938) and *Oxford Progressive English for Adult Learners* (Hornby 1954), both of which announce themselves clearly as textbooks. The *Streamline English* course, which first appeared in 1978, was certainly part of this trend. The four books in the course, each with a cover design based around an image of rail travel, were entitled *Departures*, *Connections*, *Destinations* and *Directions*. The implied link between the learning the student undertook within the pages of the books and a metaphoric journey (into English and beyond) was typical of this kind of title change. But it was not only titles which were changing, the nature and quantity of artwork and the increasing use of colour were also changing. In this respect the *Streamline English* course may be said to have led the way and it is for this reason that I begin with artwork, given its salience in *Connections* and its role in indexing key elements of content.

The role of artwork and the use of colour

Like many coursebooks from the mid-1970s onwards, *Connections* makes considerable use of a range of artwork. However, it is the extensive use of colour which immediately distinguishes it from other coursebooks published during the same period (e.g. O'Neill 1971, 1973). Out of 80 units, 39 are in colour and the blurb draws attentions to the way in which *each* page 'is attractively illustrated with drawings or photographs'.[1] In his account of the history of the course, Peter Viney (2004) tells how, at the pre-publication stage, the authors switched from one prestigious academic publisher to another at the prospect of a colour edition. 'Oxford got in at the last moment, and their trump card was the offer of colour, which we had been holding out for', he relates (ibid.). Viney does not say why colour was so important, but certainly when we look at its deployment in the coursebook we can see that its signifying potential is both powerful and complex.

Connections features photographic artwork in 30 units, with the remaining 50 consisting largely of graphics (e.g. mock-ups of forms, letters, etc.) and line drawings. One of the distinguishing features of the latter is the pervasive use of a ludic style reminiscent of British children's comics, whereby the represented participants are generally depicted as brightly coloured, with minor anatomical exaggerations, often with comical names (e.g. the pop singer Elton Kash), curiously dressed, or in situations which might be deemed amusing (e.g. buying a pet from a bandaged pet shop owner who has clearly been bitten by much of his stock). Such artwork is typical of what has been referred to as 'play' text (Hodge and Kress 1988: 130) in which the overall low modality of the drawings suggests a fictionality congruent with, in this case, the contrived nature of the accompanying written texts. This art-work also tends to make explicit a comic element already present or implicit in the written texts, and in turn is often reinforced by the voices on the tapes which may be exaggerated or modified in some way so as to sound funny (e.g. the way in which the voice for the fictional boxer Brutus Cray deliberately imitates that of Muhammad Ali). At least 32 units may be said to include some element of comedy, the function of which is clearly to entertain both students *and* teacher.[2] This light touch also applies to the coursebook's approach to language. The introduction to the teacher's edition spells this out as follows:

> [T]he student's book does not include linguistic description either of the traditional grammatical kind (the present perfect progressive, the passive, etc.) or of the functional type (inquiring about intention, expressing gratitude, etc.). Such descriptions can be of value to the teacher and are confined to the teacher's book. They may be con-fusing to the students and we would not recommend exposing the students to them. (Hartley and Viney 1979: 7)

As the index to the teacher's book shows, what *Connections* offers is a traditional grammar syllabus with an up-to-date (for the time) functional strand – both of which have been comprehensively disguised in what the introduction claims are 'interesting contexts' (ibid.: 5). In his study deconstructing the professional discourse of TESOL, Christopher Anderson (2002: 215) suggests that 'a light fun approach' with little intellectual challenge is a defining feature of much ELT classroom practice and certainly the salient and predominantly colourful ludic strand in the artwork in *Connections* resonates with this assessment. Interestingly, Viney (2004) reports that it was a perceived lack of seriousness which caused the course to undersell in the German market.

In contrast, photographs are used throughout to imply a different type of correspondence with the world beyond the coursebook – thus we find colour photography used in units on the 1976 Montreal Olympics, traffic problems in Oxford, the life of Elvis Presley and accounts of various kinds of disaster. As we saw in Chapter 3, from the perspective of social semiotics, high modality colour photography (in which the colour is neither drained nor super-saturated) functions as an adequate stand-in for what might be seen by the human eye. However, *Connections* also makes use of black-and-white photography to refer to the world beyond the coursebook in ways which are meaningful, particularly with regard to the referencing of certain aspects of language-in-use.

At the same time as disguising the syllabus through the avoidance of all grammatical terminology, *Connections* deliberately seeks to foreground visually its treatment of functional English. The blurb on the back of the book states that 'units of everyday conversation have been included to underline the practical nature of the language being taught.' These units, of which there are only 11 (out of a total of 80), are differentiated from all others, not only in terms of their linguistic content, but also through the specific modality of the accompanying artwork. This functional strand is largely focused on the language of service encounters. Each of these units has exactly the same layout – namely, three or four short dialogues which run down the left hand side of the page with corresponding artwork on the right. Altogether the artwork for this strand consists of 40 black-and-white photographs. These are characterized by what might be called a 'social realist' style in which the represented participants have the look of everyday people of the period (rather than actors) engaged in largely ritualized service encounters:

A   Next please.
B   I'd like to cash this cheque, please.

A   Yes, madam...£30. Oh! You haven't signed it yet, madam.
B   Haven't I? Oh, I'm terribly sorry...here you are.
A   Thank you. How would you like the money?
B   Four fives and ten ones, please. (Hartley and Viney 1979: Unit 18)[3]

It will be recalled that black-and-white images predominated in newspapers of the period, while Sunday supplements and magazines made greater use of colour. This use of colour, I would suggest, often but not invariably carried strong associations with leisure and/or entertainment (as in the aforementioned ludic strand), while black-and-white more often signified seriousness and/or everydayness. The choice of black-and-white photography for these units might thus be said to connote a (historically specific) degree of seriousness and to underline the everydayness and practicality of the language in these particular dialogues.[4] In social semiotic terms we can say, with regard to representational meaning, that each photograph has a narrative structure (the represented participants are shown interacting). With regard to interactive meaning, each photograph is an offer (the represented participants do not demand anything by meeting the viewer's gaze, but instead offer information about the type of interaction); the distances are those of medium shots; and the point of view depicts the represented participants more or less at eye-level (although the action of cashing a cheque is clarified by a slightly vertical angle). Overall, the viewer is positioned for detached observation of the situation. With regard to compositional meaning, the artwork for each speech event is separately framed – thereby underlining the discrete nature of each routine and there is a left (text)/right (photograph) arrangement. The teacher's book indicates that the text is to be masked in the initial stage of the lesson while the tape is played. In this way, any new linguistic item is heard in context and linked with the accompanying photograph before being seen in the written form. Thus the student is encouraged to draw on pre-existing linguistic knowledge (given) and the situational information contained in the artwork (new) to make sense of the new piece of language.

Although the teacher's book shows that a total of 44 units contain various types of fixed expressions, many are embedded in the 'interesting contexts' referred to earlier. What is different about the everyday conversation units is that they feature situations in which students visiting the UK might theoretically find themselves, and I would suggest it is for this reason that a social realist modality is used. The artwork may be said to reference a high degree of correspondence between the language found in the dialogues and that likely to occur in similar situations in the world outside the classroom – for example, 'Next, please', 'How would you like the money?' and so on. Unlike most other dialogues in the coursebook which are typified by target structure repetition and the kind of over-explicitness often noted by commentators (e.g. Wajnryb 1996; Thornbury 2005), these are designed to focus on how many setting-specific interactions rely on 'ready-made' language. In this way, by reserving a particular style of artwork for a specific type of language use, the relatively small functional strand is made salient and its 'practical nature' is underlined. That said, the overall comic thrust of *Connections* is such that even in these units there are occasional elements of comedy (e.g. a short-sighted customer at the optician's attempts to leave via the window). As we shall see, this will prove to be a recurrent element in the other aspects of content to which I now turn.

A variety of voices

As suggested earlier, work done under the auspices of the Council of Europe during the 1970s made a considerable impact on the content of coursebooks for the teaching of English. The Threshold Level (van Ek 1975) for adult language learners and a separate version for school learners (van Ek 1976) proposed a notional/functional syllabus, semantico-grammatical categories deemed common to all European languages and situational content – based on the roles students might be expected to play, the settings in which language might be used and the topics which students might be expected to address. John Trim (in Hopkins 2001: 46–47) assessed it thus:

> The impact of the Threshold Level on the teaching of English as a foreign language was immediate and very powerful. By the end of the 70s most textbooks were organized according to themes and functions and most examining bodies had made corresponding changes to their syllabuses.

That said, *Connections* was not written to enable students to meet Threshold Level requirements but it does reveal signs of the impact referred to by Trim. Although no mention is made on the blurb or in the notes to the teacher regarding the variety of English it purports to teach, the standard British dialect in terms of grammar, spelling and lexis is clearly (and unremarkably) what is on offer. With regard to phonology, no specific attention is paid to segmental or suprasegmental features – although choral and individual drilling is the predominant form of all types of controlled practice. What is of note is the range of accents on the tapes which accompany the coursebook and the ways in which these contribute to the representational repertoire. Interestingly, the introduction explains this range as follows:

> The obvious advantage of exposing the student to a variety of voices is that in any authentic situation the student will have to cope with such variety. (Hartley and Viney 1979: 7)

What is interesting about this from the perspective of the twenty-first century is that the authentic situations envisaged overwhelmingly involve British 'native speakers' interacting in Britain. The descriptive framework reveals that RP/modified RP accents are the most salient.

Table 4.1   *Connections*: Total numbers of units according to range of accents

Accent	Advanced RP	RP/ modified RP	Regional UK	International inner circle	Outer/ expanding circle
Exclusive occurrences: number of units	–	25	3	2	1
Co-occurrences: number of units	4	38	32	6	5
Occurrences: total number of units	4	63	35	8	6

Out of a total of 71 units with recordings, those on the RP continuum feature in 63 units and of those they feature exclusively in 25. This is followed by regional UK accents which feature in 35 units, almost always co-occurring with RP/modified RP. A closer examination of how these and other accents are deployed reveals a number of significant features. For example, outer/expanding circle accents are associated with foreign students studying in the UK, waiters, individuals working in the tourist industry abroad and a fictional Secretary General of the UN. Significantly, in spite of phonological variation, there is no variation at the lexical or syntactic levels in the speech of these individuals – although it could be argued that students might, even in 1979, have had to cope with variation here too. The use of advanced RP is linked entirely to the comic strand and is used mainly by characters whose overall situation is represented as 'amusing' (e.g. a British man with advanced RP is repeatedly ignored by a foreign waiter who is more intent on talking to a female customer than bringing him a menu). International inner circle accents occur in settings featuring tourists and in the few units which deal exclusively with US subject matter.

However, the surface variation in the representation of English phonologically does not imply equality of status for all accents. This can be detected in the distribution of regional UK and RP/modified RP accents with regard to speakers whose jobs are clearly identified. Although Table 4.2 shows that several speakers whose jobs are not generally regarded as being particularly high status have RP/modified RP accents – thereby making the point that this accent range does not automatically presuppose a high-status job – it is also clear that higher-status jobs *tend* to be accompanied by accents on the RP continuum and that regional UK accents are more clearly associated with blue-collar employment.

Table 4.2   *Connections*: Distribution of jobs according to RP/modified RP and regional UK accents

Jobs in which speakers have RP/modified RP accents	Jobs in which speakers have RP/modified RP and regional UK accents	Jobs in which speakers have regional UK accents
All television jobs (presenters, newsreaders, commentators, interviewers, weatherman, 'expert'); import-export company boss; import-export company employee; interviewer and interviewee for export salesman job; interviewee for export manager's secretary; airline pilot; airport security man; airline check-in person; lawyer; tour guides; ship's captain; pharmacist; waiter; travel agents; office 'boss'; doctors; bank manager; ticket sales assistants; hairdresser; receptionists; nurses; radio presenter; trainee journalist	Shop assistants; telephone receptionists for police, fire and ambulance services/commercial enterprises; bank clerks; secretaries	Army sergeant; army recruit; chef; waitress; farmer; maid; chauffeur; mechanic; football manager; football player; fisherman; guesthouse landlady; petrol pump attendant; office workers; newspaper editor; air-sea rescue crewman; traffic warden; policemen; teacher; estate agent

Furthermore, RP/modified RP accents function as the authoritative or 'teacherly' voice of the coursebook – being used to 'frame' units by announcing the number and title of each one; to narrate those passages of text which precede or link sections of dialogue; and to narrate those units which feature a single narrative voice (exceptions are two units which deal exclusively with US subject matter). Finally, a small number of gullible and criminal characters have regional UK accents – something which, as we shall see, is a recurrent feature of ELT coursebooks. Overall, the RP cluster of accents may be said to occupy a privileged position in the phonological representation of English in *Connections*.

'Interesting contexts' and the representation of gender, age and race

The Threshold Level (van Ek 1975: 14–16) suggests the following set of core topics as appropriate for students working towards a basic level of foreign language proficiency: personal identification; house and home; trade, profession and occupation; free time, entertainment; travel; relations with other people; health and welfare; education; shopping; food and drink; services; places; foreign language; and weather. When they are used to categorize the units in *Connections* we can see in Table 4.3 that almost half fall outside the range of suggestions.

Units categorized under 'other' feature a range of topics which include the following: the 'discovery' of the earth by beings from another planet; a story about a serial killer; getting caught taking a day off work while pretending to be sick; natural disasters; spotting a UFO; and a ghost story. These topics, I would suggest, are precisely what is meant by the 'interesting contexts' for introducing new language referred to earlier. Against this background of diverse topics is a correspondingly large cast of fictional and non-fictional characters. With the exception of Elvis Presley, who is the subject of an entire unit, non-fictional characters feature only in passing, and then predominantly in controlled practice activities. Reference to such characters in many cases presupposes a degree of familiarity with mostly male iconic figures in British/North American public life. Examples include Paul McCartney, Rockefella, James Hunt, the Queen and John F. Kennedy. However, the majority of characters who people the pages of *Connections* are fictional and what is immediately noticeable is that they are overwhelmingly male. Table 4.4 provides a breakdown of the total numbers of male and female representations in the reading and listening texts, in the artwork and on the tapes. (Artwork figures are necessarily approximate as I only counted those represented participants who were clearly visible.)

Table 4.3 *Connections*: Number of units in which Threshold Level topics are addressed

Topic	Personal identification	House and home	Trade, profession and occupation	Free time, entertainment	Travel	Relations with other people	Health and welfare
Number of units	1	1	12	6	9	5	1
Topic	Education	Shopping	Food and drink	Services	Places	Weather	Other
Number of units	1	5	3	5	1	1	39

Table 4.4   *Connections*: Numbers of male and female representations

Sex of represented participants	Texts	Artwork	Tapes
Male	229	245	192
Female	136	138	120

Such disproportionate representation of women is generally understood as sexism – that is, discrimination (in this case by omission) against women on the basis of gender. In addition, as Table 4.5 shows, men are represented as occupying a wider range of jobs/roles than those occupied by women.

Table 4.5   *Connections*: Fictional characters according to jobs and sex

Male characters	Female characters
Ship's captain; bank worker; television 'expert'; television newsreader × 2; television sports commentators × 3; Olympic athletes × 3; television interviewer; UN Secretary General; pharmacist; butler; chauffeur; waiter × 3; astronaut; army sergeant; army recruit; emigration officer; electrician; bank clerk; tour guides × 2; sailor; students × 5; construction workers × 2; import-export company employee; businessman; job interviewer; interviewee for export salesman job; farmer; office worker × 2; pilot; security guard; rock/pop musicians × 4; racing driver; television/radio presenter; security guard; policeman × 6; journalist; football manager; football player; television presenter; customs officer; truck driver; lawyer; doctor × 4; fisherman; bank manager; petrol pump attendant; tour guide; school headmaster; teacher × 3; hairdresser; television weather man; chef; bus driver; air-sea rescue crew member; newspaper editor; singer; mayor; mayor's secretary; assistant hotel manager; fireman; ambulance service man; teacher; shop assistant × 4; estate agent; football player; film director; film producer; writer × 2; composer; record producer; mechanic × 2; engineer; bin-man; taxi driver; detective; boxer; travel agent; tailor; supermarket manager; caliph; servant	Waitress × 2; telephone receptionist × 4; housewife × 6; Olympic athletes × 2; shop assistants × 5; maid; astronaut; bank clerk; travel agent; typists × 2; interviewee for export manager's secretary; student × 3; airport check-in staff; television game show contestant; television game show score keeper; personal secretary; guesthouse landlady; office workers × 3; salesperson × 2; secretaries × 2; receptionist × 2; radio newsreader; doctor; nurse × 2; traffic warden; television newsreader; singer; documentary director; box office sales person; trainee journalist; store detective

However, it is in the actual representation of individual women that the sexism of the coursebook becomes more apparent. This takes a variety of forms – for example, in a unit about job interviews, a male candidate is interviewed for the post of export salesman, while a female candidate is interviewed for the less important post of export manager's secretary (Unit 22). In the accompanying artwork the female candidate's application form, which is made less salient by being partly covered by the male candidate's, shows that she has a lower level of education. Women are also represented as emotional and complaining in ways that men are not. The causes are linked to unhappiness with their domestic situation or to their male partner's behaviour. Such representations are also part of the coursebook's overall comic approach to content, as the first four lines in the following dialogue illustrate:

A   Tom! You never talk to me nowadays.
B   What did you say?
A   ... and you never listen to me, either.
B   Pardon?
A   You used to take me out, you used to buy me presents, and you used to remember my birthday.
B   But I always remember your birthday, darling.
A   Do you? Well, it was yesterday! I'm going home to mother! (ibid.: Unit 34)

Tom's sleepily delivered 'What did you say?' and 'Pardon', as revealed on the accompanying tape, comically underline his initial obliviousness to the content of the utterances made by the emotional female voice. Elsewhere a housewife complains repeatedly to her husband that her life is boring (Unit 6), and a footballer's wife is angry that her husband has left her for a Swedish actress (Unit 30). A woman complains to her mother about her inability to cope with a constantly crying baby and the amount of housework she has to do (Unit 34), while another complains to her friend at a social event that her husband has spent the evening dancing with other women (Unit 40). In all instances the voices on the tapes reinforce the speakers' emotional state and in two cases the dependency of children on women is suggested through the addition of crying babies in the artwork. Erving Goffman (1979: 28), writing about gender stereotyping in advertising, suggests that when men and women are involved in the same activity the man is generally shown to assume the executive role – an observation which is borne out in several instances (e.g. Unit 3, Unit 12, Unit 49, Unit 52). By way of example, in the following extract a pressurized male chef tells a female waitress how she can help him:

Chef Have you put the sauce on yet?
Waitress Eh? Oh no, I haven't. Where is it?
Chef Here it is.
Waitress Oh, there isn't quite enough sauce here.
Chef There's plenty in that pan over there.
Waitress Ah, yes... I've got it.
Chef Now you can begin taking the plates to the customers.
Waitress Ow! They're hot!
Chef Well, use a cloth... and don't carry too many plates. You may
    drop them. (Hartley and Viney 1979: Unit 49)

At the same time, women are represented as being easily frightened – by UFOs (Unit 52) and ghost stories (Unit 62), and as fearful of gaining weight (Unit 38).

While some women complain about men, others are represented as duplicitous in their dealings with them. One woman fails to meet the man she has a date with when she receives a better offer. Later she pretends not to know who he is when he telephones to find out why she did not arrive (Unit 14). In another instance a teenage girl repeatedly lies to a man for her own amusement (Unit 42). Women are also a source of comedy – an unmarried bespectacled would-be emigrant to Australia says hopes to meet the right man there, having failed to find a husband in England (Unit 17); an aristocratic young woman gets a Ferrari for her birthday and then decides to change it for one in a colour she likes (Unit 32); the waitress from the previously quoted extract ignores the chef's advice and attempts to carry too many plates, which she then drops (Unit 49). The cumulative effect of these representations, in addition to numerical under-representation and the association of women with lower-status jobs, may be said to reinforce their secondary role in the coursebook overall.

With regard to the age of characters, all units feature adults. Although the high incidence of low modality artwork makes it difficult to make accurate statements about the age of represented participants, it is possible to state that about a third of all units depict or refer to characters who might be described as middle-aged (more or less 40–60) or older, with the remainder featuring younger adults. Young children and teenagers are depicted or referred to infrequently. Given that the introduction to the teacher's book points out that *Connections* is aimed at 'adult and young adult' students (Hartley and Viney 1979: 5), the characters may be said to reflect the broad age range of the target audience.

In contrast, the representation of race is more limited. Almost all represented participants are white. In fact there is only one colour photograph of a black character – an unidentified male athlete receiving an Olympic medal. A further four units represent ethnic difference through the use of low modality colour drawings. Apart from Dr Sowanso, the fictional head of the UN, who features in two units, representations of race other than white British appear mainly to have the function of signalling that the action takes place outside the UK. There are no representations of black British or British Asian characters and no representations of women who are not white. Although the notes in the teacher's book and specific units in the student's book draw attention to aspects of life in the UK (e.g. bank opening and closing times are given), there is no suggestion that Britain, where *Connections* is predominantly located, has large established ethnic minority populations.

Authorial point of view

All reading and listening texts in *Connections* are written specifically for teaching purposes. With regard to authorial point of view, Risager (1991: 188) concluded that the coursebooks in a survey which she carried out tended to be 'objective' and 'to avoid expressions of attitude' towards the people and events described. Similarly in *Connections* the predominant authorial voice used to introduce units, to provide links between sections of dialogue, and to tell stories is that of a detached observer who describes without any significant evaluation. Paul Simpson (1993, following Roger Fowler [1986]) refers to this as an absence of authorial modality. Point of view in these parts of the material (unlike that in many of the aforementioned dialogues and artwork) might thus be described as overwhelmingly 'neutral'. The exception to this is the unit on the life of Elvis Presley, which is told in largely celebratory terms (Unit 68). Elvis is introduced as a 'superstar' whose significance was such that 'radio and television programmes all over the world were interrupted to give the news of his death' (ibid.). In the US it is said to have warranted a presidential statement to the effect that 'Elvis Presley changed the face of American popular culture' and that he was 'unique and irreplaceable' (ibid.). The rags-to-riches treatment of the story begins with his death which is presented as the apotheosis of his career – instanced by a funeral with 80,000 mourners, traffic jams, television and radio output dedicated to his films and music, followed by record sales of a hundred million in the year after his death. The celebratory point of view is reinforced by the overall sensory orientation of the artwork, with the text and a series of photographs from different moments in Elvis' life arranged against a salient pink background. The text, which is the longest single reading in *Connections*, is also the first instance of the extended treatment of celebrity that I have found in a coursebook from the period. As such, it may be said to mark the beginning of a trend which was to develop over the following 30 years, whereby celebrity comes to assume much greater importance in ELT materials.

Student identities

In Chapter 3, I stated that one of the aims in applying the descriptive framework was to explore those identities which are associated with English. This includes not only the identities which are represented *in* the material but also those which are implied or posited for the learner *by* the material. From the perspective of cultural studies, identity is seen as both plural (we do not have one only) and unstable (they exist in a state of change). As Kathryn Woodward (1997) argues, in the contemporary world identities may derive from a multiplicity of sources, such as nationality, religion, sexual orientation, employment, parenthood, consumption practices and so on. And it is not only in cultural studies that such ideas have gained currency. The economist Amartya Sen (2006: xii–xiii) argues that

> The same person can be, without any contradiction, an American citizen, of Caribbean origin, with African ancestry, a Christian, a liberal, a woman, a vegetarian, a long-distance runner, a historian, a schoolteacher, a novelist, a feminist, a heterosexual, a believer in gay and lesbian rights [...] Each of these collectivities, to all of which this person simultaneously belongs, gives her a particular identity. None of them can be taken to be the person's only identity or singular membership category. Given our inescapably plural identities, we have to decide on the relative importance of our different associations and affiliations in any particular context.

This raises at least two issues. On the one hand, particular affiliations and senses of self can come to the fore in different settings – recall my earlier quotation from Apple (1992: 10) on the way in which students and teachers bring their 'classed, raced, and gendered biographies' with them into the classroom. Different affiliations or subject positions can be called into play by ELT materials, whether covertly, as Canagarajah (1999) has shown in his analysis of textbooks defaced by students, or more overtly, as in the case of a hypothetical student who in a free-speaking activity, drawing on her own affiliations, says what she thinks about the content of a particular reading or listening text. On the other hand, the quotation from Sen suggests that new identities can be constructed and, as has been shown, second language learning can play a key role in this (Joseph 2004; Block 2007). In learning a language then, students may be expected to respond to aspects of coursebook content in ways which invoke a variety of subject positions *and* which allow them to engage in activities in which they may rehearse and experiment with unfamiliar identities – for example, through role play.

When we look at the productive skills activities in *Connections* we see that they are invariably related to the topic of the unit in which they occur and overwhelmingly focused on speaking. These are of three types: personalization activities; role plays; and 'free reproduction' in which students use the pictures accompanying the text to retell the story. Personalization activities take two forms: those which require students to speak as individuals (e.g. 'Do you like science fiction stories?': Unit 12) and those which ask them to speak as informants about uncontroversial aspects of their own country (e.g. 'What's the weather like in your country at this time of the year?': Unit 48). Students are also asked to talk about their likes and dislikes, to discuss each other's possessions and the things they have bought, to discuss travel and leisure activities and to elicit such information from each other. In spite of the case made for the value of personalization in the introduction to the teacher's book – 'Whenever possible the student is encouraged to use the newly-acquired language in some way meaningful to him/her' (Hartley and Viney 1979: 7) – students are not asked to respond to content or talk about themselves in ways which might draw on, for example, their classed, raced and gendered identities. Hall (1996: 4), it will be recalled, argues that identities are constructed within the representations we make of ourselves and, echoing Anthony Giddens (1991), through what he calls 'the narrativization of the self'. Giddens (ibid.: 32) has similarly referred to the 'reflexive project' of the self in late modernity, whereby individual identity is located in 'the capacity to keep a particular narrative going' (ibid.: 54).[5] It could be argued that the narrative of the self which *Connections* calls in to play is one in which class, race and gender are all but abolished. At the same time, the everyday conversation units and their focus on scripts for changing money, booking tickets and asking for directions may be said to posit an L2 speaker identity for students which is based on a limited range of tourist-type interactions. Role plays, generally associated with freer speaking activities in which students have some degree of control over the language they produce, occur infrequently (there are only five) and are similarly oriented.

Altogether productive skills practice activities posit a very limited range of subject positions for students, something which cannot be accounted for by the level of linguistic proficiency assumed by the coursebook. At the same time, students are construed overwhelmingly as being in need of content which is maximally entertaining. This is instanced by the pervasive comedy (which operates at the phonological, lexical and situational level), the ludic style of much of the artwork, the choice of topics for language practice and the avoidance of all metalanguage. Such an approach might be described without too much exaggeration as an 'edutainment' view of language teaching in which, as Anderson (2002) has suggested in his discussion of the way in which the field has developed, the student is construed primarily as a customer – an identity which is discussed in greater depth in Chapter 6.

Building Strategies

The *Strategies* course had its origin in a single pre-intermediate book named *Strategies* (Abbs *et al.* 1975) – the notional/functional material for which, the authors state, was based on work done by David Wilkins for the Council of Europe Committee for Out-of-School Education and Cultural Development. In its final form the series consisted of four titles – *Opening Strategies, Building Strategies, Developing Strategies* and *Studying Strategies*. As with the *Streamline English* course the individual titles revolve around a single metaphor, in this case one which may be said to connote stages in an overall goal-oriented process. In the teacher's book for *Building Strategies* the authors state that although the organization of the material is 'based on notional/functional categories of language the forms of English are also taught' (Abbs and Freebairn 1984b: v). These, however, are not addressed in isolation as they might be in a straightforwardly structural course, but are linked instead to contexts of use. The contents page in the student's book describes the linguistic content exclusively in notional/functional terms, and corresponds closely with the Threshold Level taxonomy of functions and notions (van Ek 1975: 19–21). Thus students are taught how to elicit and offer personal information; elicit and express opinions and attitudes; elicit and express likes, dislikes and preferences; make suggestions and polite requests; ask for and refuse permission (formally and informally); make and refuse invitations politely; make and accept excuses and apologies; and express agreement and disagreement. These functions are also linked to vaguer notional categories such as time, location, distance and quantity.

Representation of language

The blurb points out that the four books in the course take students to First Certificate level and that *Building Strategies* prepares them for the RSA Communicative Use of English examination – not surprisingly, given this focus on British tests, the focus is predominantly on British English. All 16 units use dialogues to introduce or practise new language. Although no specific attention is paid to the grammar of spoken English beyond highlighting the use of relatively fixed expressions in functional exchanges, *Building Strategies* consistently represents spoken English as different from written English, as the following extract illustrates:

Paul: What do you do?
Rod: Work. Down at Western Aeronautics. I'm an electrical engineer. I come from Canada. Came over a few weeks ago. What about you? What do you do?
Paul: I'm studying, actually, at the Poly, Polytechnic. Naval engineering and maths. It's OK.
Rod: Sounds interesting. Look, why don't you come round and see the flat? ...
Paul: Yes, er – may I come round and see it straightaway – like, now, this morning? (Unit 5)

Here we see an attempt to represent many of the features often found in conversation between 'native speakers', for example, pervasive ellipsis (Work; Came over a few weeks ago; Sounds interesting; etc.); reformulation (Poly, Polytechnic); and hesitation (Yes, er). Significantly, although such features are represented, the accompanying tasks do not draw students' attention to them. The overall aim, it would appear, is to sensitize students indirectly to aspects of 'native speaker' production while focusing on the use of functional exponents and appropriate replies as the goal of student production.

The teacher's book explains that lexical selection is based on three criteria: words with high frequency value; words which can be linked to the topics of the units; and 'words which are abstract but useful in any discussion of day-to-day life and current affairs, e.g. *career, tax, redundant, politician, election* and so on' (Abbs and Freebairn 1984b: vi). These examples can be seen as an indication of compatibility with Threshold Level aims to 'enable the learner to cross the threshold into the foreign-language community' (van Ek 1975: 10) – that is, to go beyond the survival level of language a tourist might require.

With regard to phonology, the introduction to the teacher's book points out that the various types of oral exercises not only provide consolidation of the functions, structures and lexis covered in the unit but 'also give consistent practice in pronunciation, stress and intonation' (Abbs and Freebairn 1984b: xi). However, no attention is paid to segmental or suprasegmental features apart from drilling. Table 4.6 illustrates the distribution of accents across the units and shows that RP/modified RP predominates. In fact, accents on the RP continuum occur in all units with recorded material and also predominate *within* each unit. The main regional UK accent is west country (the coursebook is set in Bristol), although there are also some examples of other regional accents. International inner accents are from Canada and the US. Those accents categorized under outer/expanding circle feature speakers from Jamaica and India, as well as speakers who are identified as language learners or appear to speak English as an additional language.

Table 4.6 *Building Strategies*: Total numbers of units according to range of accents

Accent	RP/ modified RP	Regional UK	International inner circle	Outer/ expanding circle
Exclusive occurrences: number of units	–	–	–	–
Co-occurrences: number of units	15	8	9	7
Occurrences: total number of units	15	8	9	7

RP/modified RP is used to frame all units, to introduce listening texts and for interviewers' voices in those texts which take the form of interviews. However, because *Building Strategies* revolves around the lives of a set of core characters, one of whom is Canadian and several of whom have regional UK accents, other accents play an important role in the representation of spoken English. This happens in two ways – firstly, core characters occur in those dialogues which are used to introduce or practise new language, and secondly, several of these dialogues have an additional recording which is paused for use in drilling. Thus students are not only exposed to a range of 'native speaker' accents, they are also encouraged to treat them equally as models for imitation. In addition, as Table 4.7 shows, regional UK accents are not so clearly associated with what might be seen as lower-status jobs. The production manager, who is one of the core characters, the radio announcer and the engineer listed below all have regional UK accents, as does a further core character, who is a naval engineering student.

Table 4.7 *Building Strategies*: Distribution of jobs according to RP/modified RP and regional UK accents

Jobs in which speakers have RP/modified RP accents	Jobs in which speakers have regional UK accents
Shoe shop manageress [*sic*]; supermarket cashier; secretaries; physicist; journalist; folk singer; radio DJ; radio announcers; radio interviewer; radio game show compere; doctor; policewoman; racing driver; novelist	Production manager for electrical components company; policemen; radio announcer; engineer; shop assistants; secretary

Outer/expanding circle accents correspond to a diverse set of high-achieving fictional characters composed of students, an Olympic athlete, a computer programmer, an agricultural botanist and a virus specialist (as well as other characters whose jobs are not stated). That said, phonological variation is not accompanied in any instance by syntactic variation.

Zero drag, gender equality and professional success

Most reading and listening texts appear to have been produced for pedagogic purposes although some of the listening texts are unscripted so as to sound less artificial and the blurb on the back of the student's book points out that 'a number of contemporary edited texts' have been included for the development of reading. However, it is not made clear

Table 4.8 *Building Strategies*: Number of units in which Threshold Level topics are addressed

Topic	Personal identification	House and home	Trade, profession, occupation	Free time, entertainment	Travel	Relations with other people	Health and welfare
Number of units	6	3	9	2	7	3	1
Topic	Shopping	Food and drink	Services	Places	Foreign language	Weather	Other
Number of units	3	2	2	4	1	1	–

what kind of editing took place or which texts are referred to. However, as Table 4.8 shows, the topics of these texts relate closely to the Threshold Level list, with individual units often featuring more than one topic.

It is clear that the topics which receive most attention are 'trade, profession, occupation', 'travel' and 'personal identification'. However, there is considerable overlap in the treatment of these and work, travel and the exchange of information about the self are closely linked throughout the coursebook. Against this background is a set of fictional core characters some of whom appear in each unit, and a number of non-fictional characters who generally, with some exceptions, are mentioned only in passing. Given their centrality to the coursebook as a whole, I shall discuss the fictional characters first.

The two central characters are Rod Nelson and Barbara Cooper. The former is a young electrical engineer from Canada who has recently arrived in Bristol. He is the first character about whom students are given any information and his centrality is signalled by the artwork. The first page of Unit 1 features only the title – 'A new start' – and a full-page colour photograph in which he is shown beginning his train journey to Bristol. Barbara is the manageress [*sic*] of a Bristol shoe shop, who becomes romantically involved with Rod. She is introduced on the facing page in a short written profile alongside a similar one about Rod – which serves to link them together. The accompanying artwork for each profile shows their faces separately framed and in close-up. Both are in their twenties, attractive and smiling. The use of close-ups and the way in which each represented participant meets the student-viewer's gaze is indicative of a personalized and direct mode of address. Following Kress and van Leeuwen (1996), this kind of demand can be seen as suggestive of social affinity. Rod and Barbara are characters with whom learners may identify – the frontality of the images facilitates maximum viewer involvement and, as we shall see, much of what happens in the units which follow is presented from the perspective of one or both of these characters.

Additional core characters are Barbara's parents, Peggy and Jack; Rod's flatmate, Paul Blake; and the couple they rent a flat from, Joan and Norman Ingrams. All have jobs – except Paul who studies naval engineering at the local polytechnic. Jack and Norman have white-collar jobs, while Peggy is a supermarket cashier and Joan is a part-time secretary. All are white and from different parts of the Anglophone world – Britain, New Zealand and Canada. The student's book informs us that Rod, Barbara and Paul are in their twenties, the Ingrams are in their thirties and the Coopers are about fifty, all of which suggests that the coursebook is aimed at a wide adult audience. What is immediately noticeable about the characterization of the fictional characters is the representation of women. Table 4.9 provides a breakdown of the total numbers of male and female representations in the texts, the artwork and the tapes.

Table 4.9   *Building Strategies*: Numbers of male and female representations

Sex of represented participants	Texts	Artwork	Tapes
Male	198	115	82
Female	203	114	85

These figures suggest an egalitarianism in the approach to the representation of women and men – in fact overall representations of women slightly outnumber those of men. Furthermore, as Table 4.10 shows, although men are represented as having a wider range of jobs, women do occupy a range of responsible positions.

Table 4.10   *Building Strategies*: Fictional characters according to jobs and sex

Male characters	Female characters
Electrical engineer; production manager; accountant; sea captain; farmer; journalist × 3; travel guide; shop assistant; radio announcer × 2; engineer; carpenter; librarian; teacher; agricultural botanist; physicist; headmaster; managing director; policeman × 2; patrolman; railway engineer; customs officer; boxer; driver; racing driver; novelist; radio game show compere; diplomat; radio journalist; fashion designer; model × 3	Shoe shop manageress [*sic*]; supermarket cashier; part-time secretary; radio reporter; typist/clerk; shop assistant; radio announcer × 2; computer programmer; hotelier; secretary; doctor; doctor/researcher; personnel director; writer × 2; teacher; policewoman × 2; shop owner; folk singer; gymnastics teacher; film star; news reader; model × 3

However, it is only when we look at actual instances that the nature and extent of this becomes apparent. Barbara plays an important role in the way women are represented in *Building Strategies*. From the start she is represented as both independent (she has a flat of her own) and successful (she manages a shoe shop). She initiates the friendship with

Rod by inviting him to visit her shop (Unit 2) and she is shown to telephone him to suggest social activities (Unit 8). Her independence with regard to relationships is underlined by her mother's comments in a letter:

> She's got a new boyfriend who works at Western with Jack. He's very nice – Canadian – but I don't think it's a very serious relationship. You know what Barbara is like. She has never been keen to settle down. (Unit 10)

What is significant about this comment is the way in which it represents Barbara as making decisions on such matters on her own terms. Although the relationship is maintained throughout the coursebook, the focus is primarily on Barbara as a working woman with a busy and exciting life. A mock-up of a magazine article in which she is profiled as 'Bristol Business Personality' of the month (Unit 9) refers to her as 'Ms' – then the relatively new title for women who were not defined in terms of their marital status. Interviewed in her flat on the 'sixth floor of a brand new apartment block with a view of the River Avon' (ibid.), Barbara refers to herself as 'a professional person' and is described evaluatively as a 'remarkable success'. In the accompanying artwork, in which Barbara lounges on her sofa surrounded by tasteful furnishings and contemporary artwork, her smiling gaze is addressed directly at the student-viewer and again is suggestive of social affinity.

Other fictional female characters with less central roles contribute to this type of representation of women as professionally successful. These include two champion swimmers (Unit 3); a computer programmer (Unit 7); two doctors – one of whom is a researcher into viruses (Unit 10); two writers – one of whom writes romantic fiction featuring a businesswoman (Unit 12, Unit 14); and a famous folk singer (Unit 14).

Of all the representations of fictional working women in the coursebook, the latter might be described as the most overtly ideological. The following exchange takes place at the end of an interview in which Laura Dennison, a Los Angeles-based folk singer, has been talking about her career to a male journalist after a performance in her native Bristol:

> Mike: And now you're a world famous star, a composer and a mother. How do you manage to do it?
> Laura: Do what?
> Mike: Combine a career with a family?
> Laura: Are you married with a family, Mr Sanders?

Mike: Yes, but ...
Laura: Well, do you find it difficult to be a journalist *and* a father?
Mike: But ...
Laura: Think about it, Mr Sanders. Goodbye! (Unit 14)

The exchange is significant because it goes beyond the type of representation referred to above in which women are shown to be generally
independent and successful. What we see here is a direct challenge
by a female speaker to the sexist assumption that having a successful
career and being a mother might be incompatible or at least present
difficulties. The exchange *is* a representation of an independent and
successful woman but it is also a representation of the ideological
challenge which feminism poses for a worldview in which such sexist
assumptions are seen as commonsensical. Interestingly, the comprehension questions which accompany the text make no reference to this
aspect of the content but refer exclusively to the singer's biographical details. Thus the comprehension questions may be said to limit
the range of possible student responses. This is particularly noticeable
here because the ideological aspect of the text is so clearly foregrounded. Reasons as to why this may be the case are explored in
Chapter 6.

At the same time the representation of men, particularly with regard
to housework and the rearing of children, is also suggestive of a more
egalitarian approach. For example, Rod and Paul are shown preparing a
meal (Unit 7), a male interviewee in a listening text lists 'washing up'
as one of his recent activities (Unit 13) and a controlled practice activity is accompanied by artwork showing a series of men, one of whom
is wearing an apron, putting children to bed, cooking, hoovering and
reading aloud to small children (Unit 8). Bessie Dendrinos (1992) argues
persuasively that the representation of Rod is consistent with an ideology of white-collar individualism. The biographical information given
in Unit 2 takes the form of a newspaper article and purports to be part
of a weekly series about people making a new start in life. The profile of
Rod – in many ways similar to that of Barbara – portrays an individual
completely in charge of his life who relocated to Bristol because he was
bored and wanted adventure. Such new starts are presented as normal
and unproblematic throughout the coursebook: the Ingrams relocated
to the UK from New Zealand; Laura Dennison and her family moved to
Los Angeles; Jack decides to apply for work relocation to the south of
France as industrial action looms in Bristol; Paul also hopes to get a job

abroad when he finishes his degree; and Barbara moves to Canada in the final unit, having become engaged to Rod. Such characters can be seen as early examples of the 'self-programmable labour' (Castells 2000) referred to in Chapter 1 – their high degree of 'zero drag' (Bauman 2007) prefiguring a proliferation of such characters in subsequent generations of coursebooks. A similar move towards equality in the representation of gender is suggested by the non-fictional characters referred to in the material. These include Prince Charles, Princess Diana, Mrs Thatcher, Queen Christina of Sweden, El Greco, Napoleon, Captain Cook, Amy Johnson and female band Bananarama. Three units also contain longer-reading texts devoted exclusively to non-fictional characters – both male and female. These are Elvis Presley, Winnie Mandela and the Olympic ice skating champions Jayne Torvill and Christopher Dean. In the case of Torvill and Dean, the point of view is celebratory of their dedication, talent and individual determination – they are evaluated positively as 'the perfect pair', who achieve 'unbelievably brilliant' competition scores and who have foregone having children and the acquisition of material comforts 'to do something different, to achieve something special' (Unit 3). Elvis Presley too is celebrated – although somewhat differently – in the words of his detractors as 'the most dangerous thing to hit civilization since the atom bomb' (Unit 14). Yet the text credits him with helping to change the attitudes of the older generation – although what these attitudes were is not explained. Both texts celebrate individualism and are accompanied by sensory orientation artwork. The Torvill and Dean reading is accompanied by a colour photograph of the skaters bathed in warm golden light underneath a headline with is suggestive of neon lighting, while the Elvis reading features a close-up of the singer's face caught in a smiling gesture of 'licensed withdrawal' (Goffman 1979: 57) as he stares into the middle distance. This term refers to a turning away by the represented participant from an element which may or may not be visible in the photograph or, as in this instance, from meeting the gaze of the imagined viewer. The effect is to mark the represented participant off as individual or somehow different.

However, the reading about Winnie Mandela is different from these in a number of ways. Firstly, the artwork connotes seriousness not only through the use of black-and white photography but also through the way in which the text appears to have been torn from a newspaper or magazine – thereby adding to a sense of the topicality of the subject matter. Furthermore, the text is about a female political figure actively engaged in the struggle against a political system which was still in place at the time the coursebook was published. The text represents her positively as 'one of the heroines of the black activist movement', 'a founder member of Soweto's Black Parents Association' and as someone who speaks out 'tirelessly and fearlessly for justice'. Authorial point of view is also clear in its attitude towards the South African authorities who 'have imprisoned her', 'stopped her from travelling', 'kept her in her home', 'searched and constantly harassed her', banished her', 'forced her to live in the Orange Free State' and 'punished her'. The text makes it clear that the reasons for this treatment are not those offered by the authorities:

> She has suffered all these things because the police say that she has broken the law. But in reality, they have punished her because she has become, like her husband, a leader of the black nationalist movement. (Unit 14)

Although the text is about a well-known figure's political struggle against an oppressive regime, as with the Laura Dennison interview, the comprehension activities do not address this aspect of content and focus instead on checking understanding of facts.

With regard to representations of race more generally in the coursebook, clearly identifiable black and Asian characters occur in a further seven units. In some cases it is simply a case of being included in artwork – for example, colour drawings feature black and Asian characters engaged in a variety of domestic activities (Unit 3 and Unit 8); a listening exercise about three athletes is accompanied by a black-and-white photograph of an unidentified black male runner (Unit 3); and at least two of the six models in a fashion show are black and Asian (Unit 16). Extended listening activities feature speakers from Jamaica, India and Japan talking about their impressions (not always favourable) of English food, weather and people (Units 2 and 12). Two short controlled practice texts feature photographs of Maria, a black student from an unnamed country, and give details of her likes and dislikes and her (generally favourable) opinions of Britain (Unit 2). In addition, there are also two black British characters, both of whom feature in photographic artwork – Barbara's friend Ruth who calls to visit her one day after work (Unit 5) and Terry (mentioned only in passing) who attended the same school when they were children (Unit 10). The teacher's book points out that *Building Strategies* aims to 'give a picture of a real community in Britain, and some cultural information about Britain in general' (Abbs and Freebairn 1984b: v). So although all the core characters are white, *Building Strategies* could be said to construct a picture of Britain – mainly at the level of artwork – in which an element of racial diversity forms part of the backdrop.

Playing Rod and Barbara

Given the focus on functional language it is not surprising that considerable emphasis is placed on various types of speaking activities. These consist of dialogue repetition, controlled practice pair work (e.g. students rehearse functional exchanges with appropriate responses), drills, role plays and discussions. Role plays are of two types – the majority are those in which students play themselves and a smaller number in which they assume the role of one of the core characters or a character referred to in the coursebook. The teacher's book points out that these are designed to enable the students to integrate the language learnt in the more controlled activities into extended speaking. Altogether there are 20 role plays and five discussions, all of which relate to unit topics. Two role plays involve students playing Rod; another involves students playing the parts of Barbara and her largely professional group of friends from school talking about where they live, their job and their 'news'; and a fourth involves the same group being interviewed for the local paper. Students are also asked to imagine themselves as either Torvill or Dean telephoning their parents to tell them of their success in the Helsinki Olympics, as a successful detective story writer and as an Olympic boxer. Individual professional success is a key factor in the majority of these roles, as is personal mobility – none of Barbara's friends lives in Bristol any longer and the Olympic boxer is about to leave Britain for a new life in Spain. Even in role plays where students play themselves mobility of various types is a key factor – so students talk about holiday plans, apologize for not have written or telephoned while they were travelling, arrange to meet at the airport and discuss moving abroad after being made redundant.

That said, unlike *Connections, Building Strategies* is more serious in terms of its content and at times this can be overtly political – as in the case of the reading about Winnie Mandela and the interview with Laura Dennison. The difference between the two coursebooks is most noticeable with regard to the representation of gender which reveals the impact of the discourse of feminism. Women, through their numerical presence in the coursebook and more particularly through the representation of Barbara, are shown as independent and professionally successful, while men, mainly in the artwork, are shown as playing an active part in rearing children and doing housework. At the same time, congruent with the Threshold Level aims to prepare students for more than tourist interactions, *Building Strategies* introduces a range of language functions that go beyond the formulaic language of service encounters, along with information on formal and informal registers and ways of expressing politeness in both speaking and writing exercises.

Overall in terms of identity, we can say that students are actively encouraged to identify with the cast of young professional and successful characters. The use of demand photographs in which Rod and Barbara meet the gaze of the student-viewer, their general attractiveness, youthfulness, independence and success, the unfolding narrative of their relationship (about which students are invited to speculate) and the fact that students are asked to assume their identities on occasion in role plays and dialogues may be said to constitute what Althusser (1971) refers to as 'interpellation' – a hailing, in this case, to both the ideological and subject position of white-collar individualism in which success, mobility, gender equality and personal satisfaction appear largely as unproblematic givens. In *Building Strategies*, English is given a set of associations very unlike those found in *Connections* and, as we shall see, these will ultimately prove more enduring.

5
Representational Repertoires 2: *The New Cambridge English Course 2* and *The New Edition New Headway Intermediate*

Introduction

The New Cambridge English Course 2 (Swan and Walter 1990a) (hereafter *Cambridge English 2*) is the second in a four-book course. Unlike the other coursebooks analyzed here, the title does not revolve around a single unifying metaphor but relies instead on the connotative power of the word 'Cambridge' to establish its identity. This is made salient on the front and back cover of each book through capitalization of the entire word and the use of larger font than that used for all other words in the title or in the blurb. Through association with the name of a prestigious university and a set of globally recognized English language examinations (e.g. Cambridge First Certificate) and English language teaching qualifications (e.g. Diploma in English Language Teaching to Adults), the title may be said to suggest a high level of symbolic educational value. A similar conclusion is reached by Littlejohn (1992), who noted that coursebooks produced by publishing houses other than Cambridge University Press to prepare students for the Cambridge First Certificate examination often featured the word 'Cambridge' more saliently on the cover than the name of the actual publisher.

A certain amount of 'untidy' natural language

The *Cambridge English* course, first published in 1984, was distinct from the outset in its incorporation of unscripted dialogues recorded in naturalistic settings. The introduction to the teacher's book points out that while most students benefit from having language 'tidied up' for them, they also 'need to encounter a certain amount of 'untidy' natural language' so as to trigger their 'unconscious mechanisms for acquiring languages' and to 'train [them] to understand natural speech' (Swan and Walter 1990a: VIII—IX). Thus the introduction draws attention to the inclusion of 'real-life' recordings so that students are exposed to 'natural speech (in a variety of accents)' (ibid.: IX). These recordings contain many of the features associated with spoken English such as hesitation and reformulation, as indeed do many of the scripted dialogues and monologues. Furthermore, some of the differences between written and spoken English are explicitly addressed. For example, Lesson 2 presents students with a list of discourse markers and fillers (explained in the teacher's notes as typical of spoken English) and asks them to identify which occur in a series of taped dialogues.[1] Lesson 8 focuses on ellipsis and the chunking of subordinate or coordinate clauses, as exemplified in the following extract:

> Lorna: And then Janet turned up. As usual. Just when I was trying to finish some work.
> George: So what did you do?
> Lorna: Had lunch with her.
> George: Where did you go? Somewhere nice?
> Lorna: No. Just the pub around the corner. A pie and a pint, you know. (ibid: 28)

The teacher's book points out that students are not required to reproduce such features, but that they should be able to recognize them in the speech of others. In this instance students are simply asked to identify all examples of ellipsis in the dialogue. Thus *Cambridge English 2* goes one step further than *Building Strategies* in the approach to the teaching of spoken language by explicitly drawing attention to this feature. The authors also make it clear in the introduction that 'the course teaches British English, but illustrates other varieties as well' (ibid.: VIII) – although it becomes clear this is only at the phonological level. They also state that the course 'presupposes a European-type educational background' (ibid.), which would appear to refer to the assumed degree of familiarity with iconic North American and European cultural figures mentioned in the units and the inclusion of what are described as 'riskier' speaking activities (referred to below).

The introduction also suggests that a 'complete English language course will incorporate at least eight main syllabuses' (ibid.). These are listed as vocabulary; grammar; pronunciation; notions; functions; situations; topics; and skills, the content of which aims to prepare students 'to understand and produce English well enough to handle a variety of everyday situations and topics with relative ease (around the level of the Council of Europe's 'Threshold' level)' (ibid.). As might be expected, given the multi-syllabus approach, both lexis and phonology receive detailed treatment. The authors state that more than 900 new words and expressions have been included and that these contribute to a core vocabulary of common and useful words, which is systematically taught. Just how this core was established is not stated but the treatment of lexis is systematic – individual units introduce topic-related lexical sets and each unit concludes with a list of items to be learnt or revised. This includes individual lexemes, various types of chunks (e.g. Lesson 1: I'd like to introduce...; so much) and complete expressions (e.g. Lesson 1: I didn't catch your name) related to the situational and functional syllabuses.

Phonology receives similarly detailed attention, and across the units – including revision and test sections – students have their attention drawn to a wide range of features. These include individual sounds; distinctions between pairs of sounds; weak forms; word and sentence stress; contractions; rhythm; intonation; the range of sounds corresponding to different letters of the alphabet; and the use of phonetic script. In general, pronunciation work is linked to the grammatical or lexical syllabuses so that, for example, Lesson 7 on past tenses includes a focus on the pronunciation of –*ed* endings. The emphasis throughout is predominantly on recognition rather than production – a point which is foregrounded in the introduction. The authors state that, in addition to being comprehensible, students must be able to understand people 'with different accents speaking in natural conditions (not just actors speaking standard English in recording studios' (ibid.). What is interesting about this is the implicit association between 'standard English' and accent – a point which is reinforced in notes to the teacher throughout the coursebook, particularly with regard to certain RP sounds. For example, the notes corresponding to Lesson 19 refer to the RP vowel sound in words such as 'know' and 'so' as 'standard British' (ibid.: 63), adding

> If students find the sound difficult, or are unwilling to make it, tell them that it is not very important for comprehensibility, and that in any case it is not used by many native English speakers except for speakers of standard British English.

The association of 'standard British English' with the RP accent runs throughout the ELT materials analyzed here. The phonetic symbols used

Table 5.1 *Cambridge English 2*: Total numbers of units according to range of accents

Accent	RP/modified RP	Regional UK	International inner circle	Outer/ expanding circle
Exclusive occurrences: number of units	16	–	–	–
Co-occurrences: number of units	17	13	11	2
Occurrences: total number of units	33	13	11	2

in *Cambridge English 2* (and indeed the dictionaries produced by the ELT industry) are a selection of International Phonetic Alphabet (IPA) symbols used for the transcription of the RP accent only. That said, a degree of phonological variation is included on the coursebook tapes. RP/modified RP is used to frame all units and functions as the authoritative voice of the coursebook. Table 5.1 above shows that accents on the RP continuum are also the most salient in the coursebook, featuring exclusively in 16 units (out of a total of 36) and co-occurring with a range of other accents in a further 17. International inner circle accents, which are exclusively North American, feature in almost as many units as do regional UK accents, while outer/expanding circle accents occur in only two units – and represent a total of two separate utterances.

Table 5.2 below shows that while RP/modified RP does not necessarily imply a high-status job, speakers with high-status jobs tend not to have regional UK accents.

Again we find regional UK accents are also used for criminal and gullible characters – in Lesson 27 Cockney van driver Frederick George Smith introduces himself as Frederick Getty Onassis (a name that could have occurred in *Connections*) to the easily impressed Janet Parker, a more Estuary-sounding shop assistant. Under the impression that he is a celebrity photographer, Janet is lured to a photographic studio and escapes an unspecified fate when the rightful owner of the studio appears. North American accents, on the other hand, are used mainly in pronunciation exercises and randomly for three attendees at a conference (Lesson 1), an unidentified shopper (Lesson 11), an explorer (Lesson 20) and an airline steward (Lesson 35), while outer/expanding circle accents are used by a conference attendee (Lesson 1) and a speaker

Table 5.2 Cambridge English 2: Distribution of jobs according to RP/modified RP and regional UK accents

Jobs in which speakers have RP/modified RP accents	Jobs in which speakers have RP/modified RP and regional UK accents	Jobs in which speakers have regional UK accents
Professor; doctor; taxi driver; BBC sports commentator; TV newsreader; explorer; 'bosses'; switchboard operator; waiters; airline check-in clerk; hotel receptionist; travel agent; railway employee; policewoman	Shop assistants	Dentist/dental receptionist; petrol pump attendant; doctor's secretary; commercial traveller; van driver

hailing a taxi (Lesson 35). In one unit, North American pronunciation is deliberately contrasted with 'northern English' and 'standard southern British' pronunciation (Lesson 8). Thus, we can say that while the RP cluster of accents retains a privileged position in the phonological representation of English, there is a clear effort in this coursebook to raise awareness about varieties of British and American accents throughout the material.

Greater inclusivity – gender, race and disability

As can be seen from Table 5.3 below, nine of the fifteen Threshold Level topics occur – with 'travel' recurring most frequently. As was the case

Table 5.3 Cambridge English 2: Number of units in which Threshold Level topics are addressed

Topic	Personal identification	Trade, profession and occupation	Free time, entertainment	Travel	Relations with other people
Number of units	1	3	2	7	2

Topic	Shopping	Food and drink	Services	Places	Other
Number of units	3	1	1	3	23

with *Building Strategies*, it is not uncommon for a unit to incorporate several topics.

However, it is clear that the majority of units address topics other than those suggested by van Ek (1975). In the introduction the authors point out that in addition to topics of general interest, the 'coursebook should include some controversial and emotionally engaging material, rather than sticking to bland middle-of-the-road topics' (Swan and Walter 1990a: VIII). They advise teachers not to 'drop a topic because it makes people angry', adding that 'rage can get people talking!' (ibid.: IX). Topics listed under 'other' include how indigenous people live; alien abduction; genetics and eye colour; surviving plane crashes; superstitions; 'tall' tales; how paper is made; and facts about famous people. Although some of these are treated lightly, the tone overall is serious and several topics would not be out of place in a geography or science textbook (e.g. the material on indigenous peoples). Such an approach is in line with the authors' view that ELT material, in addition to including content which is fictional and which draws on personal experience, should also include fact and allow for impersonal discussion.

There is also no storyline in *Cambridge English 2* – so characters are not developed and tend to occur in only one unit. Given the remarks made in the introduction about the material being geared towards students with a European-type educational background, it may be assumed that such references have been chosen with potential schematic knowledge in mind. In fact, the notes to the teacher suggest that if the famous people who form the basis for many of the activities in Lesson 26 are unfamiliar, they can be replaced with more familiar characters. These comprise mainly historical figures, artists, inventors and explorers, rather than contemporary celebrity-type figures – Queen Elizabeth I, Marconi, Louis Armstrong, Margaret Mitchell, Cervantes, J. F. Kennedy, Charlotte Bronte and Pierre and Marie Curie. Altogether, these elements combine to give the coursebook more of an 'educational' flavour in places – certainly more than in *Connections*.

In terms of representations of age, it is perhaps no surprise, given its overall adult orientation, that most units revolve around the activities of young and middle-aged adults. What is interesting about the non-fictional characters referred to is that they are predominantly male. Indeed, as Table 5.4 below shows, the majority of the represented participants throughout the coursebook are male.

However, the actual representations of women and men show that the influence of feminism is more pervasive than these figures might suggest. Women are represented or referred to consistently as professionals

Table 5.4 Cambridge English 2: Numbers of male and female representations

Sex of represented participants	Texts	Tasks	Tapes	Artwork
Male	76	54	171	260
Female	47	48	133	165

or as occupying positions of power in the workplace. Thus, students practise a jigsaw dialogue in which a character at a conference is told that his sister is 'a fine doctor' (Lesson 1). Businesswoman Lorna arrives home from work and tells partner George about her busy day at the office (Lesson 8). Mrs Rask, president of the fictional country Fantasia, is also a 'distinguished physicist' and 'former Olympic athlete who won a silver medal for the high jump' (Lesson 14). The changing role of women is suggested in the statistics provided about Fantasia. These show that the average number of children per family has fallen from 4.5 in 1900 to a current figure of 2 and that the percentage of women in paid employment has risen from 18 per cent to 79 per cent over the same period (Lesson 14). Elsewhere, Barbara, who is good at tennis, swimming and dancing, is also identified as a university physics lecturer (Lesson 19). And finally, in a number of short texts, women are referred to as bosses (Lesson 22).

Women are also represented in less traditional roles: for example, leader of an assault course for members of a youth club (Lesson 3); taxi driver (Lesson 13); explorer and pilot (Lesson 20); and, in the domestic sphere, painting and decorating (Lesson 30). They are also shown to be brave and determined. Thus, 17-year-old Juliana Koepke, sole survivor of a plane crash in which her own mother dies, makes her way out of a jungle after a 10-day ordeal involving wild animals, physical injuries, broken glasses and no shoes – in addition to a lack of food (Lesson 7). On another occasion, female calm in the face of danger is contrasted with male panic (Lesson 20). In the following listening text, A (female) and B (male) are explorers whose plane is in difficulty:

A: We're in trouble, Pete. The engine's breaking up.
B: Oh, God! We're going to crash!
A: There goes the engine.
B: We're going to hit those rocks!
A: No, we're not Pete. We're OK. I'm going to take us down, all right?
B: What are you doing? The plane's turning over!

A: Relax, Pete. I know what I'm doing, right?

B: Relax? Relax? What do you mean, relax? We're both going to die! I don't want to die! I'm too young to die!

A: Nobody's going to die, Pete. You've got to keep calm. Now listen. I'm going to try to put the plane down over there.

B: Over where?

A: On that patch of hard sand, just ahead. But it's going to be a rough landing. So put your head down, and put your arms over you head. Landing in ten seconds.

B: Oh, God! We're going to crash! I'm not going to look!

A: Landing now, Pete.

B: (*Screams*). (Swan and Walter 1990a: 65)

The woman's voice on the accompanying tape remains calm throughout, while that of the man becomes increasingly hysterical. It is interesting to note that, in addition to landing the plane successfully, the woman also has the time and the presence of mind to give the man advice for the crash landing. Elsewhere, particularly in the artwork, men are shown pushing a pram (Lesson 10); looking after small children (Lesson 13); ironing, cooking, washing dishes and shopping for food (Lesson 30). As can be seen in Table 5.5, although men occupy a wider range of jobs overall, women are also shown to occupy positions of responsibility.

These representations of women and men contrast strongly with those of so-called traditional peoples elsewhere in the coursebook. Lesson 4, in which the linguistic focus is the use of the present simple for

Table 5.5   *Cambridge English 2*: Fictional characters according to jobs and sex

Male characters	Female characters
Doctor × 2; BBC sports commentator; footballer × 5; shop assistant × 6; President; dentist/dental receptionist; petrol pump attendant; waiter; TV newsreader; bus driver; university lecturer; explorer × 2; waiter; boss × 4; commercial traveller; airline check-in clerk; van driver/photographer; bank worker/soldier; railway employee; airline check-in clerk; policewoman; airline steward	Professor; shop assistant × 5; taxi driver; President/physicist; hotel receptionist; airline check-in clerk; university lecturer; explorer × 2; boss × 2; switchboard operator; doctor's secretary; travel agent

habitual action and factual statements, features a jumbled text about Australian Aborigines and Amazonian Indians.[2] The accompanying artwork consists of two separately framed colour photographs. The first depicts an all-male group of near-naked Aboriginal men dancing and playing musical instruments, while the second shows two near-naked Amazonian women, each with a baby, and includes no men – an arrangement which might be said to imply indirectly a strict division of gendered roles in such societies. In fact, the gendered division of labour is made explicit in a colour drawing of Inuit men and women which accompanies the controlled practice activities. In social semiotic terms the drawing is largely conceptually structured – that is, the represented participants are arranged in such a way that they suggest essential characteristics of Inuit society. Thus a foregrounded man is shown about to harpoon a seal, while a woman sits cross-legged and sewing outside an igloo in the middle-ground of the drawing. This arrangement associates the woman more closely with the home and domestic work while the man is associated with the provision of food. Unlike the majority of professional, stereotype-breaking women featured in other units, these indigenous women (and men) are emblematic of ways of life which may be said to exist *beyond* the predominantly English-speaking world represented throughout the coursebook, in which gender roles are shown to be less strictly delineated. Interestingly, the lesson concludes with a discussion in which students are asked to speculate on how Eskimos live today. The teacher's notes point out that the 'large majority of Eskimos have never seen an igloo' (Swan and Walter 1990a: 15) and nowadays live in houses and travel by car. Thus the traditional way of life represented in the artwork is explicitly associated with the past, or, in the case of the Australian Aborigines and the Amazonian Indians, living the past in the present.

At the same time *Cambridge English 2*, which is located predominantly in Britain, goes further than its predecessors in its inclusive representation of race *within* the English-speaking world. Lesson 19, entitled 'Their children will have blue eyes', focuses on 'will' and 'may' for prediction in the context of a text about the genes related to eye colour. The text and accompanying exercises are illustrated by two colour drawings of heterosexual couples in which the women are pregnant. In the first of these, Lee, a young black man, stands behind Carol, his pregnant white partner. One hand rests conventionally and protectively on her shoulder, while the other holds a bag of shopping. Less conventional, certainly for a coursebook published in 1990, is the representation of a couple as being composed of a white woman and a black man.

It will be recalled from Chapter 1 that the first snapshot was also from this coursebook and featured a white man borrowing money from a black friend. I suggested there that the image was representative of a stance being taken on multiculturalism by the publishers. Multiculturalism is a contested term and very different typologies have been produced (e.g. Kincheloe and Steinberg 1997; Parekh 1997). Block (2006) suggests that interpretations tend towards either a static or a reified view in which society is understood to comprise sets of culturally distinct groups with fixed boundaries between them, or a more dynamic or processual view which implies not only porosity between groups, but the emergence of new and hybrid cultural forms and practices. The latter view, often labelled 'critical multiculturalism' (Kincheloe and Steinberg 1997; Parekh 1997), entails the abandonment of monolithic views of national culture and a concomitant concern with the distribution of power as related (in particular) to the ethnically distinct groups within such societies (O'Sullivan *et al.* 1994). It is a view which suggests the transformation of dominant cultures and the status quo (and by implication the minority cultural groups as well), rather than the straightforward integration or absorption of such groups.

Images such as those of Lee and Carol, essentially of inter-racial contact and harmony, may be said to draw predominantly on a discourse of 'liberal multiculturalism' (Kincheloe and Steinberg 1997) – a position which ignores issues related to power while maintaining the sameness and equality of human beings everywhere regardless of the superficial differences which may exist between them. In the 13 units which feature black, Asian and/or characters from so-called traditional societies there are no references to issues related to power or its unequal distribution in the societies inhabited by these represented participants.

A second couple in Lesson 19 is also of interest with regard to the representation of race. Both partners are black and both have jobs which might be seen as characteristically middle-class – Milton teaches economics at a university and Barbara is a physics lecturer. The arrangement is similar to that in the drawing of Lee and Carol. The man stands behind his partner with one hand protectively on her upper arm, while the woman rests a hand on her abdomen. Goffman (1979) suggests that such self-touching gestures are typically associated with representations of women and can be read as an indication of the represented participant's sense of delicacy or self-worth. As with Carol and Lee, Barbara and Milton hold their bodies erect and smile confidently at the viewer.

Hall (1997b) argues that historically European representations of blackness – whether in the quantities of texts of various kinds produced under colonialism or in more contemporary media and advertising texts – have been characterized largely by stereotyping. This is understood as the 'exercise of symbolic violence' (ibid.: 259) against black people which reduces and essentializes their perceived differences to a set of simplified, fixed and exaggerated characteristics. Hall suggests that contestation of such practices has taken a number of forms, one of which is the celebration of difference. He offers, by way of example, the 'United Colours of Benetton' advertisements in the 1990s. In these, ethnically diverse models are used to construct a series of images in which difference and hybridity become signifiers of beauty and – precisely because of the existence of racism – suggestive of an alternative more harmonious view of race relations. Thus the Benetton brand associates itself with what Kincheloe and Steinberg (1997: 15) refer to as 'pluralist' multiculturalism in which the focus is on difference and where issues of power are elided in favour of an idealized and colourful egalitarianism.

Clearly the artwork described here has none of the allure of the Benetton advertisements. These are line drawings, not high-tech, high-modality advertisements for a global company – although I will suggest later they do have a promotional dimension. However, the frontality of the images and the smiling demands of the represented participants are suggestive of social affinity. They can be said to constitute a deliberate contestation to stereotypical representations of blackness in the sense that one is a positive image of racial harmony, and the other is a positive image of black people in which the focus is on achievement. Milton and Barbara are lecturers in established academic disciplines, and, interestingly, the biographical information about the first couple reveals that Lee, a bus driver, also studies mathematics at night school – a fact which might be said to suggest his commitment to self-improvement. Taken alongside the other representations of race, they form a visually salient element in the coursebook's representational repertoire.

At the same time, *Cambridge English 2* also includes representation of disability. The artwork in Lesson 28 on physical description features a diverse set of characters which includes a woman in a wheelchair. This is the only representation of disability in the coursebook but it is noticeable nonetheless, precisely because such images are rare. In fact, it is the only image of disability in a coursebook of the time that I am aware of. But equally significant in my view is the fact that the word 'wheelchair' does not appear in the exercise itself. Furthermore, it appears neither in the list of lexical items at the end of the lesson, nor in the teacher's notes. On the one hand, the artwork can be seen as exemplifying an inclusive representational practice – that is, one which seeks to include a wide cross-section of society, and similar in many ways to the afore-mentioned representations of gender and race. On the other hand, the exercise is silent about the represented participant's disability – the precise reason the character has been included – which means she must be described mainly in terms of clothes and hair. Such an approach is congruent with liberal multiculturalism, which Kincheloe and Steinberg (1997: 10) say is typified by 'colour blindness'. By the same token, the artwork here can be read as an example of disability blindness – that is, the disability is represented visually but is not referred to verbally. As we shall see in Chapter 6, the interviews with the publishers serve to shed some explanatory light on the infrequency of such representational practices.

I conclude this section with a brief comment on the artwork over-all. It is entirely in colour – however, although production values are clearly high (e.g. glossy cover, good quality paper), little use is made of photography and most artwork consists mainly of realist-style drawings. Given the overall success of the first edition of the course, it is highly unlikely that a second edition was seen as a financial risk necessitating less expensive artwork. Rather, I would suggest the drawings are signi-fiers of overall continuity between the two editions. The first edition relied heavily on line drawings – as indeed did many coursebooks from the period. In fact, many of the same drawings from the first edition reappear in the second edition. What is different in terms of 'look' is the pervasive use of colour and a new A4 size. In this way, it could be suggested, *Cambridge English 2* more closely resembles the newly success-ful *Headway* course, while still retaining key elements of an established brand image.

Talking about the self

In common with the coursebooks surveyed so far, speaking activities often involve students talking about themselves. Thus students elicit and exchange information about their leisure activities, days in their life when everything went wrong, similarities and differences between them and other members of the class, preferences, travel and food expe-riences, their views on superstitions and important facts about their own life/important events in their own life. They also engage in controlled practice dialogues in which they rehearse functions such as requests, offers and making arrangements, along with discussions (e.g. what to take from a selection of supplies in the event of a plane crash) and short role plays related to service encounters, the above-mentioned functions, talking about a day at work and a job interview. In addition, students have their attention drawn to formal and informal expressions and degrees of politeness (e.g. 'Have you got a fiver?' contrasted with 'Could you lend me a fiver?'), while writing activities function mainly to provide further practice of language points. Thus students produce reports on the personal habits of members of the class, notes to friends in which they make requests and offers, descriptive accounts of aspects of their town/country, a poster advertising their country as a tourist destination and a job application letter.

Overall, these speaking and writing topics are broadly similar to those described in Chapter 4 – although there is (along with an absence of drills) a tendency, concomitant with the communicative methodology referred to in the introduction, towards greater exploitation of the naturally occurring information gap between students. It will also be recalled that the introduction points out that the material is aimed at students with a European-style educational background. While presupposing a certain type of schematic knowledge, this seems also to mean the inclusion of some slightly 'riskier' topics. So, for example, students are asked to discuss if they would tell their married partner if they fell in love with someone else (Lesson 30), and in another exercise they are asked to write a short speech to try and convince their peers to do things such as change their religion (Lesson 23). Elsewhere the teacher's notes suggest students might be asked to speculate about the kind of children that would result if pairs of students were to get married (Lesson 19). Such activities are held to be 'important both pedagogically and psychologically' (Swan and Walter 1990a: 71), as the authors suggest students are motivated by being given the opportunity to use English to entertain, surprise, inform and move each other. They are also, as Anderson (2002) and Kullman (2003) have suggested, typical of an increasingly learner-centred pedagogy in which certain limited aspects of students' lives come to form the basis of much of what goes on in the classroom.

In conclusion we can say that *Cambridge English 2* builds on the representational repertoires established in *Building Strategies*. Although few places are mentioned, the preponderance of British characters suggests the coursebook is located mainly in Britain. The representation of these characters in terms of gender and race (and to a much lesser extent, disability) forms a distinctive element in the representational repertoire. The representations of race within the English-speaking world may be said to draw on a discourse of liberal multiculturalism in which inter-racial harmony and personal success are emphasized. Similarly, although overall the number of women is lower than the number of men, the representations of women emphasize their professional success, in addition to their physical strength and bravery.

The *Headway* course

The *Headway* course is generally seen by the ELT industry as a remarkable publishing phenomenon. Holliday (2005: 41) uses the term 'cultural icon' for certain concepts, individuals and artefacts which are revered and sustained within, what he refers to as, the ideological structure of Western TESOL, and he suggests, justifiably in my view, that one such cultural icon is the *Headway* course, which first appeared in 1986. Anderson's (2002) observation that it was used in every school he taught in resonates with my own experience of teaching and training in several different international settings over a number of years. One OUP editor I spoke to told me it is so successful that sales from the course alone could fund an entire publishing house (personal communication, OUP, 2000). At the time of writing, the *Headway* course is in its third edition and consists of five levels. The overall title may be said to connote progress, with the individual component titles suggesting incremental steps along the way (e.g. *Headway Pre-Intermediate, Headway Intermediate*, etc.).

Primacy of the RP cluster of accents

The New Edition New Headway Intermediate (Soars and Soars 2003) (hereafter *Headway Intermediate*) has a clearly foregrounded grammar syllabus. The detailed contents pages in the student's book lists grammar first in the breakdown of content for each unit (followed by vocabulary, everyday English, reading, speaking, listening and writing) and each grammar point is made salient though the use of headings in differently coloured font. Vocabulary is treated systematically. Each unit has a vocabulary section in which lexical sets related to the thematic content of the unit are introduced and practised. In addition, individual units address areas such as collocation, compounding and idioms, as well as providing information on how vocabulary can be recorded by students. Each unit ends with a section entitled 'Everyday English'. Altogether these focus on a disparate range of items which include functions (e.g. requests and offers); notions (e.g. expressing quantity); 'social expressions' (e.g. Take care!); numbers and dates; setting specific language (e.g. Hop in!; Just looking, thanks); telephone language (e.g. The line's busy at the moment); signs (e.g. Please wait to be seated); and informal British English (e.g. These trainers cost ninety quid!). The tapescripts for these

Table 5.6 *Headway Intermediate*: Total numbers of units according to range of accents

Accent	RP/modified RP	Regional UK	International inner circle	Outer/ expanding circle
Exclusive occurrences: number of units	–	–	–	–
Co-occurrences: number of units	12	12	10	6
Occurrences: total number of units	12	12	10	6

sections and for the scripted dialogues which occur throughout each unit include limited representation of features of spoken English such as ellipsis, fillers, hesitation and so on, although the accompanying activities do not draw students' attention to these.

With regard to the phonological representation of English, Table 5.6 shows the breakdown of the range of accents deployed.

As with the other coursebooks surveyed, RP/modified RP is used to frame all units and also predominates within each unit. However, all units feature regional UK accents and all but two units feature international inner circle accents – most commonly from North America. Although six units contain outer/expanding accents, only three feature speakers with extended turns. The same voice, most probably that of an actor, appears to be used for a Japanese speaker in one unit and for a Korean in another and in neither case is there any syntactic variation. Elsewhere, a speaker who is clearly labelled as being from an expanding circle country speaks with an RP/modified RP accent (Unit 10). Although the RP cluster of accents is used for a wide variety of speakers with different types of employment, as can be seen in Table 5.7 below the tendency is for speakers with higher-status jobs not to speak with regional UK accents.

In line with *Connections* and *Cambridge English 2* regional UK accents are also used to index criminality and antisocial behaviour. Thus a woman in Unit 12 who is sent to prison along with her drunken unemployed husband for antisocial behaviour has a clear regional UK accent. Her speech contrasts with that of a neighbour whose accent is more noticeably on the RP continuum. The differences between the families are also reinforced through the artwork. The RP-speaking woman

Table 5.7   *Headway Intermediate*: Distribution of jobs according to RP/modified RP and regional UK accents

Jobs in which speakers have RP/modified RP accents	Jobs in which speakers have RP/modified RP and regional UK accents	Jobs in which speakers have regional UK accents
Interior designer; 'clown doctor'; manager; fast food sales assistant; waitresses; weatherwoman; airline check-in person; airhostess; newsreaders; barman; cellist; businesswoman; personal assistant; professor	Telephonists; taxi drivers	Shop assistants; bus driver; job interviewer

is pictured holding a baby in her kitchen, while her male partner does the washing-up. In a separate photograph the regionally accented couple are pictured scowling at the camera, with the man leaning forward aggressively towards the imagined viewer. As with all the coursebooks surveyed, the RP cluster of accents continues to occupy a privileged position in the phonological representation of English.

Choice, travel and spectacularly successful cosmopolitans

From its first appearance the *Headway* course was distinguished by the use of long texts to provide reading and listening practice. The blurb draws attention to the fact that these are 'up-to-date' and have 'global appeal'. Table 5.8 below shows that, of the Threshold Level topics, 'travel' receives the most attention. In fact, in addition to being a major topic in seven units, it also occurs in all 12 units. The topics grouped under the heading of 'other' include the wonders of the modern world; a Native American folk tale; the lives of two famous artists; teenage life; relocating to Spain; winning the lottery; charity appeals; various types of obsessive behaviour; a profile of Madonna; facts about the world; problems associated with modern lifestyles; and birth, marriage and death.

As is the case with most contemporary coursebooks (e.g. *Inside Out* by Kay and Jones (2000); *Natural English* by Gairns and Redman (2002); *New Cutting Edge* by Cunningham and Moor (2005)), *Headway Intermediate*

Table 5.8 *Headway Intermediate*: Number of units in which Threshold Level topics are addressed

Topic	House and home	Trade, profession and occupation	Free time entertainment	Travel	Relations with other people
Number of units	1	4	4	7	1
Topic	Shopping	Food and drink	Places		Weather Other
Number of units	1	2	3		1 7

has no storyline and units revolve around the aforementioned topics and an accompanying set of fictional and non-fictional characters. The latter include Neil Armstrong, Tom Cruise, Nicolas Cage, J. K. Rowling, Madonna, Guy Ritchie and Frank Sinatra. With the exception of Picasso and Penelope Cruz, it is clear that the list draws primarily on iconic Anglo-American figures and that it is also more of a celebrity list than those found in the other coursebooks in this study.

By now it will be clear that feminism has made a significant impact on the representational repertoires in successive generations of ELT coursebooks. This is a trend which is continued and nuanced further in *Headway Intermediate* – despite the fact that, as Table 5.9 shows, men predominate numerically. The only exception to this is the greater number of women's voices on the tapes.

Table 5.9 *Headway Intermediate*: Numbers of male and female representations

Sex of represented participants	Texts	Tasks	Tapes	Artwork
Male	147	145	237	241
Female	113	115	251	191

As might be expected, women are consistently represented in positions of power and prestige. So, for example, students read a lengthy text about Karen Saunders who runs her own London-based travel agency specializing in sending people 'all over the world on their dream holiday' (Soars and Soars 2003: 43). It is a glamorous job which involves 'working holidays four or five times a year' (ibid.) and provides Karen with multiple opportunities for exploring new places and shopping.

Table 5.10   Headway Intermediate: Fictional characters according to jobs and sex

Male characters	Female characters
Lawyer; paperboy; teacher; manager; fast food sales assistant; airline check-in clerk; taxi drivers × 2; telephonist; shop assistant; job interviewer; newsreader; meteorologist; ironworker; cook; sailor; actor × 2; conductor; bank employee; hotel receptionist; radio presenter; professor; policeman; lifeboat captain; lifeboat crew	UN Goodwill ambassador (film star, writer); interior designer × 2; 'clown doctor'; teacher; businesswoman × 3; waitress × 2; travel agent; weatherwoman; bus driver; telephonist; air hostess; shop assistant; interviewee for journalist job; newsreader; lawyer/trapeze artist; newspaper agony aunt; veterinary assistant; cellist; midwife × 2

As can be seen in Table 5.10 above, women in *Headway Intermediate* occupy a wide range of jobs.

In many cases attention is also drawn to the personal achievements of such women. It is worth detailing what this involves in some cases – for example:

- Kaori Sato holds an honorary position at the UN and has a special interest in children's health and education, a role which takes her to Africa every year (Unit 1). In addition to being a famous film star, she is a graduate of Tokyo University and the Tokyo Theatre School. She is also a best-selling author, and is married with two children.
- Nancy Mann applies for a job as a Geneva-based business journalist (Unit 7). Nancy was born in Argentina, and went to school in Buenos Aires. She studied modern languages and journalism at University College, London; spent a year working in Berlin for the BBC; and has travelled extensively. She also worked for a company called Intertec which involved trips to Japan to 'interview some Japanese business leaders' (ibid.: 55). She has been married twice.
- Swedish cellist Astrid Johnsson, we are told, 'has had an interesting life so far' (ibid.: 80). This has involved winning Young Musician of the Year when she was only 8; a scholarship to study at the Royal Academy of Music, London; and a Master of Music degree. She got married at 21, had a daughter at 23, divorced at 29 and remarried at 38. After her divorce she bought a flat in New York but moved to Paris when she met her second husband. She is currently based there where she lectures and teaches the cello. A successful composer, she has also won a prize for the Best European Film Soundtrack.

What makes these women different from those featured in the other coursebooks in this study is that their successes are so spectacular and that they themselves, in many cases, are cosmopolitans from expanding circle countries who are at home anywhere in the world. Such representations, I would suggest, serve to link English with a new kind of cosmopolitan identity in which spectacular success and mobility are the other key components.

Another development in the representation of women in this coursebook is that many of them are explicitly identified as mothers. It will be recalled that female representations in *Connections* were predominantly sexist and that the dependency of children on women was reinforced through the artwork. *Building Strategies* saw the appearance of a different type of woman. Barbara, the main female character, was single, childless, career-minded and not interested in 'settling down' – although the professionally successful Laura Dennison was identified as a mother (but, significantly, she was not depicted with children in the artwork). In fact, in *Building Strategies* and *Cambridge English 2*, where babies and children did feature, they were mostly associated with men – particularly so in the artwork. In contrast, *Headway Intermediate* repeatedly draws attention to the fact that professional women are often mothers. In her work on historical representations of motherhood in British women's magazines, Woodward (1997) notes a tendency from the 1990s onwards to represent women as both professionals *and* mothers. She also notes that such representations tend not to feature men. The figure of the 'independent mother' (ibid.: 265), she suggests, is 'partly a fantasy figure' who can 'have it all' (ibid.: 272), adding the following:

> This new 'figure' incorporates different elements of previous maternal subjectivities, drawing on different repertoires. For a woman to have a child without male support is not only more likely at this historical time, but also a more attractive and desirable proposition in terms of this representation of motherhood without stigma, although the magazines underplay economic problems. The addition of agency and sexuality to maternal identity make it especially attractive. (ibid.: 280)

Headway Intermediate does not go quite this far. Not surprisingly, all references to sexual independence are eschewed. However, husbands may be referred to, if not always represented in, artwork. A good example of this is provided in the profile of businesswoman Karen in Unit 11. In the first of two dialogues we see her in her role as mother, spending time playing the piano with her 4-year-old daughter and, in the second, we see her as suited boss, checking her busy schedule for the day with her assistant. Although the first dialogue refers to 'daddy', there is no visual representation of a man and the artwork clearly serves to reinforce the compatibility of active motherhood with a career outside the home (warm golden tint for the domestic photograph, naturalistic orientation for the much larger office photograph).

At the same time, elsewhere in the coursebook, a Native American folk tale is used to make an overtly feminist point – namely, that a boastful warrior, for all his bravery and ability to fight, can easily be defeated by a screaming baby (Unit 3). The implication is that it takes another kind of bravery to deal with small children – a fact already known to the woman who sets the challenge. Although men *are* also shown as caring fathers, overall it could be argued that the coursebook reasserts the right of career women to be represented as actively 'mothering' – but in such a way that this is not shown to compromise their right to power and prestige in the workplace.

The world of work features throughout *Headway Intermediate*, although it is a main topic in only four units. Work is repeatedly represented as a privileged means for the unproblematic realization or reinvention of the self along lines determined purely by personal choice. Such a view is concomitant with Giddens' (1991: 82) view that 'choice of work and work milieu forms a basic element of lifestyle orientations in the extremely modern division of labour.' Thus, three reading texts on 'dream jobs' in Unit 7 feature interviews with individuals who obtain a high level of personal fulfilment from doing unusual jobs. Stanley Karras relocated from London to Florida and became a 'hurricane hunter' after seeing a television programme. Linda Spelman gave up life as a lawyer to become a trapeze artist and travel the world. She advises readers to 'Go for it! You only live once, so why stay in a boring job?' (Soars and Soars 2003: 59), while Michael Doyle, a New York construction worker, is referred to as a 'cowboy in the sky' (ibid.: 59). Although dangerous, his job is well-paid and a source of pride and comradeship. The artwork shows Michael astride a girder staring into the middle distance in a gesture of 'licensed withdrawal' (Goffman 1979: 57), thereby signalling his uniqueness.

Elsewhere, individuals are shown to choose quality of life over 'life in the fast lane' – hence a listening exercise about a 45-year-old college graduate who is happy working as a 'paperboy' because it allows him to spend time with his family (although it should be pointed out he manages to earn $60,000 a year) (Unit 2). In the same unit there is a reading about a young woman who works as a clown in a hospital for sick children. Although the job is physically and emotionally demanding, it provides her with a deep sense of personal satisfaction. In another unit a couple decide to forego the good salaries and bad weather of England for the riskier prospect of growing lemons in Spain (Unit 8). The common thread in all these situations is choice. These individuals are, to borrow a term which Elspeth Probyn (1990, in Woodward 1997: 280) applies to the figure of the independent mother, members of a 'choiceoisie' – people whose lifestyle choices are unaffected by personal, financial or social constraints of any kind.

With the exception of the middle-aged paperboy, the above are all young adults. However, an interesting development in *Headway Intermediate* is the representation of middle-aged and elderly people as leading active and fulfiled lives – doing aerobics, travelling and meeting new people. These representations can also be combined with a clear feminist message – for example, in a writing exercise on 'describing a person' (Unit 9) students are presented with a model text about Emily Morgan. In her late fifties, she lives alone and has never married. Emily is described as 'quite young in spirit', with a 'warm, friendly smile' and 'still rather attractive' (Soars and Soars 2003: 116). Her days are spent reading, gardening and walking her dog – in addition to helping others in the village. Her niece, who provides the description, concludes by saying 'I hope I am as contented as she is when I am her age' (ibid.). This celebratory representation of a single contented woman is reinforced with sensory orientation artwork of a smiling Emily walking her dog in the park. The scene is appropriately autumnal, with shades of yellow and russet predominating.

On the subject of artwork, it should be pointed out that *Headway Intermediate* is the 'glossiest' of the coursebooks surveyed. All units are in full colour with the majority of artwork consisting of photographs, many with sensory rather than naturalistic orientation. A considerable amount of colour and shading is also used on the page to frame sections, to make examples and grammar points salient and to direct students to other part of the book. However, a more important feature is the fact that demand photographs occur in all units, with the exception of one. Students are repeatedly addressed directly through gaze by coursebook characters and, in social semiotic terms, are thereby encouraged to feel social affinity with a range of successful, individualistic, generally attractive, fun-loving and well-travelled English speakers.

It will be recalled that in *Building Strategies* this type of gaze was associated mainly with the central characters, Rod and Barbara – both of whom were from inner circle countries. One significant feature of the deployment of this type of artwork in *Headway Intermediate* is that such demands are made by a much wider range of international characters. Students, I would suggest, are no longer invited to feel affinity solely with English speakers from inner circle countries but also with cosmopolitan English speakers from the expanding circle. One typical example of this type of artwork is found in Unit 6 and features two Polaroid-type photographs which have been included in a letter from Soon-hee, a Korean language student from Seoul, to her friend Sandy in Melbourne, thanking her and her family for their hospitality on a recent study trip. The letter contains details of a subsequent trip to Perth and plans for future trips. The snapshots, which show Soon-hee individually and with her brother Sang-chul, are each examples of what Goffman (1979: 10) calls a 'private picture'. Such photographs, he suggests,

> are those designed for display within the intimate social circle of the persons featured in them...[in which]...[t]he individual is able to catch himself [*sic*] at a moment when – for him – he is in ideal surroundings, in association with socially desirable others, garbed in a self-enhancing way...and with a socially euphoric look on his face...[a] moment, in short, when he is in social bloom. (ibid.)

Thus a commonplace artefact such as the snapshot allows for the presentation of private aspects of the self, and when distributed among friends and family functions as an invitation to share something of the life of the represented participants. Such artwork may also be said to include the student-viewer in the intimate social circle of the cosmopolitan represented participants. Needless to say in both photographs the represented participants meet the gaze of the imagined viewer.

Concomitant with the tendency for more demand-type artwork and an increasingly cosmopolitan 'summoning look' (Goffman's term for gaze, 1979: 16) is, what might be called, a greater globalizing of content. Elsewhere I have suggested (Gray 2002: 157) that contemporary coursebooks show signs of being 'subtly deterritorialized' – by which I meant the way in which they are increasingly less exclusively located in the UK. This is true of *Headway Intermediate* which, while continuing to locate characters mainly in English-speaking parts of the world (e.g. the UK, the US and Australia), constantly refers to their experiences in other places or their plans to visit them (e.g. Mexico, France, Spain, Thailand, Japan, Brazil, Dubai and Tanzania – to list but a few). Linked to this are the 'up-to-date texts with global appeal' advertised in the blurb.

These are essentially celebrations of the benign version of globalization referred to in Chapter 1. For example, the main reading text in Unit 1, which is entitled 'It's a Wonderful World!', suggests that the technological and scientific achievements of the last 100 years constitute a set of wonders to rival those of the ancient world. These are the Internet, space travel, advances in health care, air travel, the Olympic Games, increased agricultural productivity and the fact nuclear weapons have not been used. The tone throughout is celebratory and replete with exclamation marks (e.g. 'Surely nothing has done more for the comfort and happiness of the human race than the advances in health care!', 'We are still here!' [Soars and Soars 2003: 10–11]).

Problems which might reasonably be associated with some of these developments are elided or reduced to as-yet-unresolved glitches in management. For example, issues around food production and distribution are addressed as follows:

> In 1724, Jonathan Swift wrote, 'Whoever makes two blades of grass or two ears of corn grow where only one grew before serves mankind better than the whole race of politicians'. In Europe our farmers have done this. In 1709, whole villages in France died of hunger. Now in Europe, we can't eat all the food we produce. If only politicians could find a way to share it with those parts of the world where there is famine. (Unit 1)

The elimination of famine is thereby linked with the ingenuity of farmers rather than with the structural changes which have taken place in Europe since the eighteenth century. As with most reading and writing exercises, student responses are largely restricted to comprehension questions which focus on retrieval of information from the text. The specific nature of the problem which politicians have not been able to solve in this instance is not made available for discussion – rather, the comprehension questions lead into a 'Talking about you' section in which students discuss topics such as their favourite website.

Other such items include a somewhat essentialist guide to good manners around the world in which a dubious set of cultural 'dos' and 'don'ts' are presented as hard and fast rules (e.g. 'In Russia, you must match your hosts drink for drink or they will think you unfriendly' [ibid.: 35]), and a celebratory biography of the pizza which suggests it is the quintessential global fast food. As with many of the reading exercises in *Headway Intermediate*, these texts are reproduced with headlines and authors' names to look as though they originally appeared in a magazine – although, in this instance, they do not appear in the acknowledgements.

A final aspect of the globalizing of content is the representation of black and Asian characters. In addition to the named characters mentioned above, much representation takes place at the level of the artwork – in fact, ten of the twelve units feature a wide range of phenotypically diverse characters. In *Connections* we saw that black and Asian characters were generally used to signal that the action was set abroad whereas *Building Strategies* and *Cambridge English 2* sought to avoid this implication by introducing black and Asian characters who appeared to be British and/or American. *Headway Intermediate* is less at pains to establish the Britishness or the Americanness of such characters – rather, through an absence of framing in the artwork, ethnically diverse characters are used to compose photographic collages which might be said to connote a specifically global type of multiculturalism. This artwork, reminiscent of the Benetton advertisements referred to earlier, may be said to connote a global multiculturalism in which all the represented participants, whatever their differences, are essentially citizens of the world – linked together through the common currency of English.

Experiences, possessions, likes and dislikes

As with all the coursebooks analyzed, speaking and writing activities, while focused firmly on the personal, generally eschew seriousness. In sections labelled 'Talking about you' students are required mainly to manipulate grammatical form in such a way that they make sentences which are true for them (e.g. 'I've known my best friend for...' [ibid.: 56]) or engage in pair work in which they ask and answer questions about experiences and possessions (e.g. '___ ever been to the United States?'; '___ you ___ a TV in your bedroom?' [ibid.: 7]). Sections entitled 'What do you think?' are mainly preparation for, or follow-up activities to, reading and listening texts and direct the focus firmly onto the personal. Thus the comprehension questions which follow the reading on fast food referred to above are followed by questions such as 'Do you like pizza?', 'What are your favourite toppings?' (ibid.: 50) as opposed to, for example, questions about health and fast food. Elsewhere students are asked, 'What were your happiest times last year?' (ibid.: 19); 'Do you know any unusual holiday destinations?', 'In your opinion, what is *the* ideal holiday?', 'Where are you going for your next holiday?' (ibid.: 42); and 'What advice would you give someone who won a lot of money?' (ibid.: 66). The 'Everyday English' section, which features in all units, practises the usual functions. As well as being introduced to more idiomatic and setting-specific expressions, students are taught how to enthuse over possessions – 'What a gorgeous coat! Was it expensive?' (ibid.: 13). Overall, the same approach extends to the writing activities – so students are asked to describe their personal experiences and recount their impressions of studying English abroad; email an old friend found on the Friends Reunited website with an update of news and plans for the future; a description of a favourite room and reasons why it is important; and the story of a disastrous holiday.

Kullman (2003: 248) comments on such activities as representative of a very particular 'discourse of identity in late modernity', which he says

> views the individual's identity as not being defined in terms of the traditional anchors of family, life cycle, social rituals, nationality, and the institutions of religion, education and the state. This involves much more than mere 'personalisation', a term which is often used to describe materials and activities in ELT. Increasingly, learners are asked to *define* themselves in particular ways, highlighting certain factors, and downplaying or neglecting others.

What is overwhelmingly highlighted in *Headway Intermediate* is the unbridled individualism of those who are motivated by choice and the quest for sensation and success and the identity of the student as consumer. What is overwhelmingly neglected is the range of other affiliations students might reasonably be expected to have or identify with. Why this should be the case is explored more fully Chapter 6. I conclude this part of the study with a discussion of what has emerged through the application of the descriptive framework to the coursebook sample.

Discussion

With regard to the representation of language, the framework shows that standard British English is the variety used as the basis in all the coursebooks surveyed. There is no indication that syntactic variation (apart from errors produced by students) is a feature of language. That said, variation at the phonological level is represented – although all regional UK and international accents, regardless of their provenance, are invariably mild. Both these features are generally in line with the Threshold Level recommendations, which, it will be recalled, are posited on the notion of interaction predominantly with 'native speakers'. These stated that the learners will be expected to understand only those utterances which are spoken in the standard dialect with either the standard accent or accents which have a slight regional, foreign, and/or socio-economic colouring. (van Ek 1975: 17)

Thus, all the coursebooks in the study privilege the RP cluster of accents and reveal a concomitant tendency to associate regional UK accents with speakers in lower-status jobs. More controversial, in the case of three of the coursebooks (*Building Strategies* is the exception), is the use of regional UK accents to reference gullible, antisocial and criminal characters. Although negative attitudes towards regional accents, particularly in the media, are changing within the UK (Jenkins 2000), as Ronald Carter (1997: 10) points out, one area in which they continue to function as very specific signifiers is the world of advertising:

Thus, standard English accents (or Received Pronunciation) are used to sell banking and insurance policies [...]; regional accents are used to market cider and beers, holiday in inclement British coastal resorts, locally bred turkeys from Norfolk and wholemeal bread [...] Given the connection between standard English, proper accents, purity and cleanliness it will not surprise us to learn that bleach is marketed in RP accents.

On the evidence presented here, it would appear that British ELT publishers are happy to participate in this signifying practice, at least to an extent. Striking too is the low number of accents from the outer and the expanding circle (although *Building Strategies* does include more). This is particularly noticeable in the case of *Headway Intermediate* which, despite a thorough globalizing of content, continues to treat superficially the kind of English its cast of global characters might be expected to produce – both phonologically and syntactically.

While all four coursebooks highlight the use of relatively fixed expressions in service encounters and informal conversational exchanges, they vary in their treatment of features such as ellipsis, reformulation and so on in the representation of spoken English. *Building Strategies* and *Headway Intermediate* include examples in some tape recordings, but *Cambridge English 2* is alone in drawing explicit attention to these (although for recognition purposes only). While there may be sound pedagogic reasons for this, it has also been suggested, as we shall see in Chapter 6, that commercial imperatives also play an important role in determining the kind of language which is contained in coursebooks.

With regard to the English-speaking world and the characters who inhabit it, a number of distinctive features emerge. The first of these is the thorough feminizing of content – by which I mean the way in which the representational practices deployed reveal the influence of feminism. The pervasive sexism of *Connections* is replaced by a feminizing of content which is instanced through the actual representations of women, and, to a lesser extent, of men, rather than through significant changes in the numerical presence of female characters overall. These involve the consistent depiction of women as successful and independently minded professionals, as brave and initiative-taking individualists and as high-powered working mothers. Men, on the other hand, are consistently shown as being involved in housework, looking after children and often as professionally less ambitious than their female partners. The feminizing of content is also responsive to historical developments in the evolving discourse of feminism – thus the figure of the independent mother said to emerge in the 1990s forms a more salient element in the representational repertoire of *Headway Intermediate* than in any of the other coursebooks surveyed.

Another distinctive feature to emerge from the application of the framework is the progressive multiculturalizing of content. Thus there is a move away from the use of black and Asian characters to signal that the scenes depicted take place 'abroad' (*Connections*) to one in which such characters, alongside others from expanding circle countries, are the main focus of the unit (*Headway Intermediate*). Such representations draw exclusively on liberal and pluralist versions of multiculturalism in which issues of power and inequality are elided. Linked to this is a concomitant globalizing of content which is most noticeable in *Headway Intermediate*. This is achieved in a number of ways: firstly, through a process of deterritorialization in which the UK ceases to function as the main locus of action; secondly, through the use of global travel as a recurrent theme; and thirdly, through the increased foregrounding of cosmopolitan characters from expanding circle countries.

There is also, what might be called, a strong celebratory strand in the content of all four coursebooks. Lives, whether fictional or non-fictional, are celebrated in terms of personal and professional success. An ideology of individualism runs through these life stories and it is no accident that the final unit of *Headway Intermediate* includes a gap-fill exercise on the song 'I did it my way', the lyrics of which can be read as a self-satisfied appraisal of a life lived to the full and according to the dictates of personal choice. At the same time, the particular world in which these characters interact is also celebrated as the object of what has elsewhere been referred to as the 'tourist gaze' (Urry 1990, 2001). This refers to the way in which phenomena (e.g. mountains, museums, people, etc.) are viewed for pleasure by tourists. John Urry (1990) argues that tourism in late modernity is a marker of status and although coursebook characters also travel for work-related reasons, like tourists they are often motivated by the desire for experience rather than by economic necessity. However, the particular type of tourist gaze afforded by the ELT coursebook is the one which is offered to the student. This is best described as 'static' – that is, it is equivalent to 'the balcony vantage point' (Pratt 1992, in Urry 2001: 4) or that offered at one remove though photographs. In the pages of these coursebooks a highly particularized representation of the world is constructed and although problems such as unemployment, famine and stress *are* mentioned from time to time, the focus overall is on the positive and the enjoyable. Essentially, I would suggest, students are offered a view onto a landscape of pleasure into which a highly particularized narrative of the self can be repeatedly projected. Fundamental to the form these representations take is the artwork. The framework reveals a number of features which have taken place over time, the most significant of which are as follows: a move towards full colour for all units; the almost exclusive use of photographs and ensuing higher visual modality; greater sensory orientation in the photography; and greater use of demand-type artwork.

All these representational practices are intimately bound up with the moment of identity on the 'circuit of culture'. As we have seen, representation and identity may be said to entail one another in a number of way. Firstly, as Hall (1996) and Ferguson (2004) point out, identity implies 'identification'. Both refer to Jean Laplanche and Jean-Bernard Pontalis (1988: 205) who provide the following dictionary-type definition:

> Psychological process whereby the subject assimilates an aspect, property or attribute of the other and is transformed, wholly or partially, after the model the other provides. It is by means of identifications that the personality is constituted and specified.

Representations, of the type found in advertising and, I would argue, in ELT coursebooks, may be said to seek to create such identifications. Students, in much the same way as viewers of advertising, are summoned to adopt subject positions through the range of semiotic resources deployed in the representation. Thus we can say, for example, that the tendency towards greater use of demand-style artwork seeks to create identification and summons students to membership of a community of speakers of English who are characterized by the success, mobility and egalitarianism referred to earlier.

At the same time, Hall (1996) argues that identities are constructed within the representations we make of ourselves, and as John Joseph (2004) points out, this is a process in which language is a key tool. However, the language which students use is, as I have suggested, particularly circumscribed. In line with the conclusions reached by Anderson (2002) and Kullman (2003), my own analysis confirms a move towards an increasingly personalized type of interaction in which students talk mainly about themselves. In addition, I would argue, that students are positioned overall by comprehension tasks and subsequent follow-up activities to respond to texts as language learners for whom only a limited range of responses are required/permitted. This is particularly noticeable in those texts (and artwork) where discussion of foregrounded ideological content is foreclosed. All such practices are essentially regulatory in nature – that is, they seek to determine the subject positions students may adopt by narrowly defining what can be said. As Hall (1996: 5–6) states, identities are 'points of temporary attachment to the subject positions which discursive practices construct for us', and what is constructed in ELT coursebooks is, I would suggest, particularly circumscribed.

To find out why the representational repertoires identified in these two chapters take the form they do, it is necessary to turn now to the moments of production and regulation on the 'circuit of culture'. Many of the issues which have been raised here will be addressed again as they are explored in the light of documentation produced by ELT publishers, through interviews with publishers and from a variety of theoretical perspectives.

6
Production and Regulation of Content

Introduction

Production, it will be recalled, is concerned with the ways in which artefacts are designed, produced and marketed, while regulation considers the factors which govern the circulation of meanings associated with them. To enable an exploration of these moments and to attempt an explanation as to why cultural content has taken the particular forms identified here, this chapter is structured in two distinct parts. In the first part I analyze the guidelines for authors produced by five leading British ELT publishers as these contain explicit recommendations with regard to the type of content to be included in coursebooks. This data set is complemented by interviews with two publishing managers and two commissioning editors at one of the largest British ELT publishing houses. In the second part of the chapter I turn to the literature on consumerism and related areas in an attempt to provide a more theoretically informed and socially situated discussion of the ELT coursebook.

Guidelines for authors

Many ELT publishers provide their authors with sets of guidelines regarding content.[1] These have tended to address two areas: inclusive language and inappropriate topics. The first of these refers predominantly to the need for a non-sexist approach to the ways in which women and men are represented (both linguistically and visually) throughout the coursebook, while the second refers to those topics which writers are advised to avoid so as not to offend the perceived sensibilities of potential buyers and users. As we shall see, the emphasis given to these two areas appears to have changed over time, with concerns about potential buyers and users coming to assume greater importance.

As a genre, the type of document analyzed here may be said to originate in the response of female ELT professionals to studies which showed that women were under-represented, trivialized and stereotyped in British and North American teaching materials (e.g. Hartman and Judd 1978; Hill 1980; Porreca 1984). A group known as Women in EFL Materials, itself an offshoot of Women in TEFL which was formed in 1986 to improve the status of women within the field, was responsible for drawing up guidelines for the representational practices to be followed in the production of ELT materials. The rationale for the guidelines states that they aim to address two issues: the extent to which negative representations of women might adversely affect female students (causing them, it is suggested, to learn less effectively), and the fact that recent language change in English reflected a move away from gender bias. The guidelines, which were entitled *On Balance: Guidelines for the Representation of Women and Men in English Language Teaching Materials* (reproduced in Sunderland 1994: 112–120), make it clear that fairness and balance should also apply to representations of age, class, ethnic origin and disability. These were accepted by the British ELT Publishers Association and in turn were taken up by individual ELT publishers (often the same women) and organizations such as the British Council who produced their own in-house versions. Jill Florent *et al.* (1994) explain that the guidelines were based on over 400 responses to a questionnaire sent to schools, universities, British-based publishers, materials writers and examination boards worldwide. The influence the *On Balance* guidelines were to have on ELT publishers is instanced by the often identical wording in the in-house documents which form part of the database for this chapter.

Such documents, at least as far as inclusive language is concerned, are not unique to ELT (see Cameron 1995; Pauwels 1998). In fact, since the 1970s they have become prevalent internationally in many publishing houses, universities, professional associations and global organizations. Anne Pauwels (1998) shows that early examples of such guidelines were produced in the US for publishing companies with substantial education lists. This is hardly surprising given the role that educational institutions may be said to play in the socialization of students and the reproduction of what Cameron (1994: 27) refers to as 'sexist ideology'. The normative practices such guidelines recommend can be understood as examples of feminist language reform (Pauwels 1998) and, as Cameron (1995) points out, they have often provoked controversy and resistance.

A sustained attack by Hughes (1993) argued that such practices were predicated on little more than substituting one word for another. However, as Cameron (1995) states, no one involved in this kind of language planning has claimed the world can be made to change *solely* by changing words. But changing words has been seen by many feminists – and many teachers, myself included – as a starting point for wider social change. With this in mind I now turn to the documents themselves with a view to analyzing more closely the reasons advanced for, and the precise nature of, the normativity being advocated for ELT materials writers. Altogether I have had access to five sets of documents, details for which are given in Table 6.1 below.

Table 6.1   Details of documents analyzed

Document	Title	Date
1	Guidelines for inclusive language for ELT authors and editors	1988
2	Guidelines for inclusive language	1990
3	Guide for authors	1991
4	Author guidelines	Late 1990s
5	Author guidelines	2006

Inclusive language

Inclusive language is explicitly addressed in Documents 1–3. Of these, Documents 1 and 2 are the most substantial in terms of detail and length and both begin with a short rationale. Document 1 states that the guidelines have been drawn up 'in response to increasing concern over discriminatory language' and that they are 'not prescriptive but reflect the current attitudes and trends in the ELT world'. Document 2 begins by saying that a 'significant and growing number of people are concerned about sexism in language' – thereby implying that the guidelines are a response to this concern. The *On Balance* guidelines similarly suggested that they reflected language change in society and that it was therefore incumbent on ELT publishers not to present students with an outdated version of English. Elsewhere (Gray 2002: 159) I have suggested that such claims are somewhat disingenuous – on the grounds that incorporating language change is indicative of a stance being taken on a contested political issue and that teaching language change necessarily entails promoting language change. What I did not consider was why the authors should seek to present their activities in this light. Pauwels' (1998) survey of 136 sets of international guidelines revealed a remarkable similarity of content and structure. One feature was a tendency to introduce guidelines as advice rather than as a set of prescriptions. Pauwels concluded her survey by outlining the recommended stages for drafting non-sexist language guidelines. She pointed out that the readership of guidelines may not always be as fully apprised of the issues as the writers, and for this reason it was advisable to avoid a didactic tone, and to provide a clear rationale for proposed changes with examples of language to be avoided and alternatives to be used instead. In the same way, by presenting recommendations as *reflecting* rather than *promoting* language change, it could also be argued that the guidelines stood a better chance of acceptance by potentially resistant elements of the readership.

That said, Document 3 eschews any attempt at persuasive rhetoric and begins by stating 'We are committed to making every effort to exclude racism, sexism and stereotyping from our books.' The use of the plural pronoun 'we', which runs throughout the document, suggests agreed company policy on these issues and there is no sense of the case for inclusive language being made to the readership. Such an approach is congruent with Littlejohn's (1992) conclusion that ELT writers were essentially agents writing to an agenda set for them by the publishers. Here they are being told what the rules are, and indeed Document 3 is aimed exclusively at materials writers and contains additional information on house style, copyright permission and so on. Documents 1 and 2, on the other hand, are also explicitly directed at a wider audience of in-house colleagues, such as editors and designers for whom advice and explanation may have been deemed pragmatically more appropriate.

All three documents cover in greater or lesser detail the following issues: the visibility of women in materials; the avoidance of stereotypical characteristics and jobs associated with women and men; honorific titles for women and the avoidance of sexist terms to describe women; the avoidance of masculine generics and those lexical items for which more appropriate gender-neutral terms exist. These issues can be seen as fundamental to feminist language reform which characterized many western societies throughout the 1970s and 1980s and it is no surprise that Document 2 includes Spender's (1980) influential *Man Made Language* on its list of titles for further reading. On the issue of visibility, Documents 1 and 2 make the point that women comprise over half the population. Both are explicit about the implications of this for ELT publishing and are worth quoting at length. Document 1 states,

> Try to maintain a 50/50 balance between the sexes – numerically and in terms of the significance and prominence of the activity illustrated. This balance is not achieved by having photos that are predominantly male in the same book with line drawings that are predominantly female.

Document 2 expresses a similar position as follows:

> Over half the population is female. To provide a balanced view of the world this must be reflected in our text books. It is important therefore to keep track of the numbers of male and female characters in the text, illustrations and recordings. Even though a simple head-count is not enough, it is a basis for ensuring a fair representation of the world.

However, although prescriptiveness is denied or elided in the introductions to Documents 1 and 2, the essentially normative nature of *all* the guidelines is immediately apparent. These quotations alone contain the imperative 'try'; the modal verb 'must'; two evaluative statements containing '[i]t is important', and 'is not enough'; and two categorical assertions – 'is not achieved', and 'it is a basis'. It will be recalled that modality is a facility of language whereby the writer's/speaker's stance vis-à-vis the truth claims or the degree of obligation contained in the message is signalled (Hodge and Kress 1988). Evaluative statements and categorical assertions are likewise indicative of authorial stance (Simpson 1993; Fairclough 2003). In fact, despite the advisory tone adopted in some introductions, all three sets of guidelines are written almost entirely in the language of obligation, using mainly imperatives and modalized statements. Fairclough (2003) points out that deontic modality – that which refers to obligation/necessity – is signalled not only through specific modality markers (e.g. modal verbs, adverbs, etc.), but can also be expressed through imperative structures. Tables 6.2 and 6.3 below provide a selection of examples from Documents 1–3, many of which are repeated word for word from one set of guidelines to another.

In similar vein, the selection of modalized statements below provides further evidence of the overall prescriptivism of the guidelines. The range of modal verbs deployed shows precisely where writers are offered some degree of freedom – for example, while it is incumbent on them to

Table 6.2 Examples of imperative structures in Documents 1–3

…do not	attribute characteristics, occupations or exclusively subservient roles to women, for example, hysterical woman driver, devoted secretary, fragile flower
Seek characters	who embody a range of human potential
Remember	that men can suffer from unrealistic sexual stereotyping too
Allow women	to be praised for boldness, initiative, assertiveness to exhibit the above characteristics as often as men to exhibit self-control
Avoid	showing men always being unable to respond emotionally
Show women	participating actively and positively in worthwhile and exciting pursuits
Show men	caring for children and competently completing household tasks
Avoid	implying that the emotional life of a family suffers because a woman works outside the home
Avoid	describing women according to marital status unless relevant to the topic under discussion, treat them as people in their own right

Table 6.3 Examples of modalized statements in Documents 1–3

Members of both sexes should	be represented as whole human beings with human strengths and weaknesses
An attempt should	be made to break job stereotypes for both women and men
…it should never	be implied that certain jobs are incompatible with a woman's 'femininity' or man's 'masculinity'
Women should not	be identified by their physical characteristics while men are defined by mental attributes or jobs
…a woman can	win an important election and display love for her children
…women as well as men can	be shown as accountants, engineers, pilots, plumbers, computer operators and astronauts
…men as well as women can	be shown as nurses, primary school teachers, secretaries, typists, librarians, filing clerks, switchboard operators and child minders

break with job stereotyping, they are under no obligation to show men specifically as nurses or women as plumbers.

With regard to honorific titles for women, all three documents mention 'Ms' as an alternative to 'Miss' and 'Mrs' for avoiding reference to marital status. Document 2 also mentions the need to avoid the term 'Dear Sir/s' as a salutation in a letter and suggests 'Dear Sir or Madam' or 'Dear Madam or Sir' as alternatives – adding that these are 'acceptable usage for EFL exams'– a remark which implies that the guidelines have been accepted by examination boards. Documents 1–3 also suggest avoiding introducing women in terms of their husband (e.g. wife of...), or as if they were possessions – 'John and his wife, Elsie' is the example provided.

As noted by Pauwels (1998), most specifically linguistic suggestions are at the level of pronoun use and individual lexemes (mainly words involving the affix 'man'), rather than at the level of syntax (e.g. the use of the passive to hide agency). Documents 1–3 provide lists of items to avoid and gender-neutral alternatives. In line with the *On Balance* approach, Document 2 prefaces this section with a rationale:

> It has been supposed that the word 'man' and other male generics include women. It has, however, been demonstrated that people do not make this assumption automatically. When told that 'man needs food and shelter to survive' the great majority of people visualise only men.

This is most probably a reference to Jeanette Silviera (1980), whose research suggested that 'native speakers' of English did not interpret generic uses of 'man' to include women. All three documents also suggest avoiding generic uses of 'he' and 'his', with Document 2 citing Caxton and Shakespeare as historical precedents in support of 'they' and 'their' as gender-neutral singular pronouns. Document 1 somewhat tentatively asks readers to 'consider the effect' of teaching 'man'-based lexemes on students – without explicitly suggesting that this may cause them to think they apply only to men. The *On Balance* guidelines suggested somewhat more explicitly that under-representation and/or demeaning representations of women might adversely affect female students. Writers such as Jane Sunderland (1994) have subsequently made a stronger case for the negative effects of sexist materials on learning opportunities for female students (see also Mannheim 1994).

In addition to these similarities there are also some minor differences. For example, Document 1 suggests that illustrations should feature 'all physical types and occasional evidence of physical handicaps, avoiding stereotyped associations with these images'. Document 2 also makes the point that sexism can be difficult to avoid in instances where there is direct quotation from original sources. It is suggested that the effect can be lessened by paraphrasing quotations, putting sexist terms in brackets, using '[*sic*]' or partially quoting from the original. Finally, Document 3 is different from the others in that it includes a section entitled 'inappropriacy'. And it is to this second strand in the publishers' guidelines that I now turn.

Inappropriate topics

Topics which coursebook writers are advised to avoid are generally referred to within ELT publishing by the acronym PARSNIP (politics, alcohol, religion, sex, narcotics, isms and pork) (personal communication, OUP, 2000). Guidelines for inappropriate content are different from guidelines governing representational practices and inclusive language – while the latter may have the stated aim of reflecting language change, excluding stereotypical representations and improving learning opportunities for female students, the former are based on customers' perceived sensitivities. In fact, Documents 3 and 4 refer exclusively to 'markets' rather than to 'students', reflecting I would suggest an increasing concern with sales in an extremely competitive market.

Document 3 is unique in that it combines a list of over 20 topics to avoid alongside guidelines for inclusive language, while Document 4 consists entirely of terms to avoid and topics to be approached with 'cultural sensitivity'. The fact that Document 4 does not include guidelines for inclusivity does not mean that such issues are perceived to be no longer important – the interview data below show that this continues to be an issue for publishers. However, it may be an indication that such practices are now so widespread within ELT publishing that editors automatically expect the material they commission to be acceptable in this area (a point made to me by materials writer Norman Whitney, personal communication 1999).

Document 3 states that 'most subjects are acceptable' in books produced for the 'UK and northern European markets' but that great care has to be taken when considering 'more conservative and religious markets'. This contrast between geographical and socio-political/religious markets is significant as it constructs the world beyond the UK and northern Europe in terms of a set of perceived sensitivities and a range of topics which cannot be mentioned explicitly. That said, geographical areas within such markets are sometimes mentioned – for example, Document 3 lists 'alcohol', 'Israel and six pointed stars', 'nudes and flesh' and 'pork' as inappropriate for the Middle East. Document 4 introduces a section on 'countries and names' in which the modality markers clearly signal the high level of publisher commitment to particular representations:

> When using names of countries and nationalities, the sensitivities of those countries and regions **must** always be taken into account. The following examples represent typical areas where great care **must** be taken (emphasis added).

In the ensuing examples writers are advised to use 'developing countries' instead of 'underdeveloped or third world countries', 'East Asia' instead of 'the Far East' and the 'USA' instead of 'America' (which, it is noted, includes South America). Interestingly, writers are also told to use 'Native American names for legendary figures, e.g. Tashunca-Uitco, not Crazy Horse'. In fact, all examples of this type refer to Native Americans and the Inuit, suggesting that the sensitivities of North American teachers may be the concern here. Whatever the reason, we can assume that the use of Native American terms for named individuals is congruent with a liberal/pluralist multicultural approach to representation. As we shall see below, publishers' sensitivities to even small sectors of the market can be acute and the tendency is to err on the side of caution.

Document 4 also includes sections entitled 'Style of dress'; 'Religion'; 'Friendship between sexes'; 'Smoking and drinking'; 'Topics likely to be taboos in most countries'; and 'Household pets'. Each is followed by a list of questions: 'Is tight or revealing clothing acceptable in all target markets?'; 'Are men and women allowed to work together in all the target markets?'; 'Are animals allowed in buildings in all markets?' These questions serve simply to raise issues which writers are advised to consider. The guidelines state that doubts about any aspect of content should be thoroughly checked by writers. While guidelines on inappropriate topics are mainly concerned with perceived sensitivities within the market, Document 4 also points out that artwork 'must be thoroughly checked for any items that may prove incomprehensible' – hence (presumably) the reference to pets, which in some markets may not share accommodation with human beings.

A final note on sensitivity to markets. I approached the publishers in 2006 for an update on their current policies. The publishers of Document 3 have since been taken over by another company and their original guidelines have been incorporated, in some cases word for word, into a new document dated 2006. The new document, referred to here as Document 5, contains 14 pages on issues to consider when producing books aimed at the North American market. The following quotation indicates the extent of current sensitivity:

> Law and politics: Along with religion, treat these topics very cautiously. Issues of public order can be difficult, **as can anything too controversial that might portray America in a negative light.** For example, a piece on the 'Guardian Angels' (the vigilante group that has as a mission the protection of people on the subway) has been criticized for making it look as if the police can't control crime and encouraging people to take the law into their own hands (emphasis added).

The publishers of Document 2, while still using the 1990 document on inclusivity, explained that

> [T]here is a more recent document from 2003 which was market research based from our main offices. This is a 15 page document which we use internally as editors [...] It contains some sensitive information which compares our products with competitors on cultural grounds etc. I cannot therefore send it out to you at the present time. (email communication, 21 July 2006)

Both these quotations are indicative of the extent to which perceived market forces are taken into consideration by publishers. The advice on the need to avoid portraying the USA in a negative light certainly represents a new element in such documentation, and one I will return to in Chapter 8. Before discussing the role such guidelines may be said to play in determining the nature of the representational repertoires identified in the previous two chapters I turn in the following section to the interviews with the publishers. These serve to shed light on their attitudes to content more generally and the ways in which such guidelines are used to inform editorial decisions.

Interviews with publishers

These interviews were carried out as background to another study (Gray 2002), and were designed to explore consideration of local – as opposed to global – issues in coursebooks aimed at the more differentiated secondary school market. They are drawn on here because much of what the publishers said can be seen as being directly relevant to this study, particularly with regard to the production and regulation of coursebook content. Firstly, they are indicative of how coursebook content is regulated by publishers; secondly, they shed light on the range of factors which inform the editorial decision making process; thirdly, they indicate the extent to which specific guidelines for inclusivity impact on content generally; and fourthly, they shed light on areas of similarity and difference between ELT coursebooks for different segments of the global market. The interviews were conducted in 2000 and to protect their privacy, the informants, all of whom were interviewed separately, are referred to as Informants 1–4 in Table 6.4 below. In the interests of readability, false starts, hesitations and repetitions have been removed from quotations, and punctuation has been added.

The first point of relevance to emerge from the interviews is the way in which the regulatory power of editors is exercised with regard to perceived market sensitivities. Informant 1 was largely concerned with coursebooks for Turkey and Greece. He explained that this meant the material he oversaw had to be suitable for the curricular and methodological preferences of those countries, but that cultural sensitivities and practices also had to be taken into consideration. This meant that the materials could contain no references to Ephesus or Graeco-Roman cities on the west coast of Turkey, as he suggested these were felt by Greece to be 'a great national loss'. The course he was working on when we spoke, although aimed primarily at the Turkish market, had also been researched in more than seven other countries. However, as the following quotation illustrates, the Turkish focus meant that content had to be carefully scrutinized with regard to the representation of Turkish characters:

Table 6.4 Details of publishers interviewed

Informant/Date of interview	Role in publishing house
1 27 June 2000	Senior Editor, Turkish/Greek market
2 as above	Senior Editor, Italian market
3 as above	Publishing Manager, Spanish/Portuguese market
4 as above	Publishing Manager, Central/Eastern European market

For example Turks are very sensitive. If we have an illustrator who draws them as Arabs, if we say 'Oh Turks, they're all Arabs, aren't they?', you know, I mean no they're not. They don't look like Arabs and the sensitivity's there, so we would bear that in mind in briefing very carefully the illustrators. That's making sure that if we have a character that is supposed to be Turkish that they look Turkish, and we will supply cast photos for example to an illustrator to make sure that that is the case. I mean I've just had a drawing which I've rejected where we asked for a civil building where someone just got married and they drew a mosque and in, thinking 'Oh this is a book for Turkey', well people do not get married in mosques in Turkey full stop. It's actually against the law erm because it's a secular state so I will, you know, make modifications on that and say no we can't do that.

Thus the regulatory role of the editor can involve briefing illustrators, giving them examples to follow and, where necessary, rejection/modification of their work. Elsewhere in the data he refers to rejecting artwork in which a woman was shown wearing a headscarf in a school, which he explains is against Turkish law. Both examples serve to underline the point made by Philip Prowse (1998) that perceptions of the market have come to dominate all aspects of ELT publishing, regardless of the sector (see also Haines 1994). Informant 2, who oversaw courses for the Italian market, made the point that publishers are 'very, very market driven' and that this can mean extreme sensitivity to diverse elements within a single market. By way of illustration she explained she had recently been told not to include Dracula on a reading list accompanying material for Italy – the reason being that references to blood might be considered offensive to Jehova's Witnesses. This group, she explained, represented the fastest-growing religion in Italy – advice which appeared to originate with the publisher's market research team. According to Informant 3, these often locally based teams act as intermediaries between the publishers and the market, producing information of this type on the one hand, and on the other relaying information from the publishers back to locally based sales teams and teachers.

With regard to the representation of gender, all informants signalled their subscription to the spirit of the guidelines and referred to storylines in their coursebooks where girls were deliberately shown to be as capable as boys. Informant 4, who was involved in drawing up the original *On*

Balance guidelines, implied that times had changed since guidelines for inclusivity were first written:

> I no longer do counts and things, in the old days I used to, I would go through a manuscript and I would sort of make sure we were doing it and I would sort of write a list of – but I think **authors and editors now are so aware** and I think in [coursebook title] we've got the first level, the storyline involves the girls beating the boys at football and I think there's a danger actually of going the other way (laughing) (emphasis added).

The comment that authors nowadays are so aware of the issue resonates with the personal communication from the coursebook writer referred to above. The implication is that inclusivity, particularly with regard to gender equality, is considered nowadays by writers and editors as a generic feature of the ELT coursebook. However, Informants 1 and 2 expressed some disquiet about the constraints on the inclusivity they felt able to incorporate into materials. The constraints are represented as originating in the market to which the publishers have no choice but to comply. Informant 2 expressed this as follows:

> Boys are interested in girls which I find [...] we're not dealing with reality there either, you know, I mean, there are other kinds of sexuality which you don't deal with, and yet you have a love interest usually in this level of coursebook [14–16 age group], we generally put a love interest in and it's always heterosexual and there tends to be a certain amount of, you know, role playing around that.

When I asked her how she would like to see sexuality addressed she answered,

> I would like there to be some question mark, and when we have all these young people, I would like to be able to make young people who are having trouble with their own sexuality find something that they could, you know, get hold of, but I think at the moment we have to leave that up to individual schools, I don't think we can do it, we couldn't possibly risk it.

'The bottom line', she added, 'is that we want our course to be bought'. Equally worrying for this informant and Informant 1 was the lack of representation of disability. Informant 1 said that disabled students tended not to be educated in the mainstream in his market and that teachers were uncomfortable in dealing with the issue – something he felt publishers had to accept in coursebook design. Informant 2 made a similar point about the difficulty of including disabled teenagers in coursebooks for her market. The problem she felt lay in the fact that 'disabled people aren't a power group like they are in Anglo-Saxon culture.' In my view this remark goes to the heart of much of the decision making regarding the construction of coursebook representational repertoires – namely, that the perception of sectors of the market as powerful affects the representational practices associated with particular groups. Elsewhere a similar point has been made by Ferguson (2004) with regard to the increased representation of black characters in contemporary advertising. He suggests that as advertisers have come to see black people with increased spending power, increased representation has ensued. And indeed Informant 2 states that as the racial composition of Italy changes there is greater acceptance of inclusivity with regard to race in coursebooks:

> I think 10 years ago it was more problematic putting a racial balance in your books whereas now because they've got an enormous amount of immigration, visible immigration with people with different coloured skin and all the classrooms have got children in them now who don't speak Italian as a first language, it's more important for the teachers to be seen to be doing something.

That said, it was clear that in some markets representation of certain groups still had to be handled with care. Informant 3 explained that as publishers they actively wanted to promote racial tolerance but that they had to consider market attitudes when deciding on content. When I pressed him for an example he said tentatively:

> I mean this hasn't come up, but I can imagine that, for example that if we had a mixed race relationship for example, you know, in our photo story, you know, we had a black boy going out with a white girl, or vice versa, that, I don't know, because it hasn't come up, but that might be seen as not being appropriate.

This contrasts with the, admittedly rare, representation of a couple composed of a black man and a white woman in *Cambridge English 2* referred to in Chapter 5. Informant 4 also stated that some markets found representations of blackness problematic – 'the teachers will not see it as being part of their reality, never mind the fact that it might be British reality.' Certain sectors of the secondary school market require 'cultural information' about life in the UK, but as Informant 4 suggested, there can be a mismatch in terms of the way in which 'British reality' is understood by the publishers and the way in which it is imagined by some market sectors. In Chapter 5 we saw that coursebooks for the adult market – certainly as represented by the *Headway* course – have moved away from an attempt to paint a picture of 'British reality' in favour of an idealized picture of an English-speaking global community. A comparison between the 1996 edition of *Headway Intermediate* and the 2003 edition analyzed in this volume clearly illustrates the nature of this shift. In the *Headway* course it is achieved mainly through the replacement of British characters with those from different parts of the world, locating more of the action outside the UK, and the addition of a wider range of phenotypically diverse characters.

Another area of compromise was mentioned by Informant 1 who explained that although they aimed for a racially mixed cross-section of represented participants, only 'attractive-looking people' were used in photographic artwork. The reason, he suggested, was twofold – agencies tended only to employ attractive models and the students 'tend to like attractive models' they can 'idolize'. However, I will suggest below there may also be other reasons why only attractive models are used and why liberal/pluralist varieties of multiculturalism have increasingly come to typify coursebooks for the adult sector of the global market.

When I asked the publishers how they responded to Gillian Brown's (1990) accusation that the English contained in coursebooks was imbued with materialist values, only one informant felt that the charge was fair. Informant 1 felt it was an oversimplification, but blamed the market for limiting the range of issues which could be addressed in coursebooks, while Informants 3 and 4 felt that the comment was more relevant to the kind of adult ELT coursebooks under investigation here. Significantly, the Brown accusation triggered references to what they all referred to as 'aspirational' content. Those interviewed felt that such content *was* motivating but that for the secondary sector it had to be balanced with educational content – which they saw as the defining characteristic of their material. When asked what 'aspirational' meant, Informant 2, who concurred with Brown (1990), said,

Something [...] which they aspire to and which therefore interests them and motivates them because motivation is a big issue for us, and making something which teachers perceive as interesting, you know, we've got units on spending money, pocket money, saving money [...] at the same time you might say well, you know, down in certain parts of Palermo the kind of way in which they spend money and the amount of money they've got, the kids just wouldn't have that, so you know, I mean, I don't know, it's difficult to avoid, we live in a capitalist society.

Talking about eastern Europe, Informant 4 admitted that aspirational content could be 'divisive' in some settings. She drew a distinction between 'rural and state school' settings where such content could be problematic and, without explicitly mentioning private language schools, referred to students in 'better-off', 'urban areas' with 'a teacher-type who is much more disposed to the methodology'. This in itself is an interesting comment, suggesting the close association of a specific kind of content with particular set of methodological practices – here clearly understood as broadly communicative. A similar type of observation was made by Jan Bell and Roger Gower (1998: 123) who noted with surprise that some east European students regarded the kind of 'fun' content often found in western materials as trivial. Whatever the views of certain sectors of the market, the concept of aspirational content is interesting: firstly, because it is clearly an in-house term for a certain type of content; and secondly, because it describes much of what was identified in Chapters 4 and 5, particularly with regard to the discourse of personal and professional success.

In light of the above, it is clear that the publishers' guidelines play a significant role in determining key features in the representational repertoires of post-*Connections* ELT coursebooks. This is particularly so in the case of the feminizing and, to a lesser extent, the multiculturalizing of content. At the same time, publishers' increased attention to the perceived sensitivities of the global marketplace has meant that many topics cannot be addressed. In this, as we have seen, they tend to blame the market and position themselves as constrained by its demands. In fact, the tension which exists between aspects of the inclusivity and the inappropriacy strands in the guidelines serves to illuminate a key feature of content identified in the previous two chapters – namely, the way in which topics may be foregrounded in reading and listening exercises, while discussion of the issues arising is foreclosed in follow-up activities. Hence, for example, the several instances of explicit stereotype breaking where an overt feminist message is made salient and is then ignored in the accompanying tasks.

However, the guidelines and the interviews do not explain many of the other features identified by the descriptive framework, for example, the particular representation of English (as syntactically invariant and a privileging of the RP cluster of accents); the move towards full colour for all units; the almost exclusive use of photographs and ensuing higher visual modality; the greater sensory orientation in the photography; and the greater use of demand-type artwork. Neither do they explain the increasingly globalized and celebratory content, nor do they explain the way in which discourses of success, mobility and egalitarianism serve to characterize the world which is constructed within the materials. To account for these features it is necessary, in the second part of this chapter, to look beyond the guidelines to the wider social context in which coursebooks are produced, disseminated and consumed.

The wider social context

In Chapter 1 I made the point that although ELT coursebooks might be designed for use as educational tools, they are also embodiments of 'particular constructions of reality' (Apple and Christian-Smith 1991: 3) and, most importantly, commodities to be traded in the marketplace – a point also made by Littlejohn (1992), and confirmed by the publishers I interviewed. I also suggested that the English language and the practices and products associated with ELT are intimately connected with the complex phenomenon of globalization. For many critics, particularly those who understand it in dystopian terms, globalization equates primarily with economic neoliberalism and the marketization of areas of life which were previously the preserve of the state – such as education and health (e.g. Berger 1998/99; Persaud and Lusane 2000). In this process students and patients are recast as consumers and the education and healthcare they receive are commodified. This aspect of globalization can be seen as contributing to the further expansion of what has been called the consumer society, which in Jean Baudrillard's (1998: 25) formulation represents 'a fundamental mutation in the ecology of the human species' and is typified by 'fantastic conspicuousness of consumption and abundance, constituted by the multiplication of objects, services and material goods'. We do not have to agree with Baudrillard on the issue of the fundamental mutation of the species to accept that contemporary post-industrial societies entail the expansion of domains in which the individual is positioned as a consumer.

One consequence of the abundance of material goods and the more recent increased commodification of non-material services is that consumers orient towards commodities no longer solely in terms of their use value but in terms of what they signify. Thus through consuming and the exercise of choice (however restricted or bogus), individuals make statements about the kind of person they are, and at the same time express affinity with those who do likewise, while signalling their difference from those who consume otherwise. In this way, consumption becomes part of culture – that is, it is co-opted into the repertoire of resources that human beings have at their disposal for the making of meaning. For Baudrillard, and those sympathetic to his analysis (e.g. Jameson 1984; Ritzer 1998), this results in both the extension and the commodification of culture. Such a view resonates with Hall's (1997a: 208) assessment of contemporary society as one characterized by 'the enormous expansion of everything which has to do with culture', leading, he adds, to 'its constitutive position today in all aspects of social life'. In Mike Featherstone's (1991) account, one feature of this process, which Baudrillard (1998: 104) refers to as 'culturalization', is that commodities

> take on a wide range of cultural associations and illusions. Advertising in particular is able to exploit this and attach images of romance, exotica, desire, beauty, fulfillment, communality, scientific progress and the good life to mundane consumer goods such as soap, washing machines, motor cars and alcoholic drinks. (Featherstone 1991: 14)

This fusion of the commodity with clusters of predominantly visual associations results in the emergence of what has been called the *commodity-sign* (e.g. Baudrillard 1981; Featherstone 1991; Goldman 1992). Examples of this include items such as the Sony Walkman, Coca-Cola, the Rolex watch (Goldman 1992) or the Big Mac (Ritzer 1998). In all these instances the use value of the item may be said to be eclipsed by its more powerful semiotic potential. Increasingly, as suggested earlier, symbolic entities such as languages can also be seen as subject to commodification (Heller 1999; Anderson 2002) and, as Block and Cameron (2002) suggest, this has implications in areas such as choice of language to study, student motivation and the allocation of institutional resources for language learning. It also has implications for the production of coursebooks, the regulation of content and the construction of students as customers – something which Anderson (2002) sees as implicit in fun-oriented learner-centred ELT methodology.

A key element in the processes of culturalization and the emergence of the commodity-sign is the role of the visual as a privileged mode of communication which is particularly intensified in the second half of the twentieth century. In his discussion of advertising which is central to these processes, John Berger (1972: 129) makes the point that

> In no other form of society in history has there been such a concentration of images, such a density of visual messages.

Similar points have been made by Fredric Jameson (1984: 54) who sees 'a whole new culture of the image' as typifying contemporary society, and Jonathan Schroeder (2002: 3) who argues that 'visual consumption' (similar to Urry's (1990) concept of the tourist gaze) is a key feature of an economy 'organised around attention'. However, Andrew Wernick (1991) argues that the imaging of commodities, although central to contemporary society, has a longer history than that generally referred to in much of the literature cited above. He locates its origins in the late eighteenth century and the practices associated with the promotion of the first mass-produced goods. By way of illustration, Wernick tells the story of Wedgwood's copy of the Portland Vase – a piece of Classical Roman glassware. The replica was considered to be such a feat of manufacturing expertise that when it toured Europe it served to promote sales of other Wedgwood products which were subsequently imbued with its allure. So although a commodity in its own right, the Wedgwood replica functioned as a unique kind of advertisement for a range of other goods. Wernick uses the term *promotional-sign* to refer to the advertising, packaging and the activities associated with the launch of a product. The function of the promotional-sign is to image the entity to which it refers and to make it mean in specific ways. When a commodity, as in the case of the replica vase, also acquires a promotional function it can be seen as a *promotional commodity* or *commodity-sign*, which, in Wernick's (ibid.: 16) view, promotes not only itself but 'all other produce to which, by brand and style, it is imagistically linked'.

Wernick goes on to argue that promotion has subsequently become 'a rhetorical form diffused throughout our culture' (ibid.: vii) and is no longer solely a commercial phenomenon – so that, as Fairclough (1993) shows, a job advertisement for a university lectureship can also be seen as simultaneously promoting the institution from which it emanates. A good example of this type of promotion is the 2003 British Council recruitment campaign for teachers. Under the heading 'Teach English and Individualism' the artwork for one advertisement comprises a photographic montage of racially diverse faces, the meaning of which is made clear in the accompanying text:

At the British Council we aim to employ English teachers from a mix of backgrounds and ages. In this way we'll send out signals that in Britain we believe in the right of individuals to pursue their particular lifestyle. (in *EL Gazette* 2003, Issue 282: 7)

At the same time as attempting to recruit teachers, the advertisement actively seeks to promote a view of the British Council and Britain as places of tolerance and diversity. It is my contention here that ELT coursebooks are similarly constructed and can most usefully be understood as examples of promotional commodities. In fact, it is only when we look at coursebooks in this way that the particular form which cultural content takes can be fully understood. In the following two sections I will suggest that the imaging of English in ELT coursebooks – that is, its construction as a commodity-sign – owes much to the practices associated with advertising in contemporary consumer society. In this the role of photography is decisive.

Artwork and advertising

As stated earlier, one of the most significant changes in coursebooks over the last 30 years is the move towards photographic artwork. Since the invention of photography in the nineteenth century, photographic images have played an important role in connoting truth and authenticity (Kuhn 1985) – despite the fact that all such images are the result of choices made by the photographer and are increasingly subject to digital manipulation. The very fact that photographs are generally referred to in English as 'taken' rather than 'made' suggests a correspondence between the image and something which was already there in the material world and available, as it were, for the taking. As Susan Sontag (1973: 5–6) suggests,

A photograph passes for incontrovertible proof that a given thing happened. The picture may distort; but there is always a presumption that something exists, or did exist, which is like what's in the picture.

More recently, Judith Butler (2009: 72) has commented on the power of photography in late modernity, with specific reference to the photographs of prisoner abuse emerging from Abu Ghraib in 2004, as follows:

When, for instance, Rumsfeld claimed that publishing the photos of torture and humiliation and rape would allow them 'to define us as Americans,' he attributed to photography an enormous power to construct national identity itself. The photographs would not just show something atrocious, but would make our capacity to commit atrocity into a defining concept of American identity.

Charles Sanders Peirce's (1955: 98–119) conception of the sign is illuminating with regard to the power of photography. In Peircean semiotics the sign is said to have three modes – the symbolic (in which the relationship between the signifier and the signified is completely arbitrary, as in the case of a red traffic light signifying stop), the iconic (in which there is a resemblance between the signifier and the signified, as in the case of a portrait painting) and the indexical (in which the signifier and the signified are more directly linked, as in the case of a footprint).[2] In Peircean terms the photograph may be said to constitute an iconic sign. However, to quote from Sontag (1973: 154) again:

> a photograph is not only an image (as a painting is an image), an interpretation of the real; it is also a trace, something directly stencilled off the real, like a footprint or a death mask.

So in addition to its iconic nature, Sontag implies an indexical dimension. Barthes (1984) adopts a similar position, arguing that a photograph 'is never distinguished from its referent' (ibid.: 5). It is 'literally an emanation of the referent' (ibid.: 80). Although Peirce (1955) states that an indexical sign does not resemble the object it represents (or at least not necessarily), he does recognize the indexical quality of the photograph. With reference to indexicality he states, 'psychologically, the action of indices depends upon association by contiguity' (ibid.: 108), and it is precisely the powerful sense of psychological contiguity which may be said to be at work when, as Barthes (1984: 5) points out, people say such things as 'Look this is my brother; this is me as a child' when talking about family snapshots. Indeed, this sense of contiguity has been a constant from the earliest days of photography. Walter Benjamin (1931/1979: 244) quotes Karl Dauthendey, one of the first nineteenth-century photographers, as follows:

> We were abashed by the distinctiveness of these human images, and believed that the little tiny faces in the pictures could see *us*, so powerfully was everyone affected by the unaccustomed clarity and the unaccustomed truth to nature of the first daguerrotypes.

The point I wish to make here is that photography, regardless of the type of photograph or the manipulation involved in its production, has generally been understood as somehow more 'real' than other representational modes, and I would suggest it is because of this combination of iconicity and indexicality.[3] Its use therefore in both advertising and coursebook texts can be seen as an important marker of visual modality – 'this exists' (or 'this existed'), the photograph proclaims, even if the colour and image sharpness have been distorted to induce pleasure or elicit some kind of emotional response from the viewer.

If we turn to the literature on advertising we find that the way in which the imaging of products is discussed can shed light on how English is constructed in coursebooks. William Leiss *et al.* (1990, in Schroeder 2002: 28) suggest that all advertisements:

- create positive associations for the product, service or organization,
- are as carefully constructed as art,
- are aimed at a specific 'target audience',
- must dwell in the future,
- propose that their product or service is part of the good life,
- influence, construct and reflect consumer identity.

The application of the descriptive framework in Chapters 4 and 5 clearly demonstrated that English is consistently endowed with positive associations and that the artwork is constructed with great care – a point which was underlined in the interviews with the publishers. The suggestion that advertisements dwell in the future and are linked to identity parallels, in my view, the aspirational nature of much coursebook content. It will be recalled that the publishers I spoke to believed that aspirational content (in many, if not all, settings) was motivating for students. For Berger (1972: 132) this is precisely how much advertising imagery works:

> Publicity is always about the future buyer. It offers him [*sic*] an image of himself made glamorous by the product or opportunity it is trying to sell. The image then makes him envious of himself as he might be.

In this way, it is suggested, consumers are motivated to literally 'buy into' the self they may become. This envy of the projected self is crucial to another aspect of the coursebook identified by Kullman

(2003), namely, that of personal transformation. Drawing on the work of Giddens (1991), Kullman concludes that coursebooks have been invaded by discourses of identity and psychotherapy in which language learning is reconfigured as part of the ongoing work of developing and sustaining a coherent sense of the self – a process held by Giddens to be a key feature of life in late modernity. For Kullman this identity work takes place largely in the speaking activities which students are asked to carry out. But it also takes place in my view at the level of artwork in a way similar to that found in advertising. In fact, Berger argues that one of the things advertising does is to suggest the possibility of personal transformation by showing us images of those already trans- formed. Thus, in the case of ELT coursebooks, the summoning look of the represented participants and the sensory orientation of much of the artwork combine to hail students to a lifestyle in which the discourses of success, mobility and egalitarianism form the basis of the promo- tional promise of English. Leiss (1983) noted a similar move away from product information towards a focus on lifestyles in television advertise- ments in the early 1980s. Commenting on this, Featherstone (1991: 86) suggests that lifestyle depictions provide the consumer with glimpses of what might be, adding that 'consumer culture publicity suggests that *we all have room for self-improvement and self-expression* whatever our age or class origins' (italics added). Thus, discourses of personal transfor- mation linking visual consumption, identity and lifestyle may be said to play a key role in both advertising and the imaging of English in coursebooks.

At the same time, as we shall see in the following section, the com- modification of social issues noted in recent advertising also finds a parallel in ELT coursebooks.

Commodification of social issues

The feminization of content is a key feature in the coursebooks ana- lyzed in this study. The dominant note in the representation of women is one of professional success, mobility and equality with men. The guidelines for authors were shown to be crucial in establishing this par- ticular representational repertoire. However, as Robert Goldman (1992) demonstrates in his analysis of women's magazines from the 1980s, discourses of feminism have been used increasingly to image products aimed at women consumers. He refers to this as 'commodity feminism' (ibid.: 130), a process whereby, in Bethan Benwell and Elizabeth Stokoe's (2006: 188–189) formulation:

signs of feminism (the briefcase, the Filofax, the suit) become commodified and incorporated [...] into advertisements for products ranging from perfume to jeans.

Significantly, Goldman argues that commodity feminism elides the challenge feminism poses for the status quo in patriarchal societies, representing it in a depoliticized form as yet another lifestyle choice. It could be argued that a similar depoliticizing takes place in the representation of feminism in coursebooks. So although the guidelines for authors *are* politically motivated, the way in which the wider social issues raised are repeatedly foreclosed as topics for discussion indicates the nature of the publishers' compromise with perceived commercial imperatives. In this way the co-opting of feminism into pedagogic materials becomes a means of aligning English with ideas of egalitarianism and harmony between the sexes – but in such a way that ideological struggle is largely written out.

The same can also be said of the versions of multiculturalism found in coursebooks. As stated in Chapter 5, the representations of racial harmony are reminiscent of the United Colours of Benetton campaign from the 1980s or advertisements for Coca-Cola in which attractive ethnically diverse characters celebrate their difference *and* signal their essential sameness through consumption (see Tinic 1997 for examples of advertisements). Marie Gillespie's (1995, in Mackay 1997: 56) interviews with young Asians in Southall found the multicultural imaging of Coke to be part of its appeal. She concluded that

> Coke-drinkers are seen to be 'happy', 'active' 'kids in America' where 'the sun is always shining', everyone is 'happy' and 'free', 'all races get on' and there are 'no signs of anger'.

By substituting 'English speakers' for 'Coke-drinkers' the quotation could easily be applied to ELT coursebooks where a similarly benign world, composed largely of attractive successful people, is similarly constructed.

However, as Serra Tinic (1997) shows, Benetton was to abandon such celebratory representations in the 1990s in favour of advertising campaigns in which social issues such as AIDS, war and capital punishment were increasingly foregrounded. These campaigns represented a departure from the practices normally associated with the imaging of products as outlined above. On the one hand they can be understood as the commodification of a wider range of social issues, but as Tinic (ibid.: 12) suggests, they were also an attempt to create a situation in which buying Benetton meant the consumer was simultaneously 'purchasing a philosophy' – essentially an exercise in branding or extending the brand. As with more mainstream advertising, ELT coursebooks have tended to steer clear of problematic social content (the Benetton advertisements were very controversial), although readings and listening on global charities tend to feature regularly, as does the environment. One of the publishers (Informant 1) mentioned the 'green issue' as being particularly appropriate for coursebooks precisely because 'it doesn't harm anyone' – it is clear, however, that the harm publishers are mainly concerned with is the potential for commercial harm to themselves.

This still leaves us with a number of other features identified by the descriptive framework which cannot be accounted for by the guidelines for authors and which are not related to the artwork. What are we to make of the representation of English as syntactically invariant, with a limited focus on the grammar of the spoken form, and a privileging of the RP cluster of accents?

The representation of English

As language users we know that language is not syntactically, lexically or phonologically invariant. Variables such as social class, gender, age, ethnicity, nationality, geography, L1, as well as a host of contextual factors impact on the way in which linguistic resources are deployed by language users. However, the representation of English in the coursebooks analyzed does not reflect variety to any great extent and the English on offer is very similar from one coursebook to another. The implication is that there is a single model of English – that contained in the coursebook – which is appropriate for all students in all contexts. We also know that spoken and written discourse are very differently organized. And while the application of the descriptive framework did show that some features of spoken English were given more emphasis in some courses than in others, overall the 'untidiness' (cf. Swan and Walter 1990a) of spoken English is kept to a minimum. Thornbury (2005: 78), commenting on the way in which the transactional function of language (i.e. getting things done) is consistently privileged at the expense of the interpersonal function (i.e. relationship maintenance), states that 'even "getting things done" involves a degree of interpersonal "grooming" and the kind of language associated with social grooming perhaps deserves inclusion, even in the most mundane exchanges.' Clearly a certain amount of tidying up is necessary for teaching purposes, particularly in the early stages of language learning. However, I would suggest the logic of consumerism also provides us with a useful heuristic for addressing this issue. Although approaching this from a somewhat different angle, Ruth Wajnryb's (1996, no pagination) critique of the kind of English contained in ELT coursebooks makes a number of points which are relevant here. Commenting on the way in which the role of context in linguistic choice is largely ignored in most coursebooks, she states,

> This process effectively turns language into a manageable, indeed a marketable product. Instead of a fragile, impressionable, context-qualified phenomenon with blurred edges, language is now more like a discrete item on a shop-shelf – hardy, portable, reliable [...] It is as if the very act of acknowledging context as significant limits the currency of the language presented [...] making it less easy to 'mount' the language as a product on the page, less easy to display.

By representing language as largely invariant, by exposing students to a very narrow range accents, by consistently privileging the RP cluster of accents and by limiting the focus on spoken discourse, English is not only simplified for the purposes of teaching and learning, it could also be argued that it is reified and stabilized (again to echo Wajnryb) for commercial reasons. Another kind of 'untidiness' which is entirely absent from the materials analyzed here (and I would venture to say from most global materials that I am familiar with) is that which can be found in the language produced by other second language speakers. As I suggested in Chapter 3, learning a language is not only a matter of learning a variety of the code, it is also about learning how to decode the language of others – many of whom in the case of English may be second language speakers from a variety of linguistic backgrounds who have varying degrees of competence. Exposure to realistic samples of L2 English, however untidy from a publisher's perspective, could be seen as increasingly essential to the development of appropriate receptive skills for students in many settings (and indeed such material is used in Business English courses).

Elsewhere, Thornbury (2000a) refers to the discrete-item approach of the typical incremental grammar syllabus as 'the grammar McNugget'. In this way, linguistic content is regulated by the publishers, made deliverable for teachers in manageable portions and finally made testable by examination. Many coursebooks (although not all the coursebooks in this study) are in fact linked to examinations or aim to prepare students for eventual examination. Thus language learning promotes testing, which in turn promotes more language teaching, as students progress through a series of carefully graded stages represented by the individual coursebooks in an English course. In this form, English is clearly an example of a McDonaldized product – that is, one which has been subjected to a process of rationalization along the four dimensions identified by Ritzer (1996): efficiency; calculability; predictability; and control. In the case of English, efficient delivery is facilitated through the discrete-item approach found in most coursebooks, the successful learning of which can be calculated through testing. At the same time, the incremental syllabus and a narrow range of accents aim to guarantee predicable learning and performance outcomes. Finally, control is exercised through coursebook activities and tasks which foreclose certain types of engagement with topics, for reasons which are largely associated with the inappropriacy strand in the guidelines for authors. In this way the coursebook may be said to allow for the effective delivery of English as a commodity. Thus a standardized product is delivered through the standardized methodology embodied in the coursebook into the global marketplace – in which all are assumed to want and need exactly the same thing. But do they? In Chapter 7 we explore teachers' thinking on the issues raised by the study so far.

7
Consumption of Content

The audience research study

Within the field of cultural studies audience research has tended to explore the consumption of the products of popular culture such as soap operas, romantic fiction, Hollywood films and teenage magazines. Data gathering has taken a wide variety of forms – for example, Ien Ang's (1985) study of why women watched Dallas was based on letters she received from viewers, while a more in-depth study of the same programme by Tamar Liebes and Elihu Katz (1990) involved video recordings of family interactions while watching the programme, focus group interviews, collective retelling of episodes and questionnaires. A similarly detailed study of a group of women readers of romantic fiction was carried out by Janice Radway (1984) and involved group interviews, individual interviews, informal chats with a 'reader' who made recommendations to other women, questionnaires and a fieldwork journal. Kay Richardson's (1994) more small-scale study of audience responses to the screening of a documentary about poverty in Britain involved post-viewing group discussions with a range of different audience-types. Whatever the methodology, all such studies reject what Thompson (1990: 306) refers to as the 'fallacy of internalism' – the idea that meaning resides exclusively in the text – and take it as axiomatic that meanings are also created at the moment of consumption.

Given my aim of exploring teachers' thinking I opted for what I have called activity-based interviews, in which teachers responded to prompts and talked about materials they had before them, rather than simply answering a pre-determined set of questions. I approached the design of the interview schedule in terms of four main activities (described below), one of which took place prior to the interview itself. In opting for such an approach I was influenced by a number of factors, the first of which was the suggestion that English language teachers often lacked a vocabulary for talking about culture in anything other than very general terms (Adamowski 1991; Lessard-Clouston 1996; Byram and Risager 1999). Certainly the interviews recorded by Phyllis Ryan (1994) as part of an in-depth study on the role of culture in ELT conducted among teachers in Mexico confirmed this in my view. A second consideration was the desire to make the interviews as informant-friendly as possible, while simultaneously providing the maximum amount of stimulus and opportunity for response.

I dealt with the first of these potential problems at the pre-interview stage by following Michael Lessard-Clouston's (1996) advice of exposing informants to a framework and vocabulary for discussing culture in ELT prior to meeting them. The framework chosen was that produced by Adaskou *et al.* (1990) (referred to in Chapter 2 of this volume) which had the advantage of having been devised for designing coursebook cultural content for use in an EFL setting – nominally the same one in which the interviews were to be carried out. The idea was not to impose the framework and its vocabulary on informants – rather the idea was to provide exposure to one way of construing the role of culture in ELT and then, in interview, to provide them with an opportunity to accept, modify or reject it. Each teacher who agreed to be interviewed was given a pre-interview activity at least a week before the interview took place. In this way it was also hoped that any possible feelings of anxiety about the interview might be attenuated through the provision of advance information (see Figure 7.1 below).

As can be seen, the activity asks informants to select and rank the 'senses of culture' in order of importance. The fact that this might prove impossible was viewed as a potential, although not necessarily undesirable, outcome. The aim was to stimulate thinking on the topic and, it was hoped, to make the interview seem less threatening through the use of activity-types already familiar from teaching. Furthermore, by inviting teachers to bring materials of their own choosing for discussion as part of the interview I aimed to give them the opportunity to take charge of a significant part of the encounter.

In addition to discussing two pieces of material provided by the teachers, I also decided to provide two pieces myself. Before deciding finally on which material to include, I invited a number of informants to participate in a group interview with a view to exploring informally key issues in their thinking about cultural content. Of those

---

Culture and English language teaching

Adaskou, K., B. Britten, and B. Fashi (1990) suggest there are four ways of looking at culture in teaching English as a foreign language. These are:

1. the aesthetic sense (e.g. information about the cinema, music, literature)
2. the sociological sense (e.g. information about the nature of family, home life, interpersonal relations, leisure activities, customs)
3. the semantic sense (e.g. words like 'cosy', the difference between dinner, tea, and supper, a bank holiday weekend, that is words or concepts that relate to a particular way of life)
4. the pragmatic sense (e.g. information about social and paralinguistic skills that make successful communication possible: exponents for communicative functions, norms of politeness, rhetorical conventions in writing)

<u>For the interview</u>:
Which of the above senses are most important for you in your teaching?
Rank the senses in order of importance.

<u>For the interview</u>:
Bring two pieces of coursebook material to talk about – one which has implicit or explicit cultural content which you approve of, and one which has implicit or explicit cultural content which you disapprove of.

Figure 7.1 Pre-interview activity

approached, five teachers, all from inner circle countries, agreed to attend. Two main issues emerged in the ensuing conversation. The first of these was the problematic nature of stereotypical representations (mainly to do with race) and how these should be addressed in the classroom. The second concerned the extent to which teachers were involved in teaching 'British culture' when they taught certain genres such as business letters. One participant made the point that perhaps it might be more appropriate for a Spanish person writing in English to an Italian colleague to use the rhetorical conventions of Spanish writing (perceived to be 'less direct and more flowery') than the style favoured in a British business letter. Both these issues fed into the design of the activity-based interview. The comments about stereotypes resonated with an earlier exploratory study which suggested that teachers often found such representations problematic (Gray 2000) and with Byram's (1993) suggestion that the exploration of stereotypes is in fact a useful starting point for enabling students to relativize their worldview. Therefore the first piece of material I chose for the activity-based interview was taken from *Headway Intermediate* (Soars and Soars 1986) and was entitled 'The average British family: A STEREOTYPE' (see Appendix 4). By including this I hoped to be able to explore in more depth teacher thinking on stereotypical representations in coursebooks.

The second piece of material I selected was a controlled practice activity from *Cutting Edge* (Cunningham and Moor 1998). In this exercise students are asked to rewrite a series of requests so that they are more polite (see Appendix 5). This choice was triggered by the comments about the relevance of teaching a 'native speaker' style of writing for lingua franca communication which I hoped would be an opportunity to allow informants to respond to the charge made by Byram (1997) that the currently dominant paradigm in language teaching aims to produce an ersatz 'native speaker'. One area in which this could be said to occur is in the teaching of politeness strategies which are modelled on 'native speaker' pragmatic norms – whether in writing or speaking. McKay (2002: 74) argues that 'there is no inherent reason why a native speaker model should inform the teaching of pragmatics in EIL', and she goes on to suggest that some studies suggest that not conforming to 'native speaker' norms can actually make more pragmatic sense. This piece of material, it was hoped, might also trigger informants' thoughts on the role of the 'native speaker' as a model in ELT more generally.

The final activity for the interview consisted of a number of statements on card which were designed to encourage informants to respond as students do to true/false statements. The statements were as follows:

1. Teaching language is teaching culture (Kramsch 1993).
2. In teaching English we can impart to learners not only the present perfect, but also the power of knowing and caring about the world they live in (Prodromou 1992).
3. The kind of English contained in coursebooks can be called 'cosmopolitan English' because it 'assumes a materialistic set of values in which international travel, not being bored, positively being entertained, having leisure, and above all, spending money casually and without consideration of the sum involved in the pursuit of these ends, are the norm' (Brown 1990).
4. In ELT coursebooks students are positioned at the receiving end of a one way flow of information (Alptekin and Alptekin 1984).

These statements were designed to explore issues, some of which have already been discussed. Statement 1 was designed to explore teacher thinking on the role of culture in ELT generally. Statement 2 aimed to explore the teachers' views on the charge of a perceived lack of an educational dimension in much ELT material (an essential component in the Humboldtian view of language teaching and learning referred to earlier). Statement 3 aimed to explore the materialistic values which it has been argued are associated with English in textbooks (Dendrinos 1992; Hyde 1994; Pennycook 1994; Canagarajah 1999). Finally, Statement 4 was designed to investigate the charge that the absence of any serious cross-cultural dimension meant that students were given little opportunity to respond to the content of the coursebook from their own cultural perspective (Alptekin and Alptekin 1984).

Informants

The activity-based interviews were all conducted with EFL teachers working in the Barcelona area.[1] The reason for my choice of location was determined by the fact that I had worked there as a teacher for many years and it was a setting in which I had easy access to a large population of teachers – both 'native speakers' and L1 Catalan and Spanish speakers. In addition, the Spanish market for British ELT materials in both the state school and the adult learning sector is known to be large. The teachers in this study all worked in the adult learning sector. I interviewed 22 teachers individually – 12 of whom were 'native speakers' and 10 of whom were L1 Catalan/Spanish speakers. All had taught for a minimum of 5 years and thus they may be said to represent an experienced group of ELT practitioners. All informants were given pseudonyms to protect their privacy and no institutions have been mentioned by name. When an informant is first mentioned in the analysis the name is followed by country of origin and years of service (see Appendix 6 for details).

In the following sections I discuss their responses to the various activities in the interview schedule.

Activity 1: Culture and English language teaching

As expected, the ranking activity proved difficult. In fact, two teachers said it was impossible as they felt the four senses were too interconnected to be separable, while a further ten felt they could identify only one or two senses as being important in their teaching. That said, the first activity overall did appear to have provoked a considerable amount of thinking on the topic. Four main points emerged from their engagement with the framework. The first was that the pragmatic and the semantic senses raised issues which were seen as being generally more

Table 7.1   Order of importance of senses of culture

Senses of culture/order of ranking	1st	2nd	3rd	4th
Aesthetic	3	1	1	7
Sociological	5	2	5	1
Semantic	4	7	4	–
Pragmatic	8	7	–	2

integral to language teaching and learning than the issues raised by the aesthetic and the sociological senses. This is not surprising, given that they are the senses most directly concerned with language. While the aesthetic and the sociological senses were seen as useful for the contextualization of language, they were also perceived as much more variable components. Table 7.1 below shows that the pragmatic sense received the highest number of first choices, and that it shares with the semantic sense the highest number of second choices.

However, even when the ranking decisions were similar for the pragmatic and the semantic senses, the reasons given suggest different orientations on the part of informants with regard to pedagogic implications. Robert (UK, 20) summed up the views of many who ranked the pragmatic sense first when he said,

> I chose that because it can cause so many confusions. I mean if they're going to interact with people they have got to get their registers right and they have got to [...] be socially appropriate [...] otherwise they can offend people. That's why I chose that as the most important of the four [...] 'cause the rules are different, the linguistic system is completely different, obviously between Spanish and English.

On the other hand, Pere (Sp., 12), who worked mainly with students of Business English, took up a somewhat different position:

> I think the semantic sense would be the most important aspect for me as a teacher because it's where most meaning is conveyed [...] my students do business with British companies and they tell them that they can't send them something because it's a bank holiday, they need to know what a bank holiday is, otherwise they can't do business, yeah. So that seems to be the most important issue here. Secondly I'd probably say pragmatic sense [...] for instance at receptive level

helping them realize that when a native English speaker begins a sentence by saying 'I'm afraid' what follows is usually bad news [...] I think at least in terms of receptive knowledge or ability that's pretty important.

What is noticeable here is that Robert's view is essentially normative, with an implicit focus on student production, while Pere sees the semantic and the pragmatic senses more in terms of understanding an interlocutor's meaning. His reference to the 'receptive level' and 'receptive knowledge' in the context of interaction with a 'native English speaker' points to a somewhat different orientation to that of Robert, whose focus is on ensuring that students get 'their registers right' and that they are 'socially appropriate'. As we shall see in subsequent sections, this productive/receptive divide points to contrary views held by many informants regarding the concept of appropriateness and the view of the 'native speaker' of British English as the only model for ELT in Spain. At the same time, the importance attached to the semantic and the pragmatic senses was seen as often being determined by specific contextual needs. Thus Bob (US, 14) felt that the pragmatic and the semantic senses assume greater importance for Erasmus students about to study in Britain, while Melissa (UK, 14) saw the pragmatic sense as 'intrinsic' to the 'actual teaching syllabus' for students preparing to take Cambridge examinations – a point also made by Karen (UK, 13).

Informants who ranked the aesthetic and the sociological senses highest were generally those who took a more topic-based view of language lessons – thus Judy (Australia, 9): 'they are the themes we teach through a lot, especially in the lower levels' and Robert, who ranked the sociological sense second: 'I mean they're the sort of things we do.' All informants were of the opinion that cultural content in the aesthetic and the sociological senses could vary considerably depending on students' interests or the context of instruction.

The second point to emerge from the teachers' engagement with the framework was the perception of a considerable degree of what might be called *cultural convergence* within the 'western world' (see following quotation). For the four Spanish teachers who mentioned it, the cultural differences between speakers of Spanish/Catalan and English were less significant than the differences in their respective linguistic codes. To quote Pere again:

Cinema, music, literature, I mean this is world culture now, I mean, I don't really see a great deal of boundaries, particularly within

Europe or the western world, you know between the kind of media culture in the Anglo-Saxon world and the media culture in say southern Europe [...] we see the same films, read the same kind of books really, so that would be the least important of all four.

Similarly Josep (Sp., 10), who, like Pere, ranked the aesthetic sense last, did so on the basis that 'we are all in the western world, I mean, they are so exposed to it... because I mean the students actually receive it from the outside.' This point was also made by Caroline (Ire., 13) and Clare (US, 18) with reference to the aesthetic sense. These comments resonate with Ulf Hannerz's (1992: 30) view that, in an increasingly globalized world, 'media contribute greatly to making the boundaries of societies and cultures fuzzy' as the same cultural products are consumed more widely by greater numbers of people. In this way, he suggests, globally dispersed consumption can lead to an increased sense of having 'more contemporaries' (ibid.) – as individuals or groups come to feel part of transnational cultural entities. Another teacher in her fifties, Pilar (Sp., 26), also felt that in her own lifetime differences at the level of the sociological sense had decreased:

I think that the differences are not as important as some years ago maybe... home life is not that different now, maybe from the time when I was a child here and maybe somebody in England. I don't think that there are as many differences now, there may be something, but maybe there are not as many now [...] it's becoming more and more general no, the European scene.

At the same time, informants viewed specifically British subject matter – in the background studies sense – with considerable reservation. This is the third point to emerge from the first task. Information of this type was seen as being largely irrelevant, except in those instances where students actively solicited it, or where it could be used as the basis for cross-cultural comparisons which might lead to classroom discussion. Here, Caroline sums up the views of most informants:

When the teachers at [institution] are looking at books to decide which one to use, we do tend to avoid those which seem to be too British culture-biased... and the thing that I've noticed, for example when I was piloting a book for Longman which is about to come out, one of the things that they asked me to look at was would it be suitable for all cultures, and so I was looking at the cultural content of that book and what I liked about it was it gave information about all kinds of different kinds of culture, not British culture, or American, I mean it gave information about American culture, African culture, Arab culture etc.

The data suggest the main reason for this attitude is that English is perceived as an international language – a point which was made repeatedly by the interviewees – and that students are mostly learning it with a view to interacting with other second language speakers. As Pere explains, this has implications for content:

> The vast majority of our students come here probably three hours a week for the purpose of learning the code so they can use it with Swiss people (laughs), so I mean they're really not that bothered about learning about the British having an average of six cups of tea a day. It's just pretty meaningless as far as they're concerned.

The example Pere uses to exemplify his point may also suggest that he sees such information as being essentially trivial in nature. Similarly Montse (Sp., 15) explained that she tried to instil in her students an awareness of English as an 'international language' by using class readers about life in Nigeria and a story about Australian Aboriginals. Apart from 'getting the students interested', she felt the benefit was that 'they get to know another culture [...] another place where English is spoken.' This is consistent with McKay's (2002) conclusion that, of the three possibilities put forward by Martin Cortazzi and Lixian Jin (1999: 205) as approaches to cultural content, 'international target culture materials' can serve to raise awareness about how English is used internationally. A similar point is made by Aya Matsuda (2006) who suggests that such content serves to challenge the view of English as an exclusively 'American' or 'western' phenomenon.

Finally, the fourth point to emerge from the discussion of the framework is that for most teachers the best starting point for any kind of focus on culture is the students themselves. For Marta (Sp., 22), echoing Holliday (1999), it was essentially a matter of the small 'culture of the classroom' taking precedence over any other kind of culture:

> The first is to create the right atmosphere in the classroom, so this is culture on its own, because it's the culture of the classroom, and it's a complex culture because every time you begin a new year you have new students, and it's where you start all your interpersonal relations,

and you establish a milieu in that place and from there you start to exchange your own experiences, and when all this begins to work is when you can incorporate things from the outer world.

Marta's idea of a 'milieu' in which an exchange of experiences might be linked to wider issues of interest to the students neatly encapsulates what most teachers appeared happiest with. A further justification for the focus being on students was also made by those 'native speaker' teachers who had spent a long period abroad. Six of them positioned themselves as no longer qualified to address many aspects of culture specifically associated with the UK or the US and/or as cultural learners themselves. This issue was originally raised in the group interview by Max (Switzerland/US, 23) where it met with the approval of the other informants:

> Our culture is so diluted, I mean I don't know where I come from anymore, and like I just deal with what they bring and we kind of do their culture in English.

On this view, culture is (partly) understood as knowledge which, in this instance, can become weakened or otherwise reduced though living abroad. Max returned to this theme again during the first task, this time positioning himself as a learner of the students' culture:

> I guess I turn it upside down, and like I'm the kind of the person who's, doesn't know, and I ask them about their culture rather than the other way round I think.

As we shall see, many of these core concerns were returned to and further nuanced in the subsequent sections as the teachers engaged with the remaining activities. In the next section I turn to the second phase of the interviews, in which the teachers discussed material they chose themselves.

Activity 2: Teachers' materials (1)

Earlier I referred to the fact that the literature on teacher thinking with regard to issues of culture in ELT suggested that teachers tended to talk about the topic in very general terms. In one study (Byram and Risager 1999), over 850 British and Danish modern languages teachers were asked to outline their views on the role of culture in language teaching through questionnaires, and over 50 were also interviewed. In the questionnaire the teachers were asked to define 'culture' and 'cultural awareness'. The analysis of the answers led Byram and Risager to conclude that most teachers understood culture in very general and 'uncontroversial' (ibid.: 89) terms. They add the following:

> There is scarcely anyone who includes thoughts about dominance, suppression, power, cultural imperialism, prejudices, stereotypes or similar concepts. (ibid.: 89)

Interestingly all these issues *were* raised by the Barcelona teachers. The reason may be related to the format of the activity-based interviews in which the teachers were asked to include material they disliked. Although I did not ask for a definition of culture, on the grounds that such a question might have been seen as daunting, I did ask the five teachers who came to the initial group interview, held at the planning stage of the activity-based interview schedule, to brainstorm the words they associated with 'culture'. The brainstorming produced only one of the terms listed by Byram and Risager, namely, 'stereotypes', while the remainder were similar to many of the general associations found in their study. At the end of the brainstorming activity, the teachers in the group interview were asked to list their first three associations. These are described in Table 7.2.

These terms may be understood as being associated with each teacher's prototypical or default view of culture. Many of them can be linked to the conceptions and ideas surveyed in Chapter 2 – that is, 'high' culture (theatre, poetry); 'popular' culture (newspapers); the centrality of language (language, jargon); the 'way of life' view of culture (traditions, food); and the notion of cultures as plural and differentiated (varied, groups, variety, society). Even Melissa's list of adjectives may be said to point to the 'exotic' – identified by Alfred Kroeber (1953, in

Table 7.2 Words associated with 'culture' by group interviewees

Teacher	Words associated with culture
Gary (UK, 9)	variety; society; stereotypes
Karen (UK, 15)	theatre; groups; culture
Max (Swit./US, 23)	newspaper; poetry; jargon
Melissa (UK, 14)	fascinating; rich; varied
Judy (Aust., 9)	language; traditions; food

Hannerz 1992: 3) as the focus of so much early anthropological interest in culture. However, when the same teachers were asked to discuss examples of cultural content in ELT coursebooks which met with their approval and disapproval they addressed a considerably wider range of issues, many of which were linked to the context of instruction. I begin with the materials they disliked, as teachers had more to say on this topic than on materials they liked.

Stereotypes

The type of materials most teachers viewed negatively were those containing stereotypical representations, mainly of nationality and gender. Thus several teachers drew attention to the representation of a North American family on a whirlwind tour of Europe in *New Headway Intermediate* (Soars and Soars 1996). This reading and listening activity, entitled 'If it's Tuesday...we must be in Munich', consists of an interview with four tourists who are confused about what they have seen.[2] Bob and Clare both found it objectionable to varying degrees. For Clare all national stereotypes were offensive and at odds with her understanding of language teaching as an activity 'to promote some sort of cultural understanding of people'. In her view, the problem with such representations was that students could have their existing stereotypes 'confirmed to some extent by seeing these drawings and things in a textbook'. Bob was more equanimous, describing them as 'a cheap shot', while broadly agreeing that they could confirm students' preconceptions about North Americans. Similar views were expressed by Montse, who said a colleague had been 'outraged' by the way in which the tourists were represented, and Pilar, who disliked the nationality stereotyping, also added that it was 'terrible' that one of the women was shown to be 'really stupid'. Pilar and Josep also felt another reading in the same coursebook about a white middle-class family living in the south-east of Britain was inaccurate. For Pilar, it painted a 'misleading' picture that would give students the 'wrong idea' about British people, while Josep felt it completely ignored the fact that Britain was a 'multiracial society'.

Melissa and Karen both drew attention to gender stereotyping – although, like most informants, they felt that coursebooks had improved greatly in this area since they had started teaching. Melissa described a listening activity as 'sexist' in which women were repeatedly represented as bad drivers and said that having used it once she would never use it again. Her answer to my question about why she felt so strongly indicates how closely teachers can identify with the materials they use and how they resist being positioned by them:

> it's as if you're giving it your seal, you approve of it, yes. If you don't approve of it you shouldn't use it because you might give the impression that you agree with, say the ideas on the cassette, or with the way the women are portrayed and I wouldn't like my students to think that I did, that I agreed with that.

Like Clare and Bob, Melissa thought that stereotypical material had the potential to reinforce ideas students might already hold. Although teacher-instigated discussion of such issues was an option, she added that it was sometimes a risky strategy as students could take the opportunity to express sexist or racist views. This was seen as problematic as it raised the issue of how to respond. In the group interview she had made the point that teachers had to be careful about how they expressed their own opinions in such circumstances:

> you have to be diplomatic [...] with students you're in a delicate situation because they're customers, clients, and you mustn't offend.

Melissa's remark is a reminder that, in some instances, particularly for those teachers working in the private sector, the marketization of language teaching can impact on pedagogic decision making. In such settings, in Eulàlia's (Sp., 15) opinion, it would be preferable if the critical perspective came from the activities contained within the coursebook itself – thereby absolving the individual teacher of appearing to follow her own critical agenda (although she lamented that this was not the case with global coursebooks).

Irrelevant content

As stated earlier, specifically British subject matter was seen as often being irrelevant in the context of instruction. Thus Max explained that while the material he brought to the interview was suitable for 'a kind of ESL situation' in the UK (using a public telephone and similar activities), it was largely irrelevant to students in Barcelona. Robert also mentioned the lack of relevance of a piece of material on the typical English breakfast in the context of a teacher training course he delivered in Romania. In the following extract he explains why he found it 'embarrassing':

> there's toast, orange juice, coffee, cheese, God marmalade, croissants (laughing), it's all there, I mean [...] for your average Romanian that

would be a sort of a wedding banquet I should think. So I mean I find it embarrassing and I don't think it's necessary [...]. There was no way that most of them were going to encounter what's on this page, and I don't think they needed to know about it really. I just can't see the relevance of it at all.

Robert returned to this before completing the activity to make the point that the material would not have been embarrassing in Spain because it would not 'insult anybody', whereas in Romania it was 'like rubbing their noses in their poverty sort of thing'. This recalls comments made by one of the editors in Chapter 6 who admitted that certain kinds of aspirational content were not appropriate for all east European contexts. Marta also mentioned the irrelevance of material on how to avoid culture shock in various British social settings – on account of the degree of cultural convergence referred to earlier. Jennifer (Australia, 18) also complained about the overall picture of Britain painted throughout the *Headway* course. In her view this was constructed around 'quaint, anecdotal, English, eccentric stories' which were 'of very little interest to the majority of students' and 'downright embarrassing' to teach.[3] Similar points were also made by Isabel (Sp., 7) and Janet (UK, 18). These references to embarrassment are suggestive of the way in which teachers can feel positioned by materials which they believe to be inappropriate for certain groups.

Gary's (UK, 9) example underlined the point that the context of instruction is a key factor in evaluating the relevance of a piece of material. He described how a listening exercise about a collective of women mechanics in Sheffield had been the basis of a 'fantastically successful lesson in Cairo' because

it generated lots and lots of fascinating discussion [...] it was a fascinating area, it prompted lots of interest, the cultural content really went down well, it got lots of discussion.

However, the same material 'died a thousand deaths' when he used it with his students in Barcelona, the reason being, he suggested, that Catalans took the view that 'everybody can do everything' and there was therefore nothing to discuss. What is also significant about this remark – something we will encounter repeatedly in accounts of what teachers approve of – is that the material's potential for generating discussion is a key factor in overall evaluation.

Discursive weight

Pennycook (1998: 2) argues that while English is not inherently colonial it remains 'deeply interwoven with the discourses of colonialism'. On this view, English and ELT, the origins of which Pennycook locates at the heart of Britain's colonial project, continue to bear what he calls a 'discursive weight' (ibid.: 8). This is instanced, he suggests, in a multitude of ways including, *inter alia*, the popular media's 'glorification' (ibid.: 156) of the distinctive qualities of English and the way in which this is frequently reproduced in ELT materials along with celebratory accounts of its global spread; the construction and the uses of the 'native/non-native speaker' dichotomy; and the essentializing of certain groups of students as passive or incapable of critical thinking. As we shall see, a cluster of themes which can be linked to the concept of 'discursive weight' were raised by a small number teachers for whom the construction of English in coursebooks was seen as problematic in this respect.

Like most informants, Caroline felt that overtly British content was best avoided. She began by suggesting that students 'like to be able to identify with things in books' and that an exclusive focus on things British is 'a bit limited, a bit boring'. Then after an initial hesitation, she added, 'I was going to say, on a personal level, it comes a bit back to the empire thing.' Her answer to my request for clarification is worth quoting at length:

> I suppose one of the things that has marked British intervention in most countries is that they do try to impose their culture on the other countries and in a way, historically speaking, that's why English is the most widely spoken language [...] historically speaking, the British have always tried to impose their language and their customs on the many countries which they tried to colonize, or did colonize. I don't think the British are very well seen in general in other countries because often people think that they're arrogant and, I'm sure it comes from this as well, thinking that well, the way they do things in Britain is better than the way they do them anywhere else. In fact I was talking to a Spanish person about this very thing last night and I suggested that the Spanish also colonized a lot of countries, but she was saying yes, but they didn't tend to impose everything Spanish on the country, OK, they took everything there was out of the country and they exploited it for material benefit, but they didn't seem to have the same arrogance where the other country had to adopt their culture. And this is the feeling a lot of people have about the, the British. In Ireland the same thing happened [...] unless you

stopped speaking Gaelic and you started speaking English you hadn't a hope in hell of getting work or being able to communicate with the oppressors.

This extract raises a number of issues – firstly, there is her own fore-grounded sense of personal involvement with the material (a feature of many teachers' choices); secondly, there is her account of Britain's colonial past which is linked with her perception of 'the British' as arrogant; and thirdly, there is the link between Britain's colonial involvement in Ireland and language shift from Irish to English. It should also be said that her initial hesitation and subsequent, somewhat vague, reference to 'the empire thing' suggested she might need encouragement to express a possibly negative assessment of overtly British content – hence my clarification request. In fact I had inferred correctly from her hesitation and the implicit hedge in 'the empire thing'. No other 'native speaker' teacher spoke about cultural content in this way, although some L1 Spanish teachers did refer to colonialism, linguistic imperialism and the notion of 'the dominant culture'. What is interesting about this highly politicized (and in places essentializing) statement is that it is offered as an explanation of why she prefers not to use overtly British material in class (although she offered no specific examples of what she meant). Pennycook (1998: 16) suggests that ELT practitioners 'walk in Crusoe's footsteps', by which he means that ELT practices are perforce linked to the legacy of colonialism, and Caroline's comments certainly suggest that for her the legacy of colonialism continues to 'adhere' (using Pennycook's term) to English. It is for this reason she says she prefers content which is 'more global' in orientation.

Pere too was aware of the adherence of colonialism – although he positions himself very differently. As an example of material he disliked, he cited a *Cambridge English 1* (Swan and Walter 1990b) text in which Zulu, Maori and Native American speakers describe their unhappy child-hoods. All three mention unkind treatment at the hands of white people. The following exchange illustrates the nature of his alternative perspective:

P: [...] and it's just kind of like 'Is this really necessary?' and I'm sure it's true and very sad and regretable, but what kind of message are the authors trying to convey here? I mean is this, the idea, some kind of penitence for my students to repent and feel guilty in class as well as learn the simple past of the verb be, you know?

J: It's an interesting area, isn't it? I mean why do you think they've put that sort of stuff in the book?

P: Because I think it makes some British people feel better about themselves (laughs) to be honest.

J: Do you mean maybe teachers?

P: Teachers, maybe coursebook writers, maybe kind of liberal professions or whatever, people who are aware of what imperial countries might have done some time ago, and the damage done etc., etc. and they try to pay back or apologise for it, which I'm not saying is a bad thing, it's probably called for, necessary, but you wonder to what extent this is really the best choice for teaching the simple past of the verb be.

Pere's point is essentially that the legacy of colonialism has nothing to do with him or his students. His rationale for its presence in a course-book also resonates with the 'guilt complex' explanation offered by Alan Pulverness (1999: 5) for the demise of background studies in British ELT materials. The reference to 'what imperial countries might have done some time ago' is indicative of his understanding of such content as essentially historical baggage which is of dubious value for contextualizing grammar. Like Caroline, he states that he prefers materials that 'address the issue of English as an international language'. For Pere this clearly involves a different type of thematic content, but he added – a point he would make throughout the interview – that it would also involve a move away from what he perceived as a narrow focus on RP and the inclusion of a much wider range of accents from around the English-speaking world.

The reservations expressed by Caroline and Pere (although somewhat differently motivated) point to a view of English as historically encumbered – and both suggest that it can, and should, be constructed differently in coursebooks for the teaching of English as an international language. Other teachers, whose views I now address, raised the issue of a different kind of encumbrance – that of the uncritical representation of what they called the 'dominant culture'.

Jaime (Peru, 20) positioned himself as having been raised in 'a very much Anglophile culture' in Lima and during the discussion of the first task he made the case for prioritizing the aesthetic sense as a way of making the language attractive to students and as means of opening up new cultural perspectives. He described his own view of teaching as 'humanistic' in which he aimed to help students become members of 'a global community'. However, as the following exchange suggests, this involves the development of critical faculties:

> Jaime: I tend to create [...] a certain distance between English as a dominant culture, in many of the places in the world I have taught English, and maybe because of personal, or for respect of my own culture of origin, for respect of my own culture of origin, I always tend to create this distance.
>
> J: Between?
>
> Jaime: Between lang-, English as a dominant, as a means of transferring a dominant culture to my students and to, even to myself.
>
> J: OK, that's very interesting Jaime, can I just ask you a little bit more about that? How do you manage to get that distance in there?
>
> Jaime: Well basically by doing the same kind of process of learning that I encourage in my students, actually processing the information I learn through language, language learning and language teaching with a critical eye, with a critical attitude.

This suggests a certain duality inherent in English – on the one hand it can facilitate entry into a global community, and on the other is it has the potential to transfer the 'dominant culture' to both teacher and students, with perhaps negative consequences for their 'culture of origin'. Such a process has been referred to elsewhere as 'ontological imperialism' (Modiano 2001: 164), whereby 'the learner's mind is colonized through the acquisition of a foreign tongue.' Jaime subsequently describes the 'dominant culture' tangentially in terms of coursebook material in which the focus is on 'glorifying a kind of middleclass' for its eccentric individualism and conspicuous wealth which he feels 'might be considered shallow' in certain educational settings. He suggests that students should be given the chance to reflect on such content, and that the teacher's role is to help them do this, while at the same time encouraging them 'to talk with pride' about their own cultural backgrounds. Such an approach, similar to that advocated by Freire (1970/1996) and Kramsch (1993), is also recommended by Martin Hyde (1994) as a means of enabling Moroccan students to resist the hypothesized potential of English to undermine specifically Moroccan values.

Eulàlia also saw glorification in the coursebooks she used. In this extract she describes how *New Headway Upper-Intermediate* (Soars and Soars 1998) represents Bill Gates:

> I think in English, in English books, there is a lot of, a lot of like the icons of the culture are like very much very present, I think. And

sometimes, I don't know if they are very critical of it, I don't think they are [...] for example in relation (to) this, here in the new Headway there is a text about Bill Gates [...] 'The man who could buy anything', I mean how powerful this guy is, and 'The richest private citizen in the world' [...] 'He has a personal fortune which is more than the annual economic output of over a hundred countries'. And I think this like, I mean there is something to be said about this, you know. I mean, obviously I'm not saying that the book, I mean it's there, you can do what you want with it, but, but the thing that, they do this a lot, they take people, maybe Americans more [...] and then they kind of glorify it a bit, and they are not very critical.

For this teacher the problem with such material, which can be seen as celebratory of individualism, wealth and celebrity, is that it is presented uncritically – 'there is no criticism [...] or no questioning [...] no discussion or anything, whether this is like morally right or not.' Other similarly glorified 'American icons' included Paul Newman, Madonna, Mickey Mouse and Coca-Cola. As we saw above, dealing with problematic content can present the teacher with a dilemma. This can be a direct consequence of the context of instruction where, for example, the student may be seen as a customer – with all the implications this has for the way in which teachers may perceive their own role. For Eulàlia, who sees the teacher's role as that of 'co-ordination', appearing to be neutral and allowing the students to do the talking is preferable, although she admitted she did not always manage to keep her views to herself. A further point, which she made repeatedly throughout the interview, was that despite her deep reservations about the celebratory representation of the dominant culture, such content often 'worked' at the methodological level – a point I will return to.

Activity 2: Teachers' materials (2)

Given the topics mentioned in the previous section it is not surprising that some informants brought along materials in which stereotypes were shown to be broken. Thus Karen and Eulàlia drew attention to representations of gender and race which they felt challenged existing stereotypes and reflected social change. A second type of content which was viewed favourably was that which was perceived to be directly relevant to students. Pere identified material on social introductions in a business setting as relevant to his students, adding that he liked 'the kind of international world culture kind of feel to it'. Similarly Jaime felt that material on how to give a business presentation would 'empower' his students to function in the 'corporate culture' in which they would use their English. Marta's material, which consisted of a listening exercise in which a number of speakers talked about changes they had seen in their own lifetimes, was described as dealing with 'the culture of life', and revolved around the topics of education, city life, food, travel and work. She also commented favourably on the way in which the speakers had accents from around the English-speaking world. Other types of relevant content mentioned by Robert and Janet were related to service encounters they felt their students might have to engage in, while Josep brought along material on music and 'the generation gap' with which he felt teenagers could identify.

However, apart from these, the remainder of the material produced in this stage of the interview fell into two broad categories – texts about cultural practices in various parts of the world, for example, contemporary life in Samoa, a dragon festival in Hong Kong, avoiding culture shock when abroad, good manners in different parts of the world and Spanish lifestyle; and, despite reservations expressed in activity 1 and the first part of activity 2, texts which were more clearly of the background studies type, for example, information about emigration to the US, the Grand Canyon, Christmas cards, New Year in the UK, attitudes to drinking tea, bonfire night and the lives of Shakespeare, Agatha Christie and Thomas Hardy. However, what is significant here is the way in which the informants discussed this material almost exclusively in terms of the activities students had to do or in terms of the linguistic outcomes – rather than focusing on the actual content itself. Teachers in fact seemed to switch to their default view of culture when asked to select material which met with their approval and to switch also to a position in which linguistic concerns were uppermost in their thinking. Terms and expressions used to describe materials included 'quite challenging' (Caroline); 'very engaging', 'very communicative' and 'very exploitable' (Pere); 'it produced a lot of [...] interesting conversations' and 'it worked well' (Max); 'you get a bit of discussion' (Judy); 'there are four shorter texts, interconnected to some extent, which in the class worked very well' (Isabel); 'it's task-based [...] it's more communicative, it integrates skills (Marc, Sp. 9); 'material which I thought worked very, very well and was good fun' (Gary); 'it actually works' (Bob); 'it can be extrapolated to the student's own experience' (Jennifer); 'it's well organized and ... has a lot of activities around it' (Clare). In many instances what made the material 'work' was an interactive element in which students exchanged information, or there was a cross-cultural dimension in which the students were given the opportunity to compare how things were done in Spain with things elsewhere, or, in the case of the text on Spanish lifestyle, to react against a stereotypical representation. Overall though, Gary's comments on the text about the collective of women mechanics referred to earlier summed up the views of most teachers:

> Basically what I hope to get from materials is a nice context for language focus and nice context which is going to animate discussion. So what I'm saying is like gender, I've learnt now as a language teacher practically in Catalonia that I'd probably not use a piece of material like this again because it wouldn't stimulate much discussion or much interest [...] what I feel is that it's probably a good topic to include in a coursebook, I think it would go down well in Brazil, it would go down very well in Egypt but it doesn't go down well everywhere and the teacher has to select according to what's going to stimulate practice.

In fact, animating discussion and stimulating practice were at the heart of most teachers' concerns in their selection of cultural content which they viewed positively. I now turn to the third phase of the interview in which the teachers engaged with materials I had selected.

Activity 3: Researcher's materials

Reactions to the first piece of material 'The average British family: A stereotype' were mixed. Just under half the teachers agreed with Marta's view that the text was 'boring', 'uninteresting' and 'unattractive' and several of them said that they would prefer a focus on a real family. Clare cited the *Material World: A Global Family Portrait* (Menzel *et al.* 1995) as an example of something which would be more interesting for students to engage with. This consists of photographs of families from around the world pictured outside their house with all their possessions on display. Others felt the focus was too narrow and that families today, both in Britain and elsewhere, were more varied units, as Edward (UK, 13) points out:

> but what about the average British family which is a single parent family, and what about the average English family where you haven't got he and she, you've got he and he, yeah?

Similar points about lesbian and gay invisibility were made by Montse, Marta and Jaime. When I asked if teachers would like to see the focus widened to include more ethnically diverse families most teachers said they would, although Pere, Pilar and Rosa (Sp., 7) felt this was somewhat missing the point. Pilar explained that for her 'the central point is language' and that if such information were to be included in coursebooks it would be more useful to include a wider range of accents and varieties from around the English-speaking world – a view echoed by Pere. Rosa explained that just as it was preferable nowadays to speak of 'literatures in English' instead of 'English literature', so too in the study of English language there was a need to amplify the subject to expose students to different varieties. Her rationale for such exposure was that it would provide students with new information about the language they were learning which she felt would be more motivating than the kind of content normally found in coursebooks.

However, over half the teachers were more positive about the material and the majority of those saw in it the potential for cross-cultural comparison and the possibility of generating discussion. As with the discussion of material they liked, teachers explained how they had used it in the past or what they would do to fully maximize its language-generating potential. Thus marked stereotypes were not necessarily rejected, but could be viewed positively by many teachers – including Bob and Melissa, both of whom had complained earlier – on account of their potential to stimulate language practice.

The second piece of material on polite language raised three issues, all of which can be related to the normative role of British 'native speaker' models in contemporary ELT. These are to do with politeness, pronunciation and idiomatic spoken British English, each of which I shall address in turn.

Politeness

Cook (1999: 190) makes the point that although the 'native speaker' has maintained a ghostlike presence in second language acquisition SLA research, the presence in ELT has been altogether more substantial. He argues that coursebooks are 'implicitly native based' (ibid.: 189), as instanced by the predominance of idealized 'native speaker' interactions as models for contextualizing language. To this we might add the use of the RP cluster of accents identified in Chapters 4 and 5 as the predominant element in the phonological representation of English and the way in which many contemporary global coursebooks include sections on idiomatic spoken British English. Although all informants (with the exception of one) felt the second piece of material *could* be used in the classroom, many were critical of the way in which it was presented and what it seemed to imply about language use. Gary summed up much of this criticism as follows:

> A criticism I have a lot, of a lot of coursebooks in the way that they deal with language, is that they say to students in x situation such and such a choice of language is appropriate, they don't say to students in x situation you have a range of choices, the liable effect of these choices on the person you're interlocuting with is liable to be boom, boom, boom because of these reasons [...] and a lot of coursebooks seem to come from the attitude of this is what you say to your dad, this is what you say to your boss, and this is what you say to your best friend, nonsense.

This is precisely the charge levelled by Leung (2005: 137), who argued that such 'reductionist and static idealizations [...] are at best partial representations of social reality', adding, with reference to *Headway* advice on greetings, that there is 'no one way of greeting people, any more than there is one way of talking to a bank clerk or an airline worker'. This was the view expressed by informants who felt the material needed input from the teacher so as not to be misleading. The exercise also triggered doubt about, or in some cases criticism of, the way in which coursebooks often devoted considerable time and space to the presentation and practice of more elaborate forms of politeness associated with British 'native speakers'. For these teachers such activities were seen as possibly unnecessary for the kinds of interaction their students were likely to engage in, that is, those involving mainly L2 speakers. Thus Pere commented,

> in terms of productive work this is where you could argue a case for saying, well look, here's your German counterpart you know, you're Spanish, why on earth should you struggle you know with these convoluted, embedded kind of phrases 'I'm really sorry to bother you, but I wondered if you could possibly' you know, which British people might choose when dealing with other British speakers. So you could argue a case, you could make a case for that, maybe that's not really necessary.

At the same time he was quick to add that such speech could be produced by an interlocutor and would have to be decoded:

> On the other hand, a lot of European students are learning English using British English as a model, so, even for productive purposes,

my Spanish manager might be faced with a German manager who does choose to say things like 'I'm really sorry to bother you, but I was wondering if you could possibly bla bla bla bla bla' in which case he or she would need to be able to understand and decode that and respond to it appropriately.

Jennifer was also doubtful of the value of teaching such forms, but pointed out that she was constrained by 'a very culture bound exam' (Cambridge First Certificate) to teach such elaborate language. Under different circumstances she said 'I certainly wouldn't give it much emphasis.' Ideally, students could be taught to produce more 'neutral' language (of the kind featured in the material from *Cutting Edge*) which she felt was more appropriate for her students who, via the Internet, were being exposed to what she called 'world hybrid English'. For such students, 'can', 'could' and 'please' provided a 'good base' and were ultimately more 'serviceable' than the culturally specific forms she was required to teach at First Certificate level. However, despite complaints about the way such language was addressed generally in ELT materials, the teachers, including Jennifer and Gary, saw the *Cutting Edge* exercise as potentially useful, particularly for Erasmus students headed for Britain or for those students aiming at a high level of perfection.

When asked about their views on the role of the 'native speaker' ideal within ELT, not surprisingly, many informants saw the term as inherently problematic but felt that when it came to matters of politeness or the expression of pragmatic meaning then issues of student choice and the context of use needed to be considered. Most took the view that if students were going to go to Britain or the US then they needed to be made aware of how their language might be interpreted by 'native speakers'. On the other hand, Melissa pointed out:

A lot of students in actual fact don't use English with native speakers [...] they often use English on the telephone, or in faxes, or emails or whatever, and they develop their own kind of lingo [...] so maybe for these people these things aren't important, but at least you give them the, in the classroom, you give them the opportunity to be, you make them aware of them, whether they choose to use them or not is up to them.

Josep and Jennifer also referred to the notion of students developing their own speaking and writing style – although they acknowledged a tension between this and the requirements of international examining bodies which, as has been pointed out (Leung and Lewkowicz 2006), remain focused on metropolitan 'native speaker' varieties of English. For these teachers the issue is essentially one of emphasis – they appear to be happier with the classroom focus on such language being on reception rather than necessarily also entailing production, which they see as a requirement only in some contexts of use.

Pronunciation

At the mention of the term 'native speaker' many informants turned to the issue of pronunciation. Here opinion was uncertain about the extent to which students should be taught to approximate some inner circle 'native speaker' model. While most teachers were critical of what they saw as the narrow range of accents contained in the coursebooks, several teachers felt that the concept functioned as a kind of benchmark around which to work. Pilar, positioning herself as a language learner, stated,

> I think we, we have to have a model […] for me it's still a model, the native speaker, but it doesn't mean that I have to be like the native speaker, it's my model, but I know that I will never be like a native speaking the language.

In Pilar's case the model was RP – 'I think that it's basic' she said, although she recognized this position was no longer widely accepted by teachers. Her view was that in the early stages of language learning students should 'follow' only one accent on the grounds that this had been important in her own learning. Pilar was the only teacher to make the case for a so-called prestige accent in this way – the remainder of the Catalan/Spanish teachers generally made the case for a wider range of accents on the accompanying tapes. Most 'native speaker' teachers took the view that their own accent functioned as a model for students and said that they also tried to expose them to other pronunciations where possible, in the knowledge that students would not end up sounding like 'native speakers'.

There were also clear signs that teachers were aware of emerging debates within ELT surrounding the issue of the teaching of pronunciation. For almost all the teachers the global spread of English and the rise in numbers of speakers of English as a second language were seen as having implications for teaching. At the same, it was also evident that the precise nature of these implications was far from clear, as the following exchange with Pere reveals:

P OK. The problem here is what native speaker? Is it British? If British, then what? RP? Or London?, because London's the metropolis or whatever, but hang on a minute there's three hundred million North American English speakers, and certainly the United States have got a much greater role in the world today than Britain, so maybe it should be American English, or some kind of American English variety that we should use as a model. I really don't know. I think somewhere, it's Crystal or Brazil or someone saying that in twenty years time there'll be more English speakers for whom English is a second language than there'll be native speakers of English. So really this might be a debate that we might be able to drop altogether in twenty years time and stop worrying about it because we'll be using a kind of toned down more international, more neutral form or variety of English as a model.

J And as a teacher you would find that acceptable?

P I would probably find it desirable to be honest, because, like I said, we teach, I don't know probably about 300 students at companies. Probably only about 15 of them have regular contact with native British speakers. So you really wonder what kind of service you're doing them by, by using British English as the only model, the predominant model, yeah, but I think it's going that way more and more so in the near future.

J Towards some kind of international ...

P Definitely, definitely newer materials like *Business Opportunities* reflect this I think quite well. And I think that's, that's a road I'd choose to take. Having said that, I mean, what is world English or international English? Is there such a thing as that? I don't know, I mean we'll probably end up using a kind of toned down version of standard mid-Atlantic speech as a model, yeah, something that's fairly neutral.

Such a view implies that the primacy of the British 'native speaker' is rendered problematic by the global spread of English, and at the same time recognizes that any replacement of that idealized model is far from straightforward. Material of the kind Pere liked frequently features key characters who speak English as an L2 with L1 accents. Similarly, Eulàlia introduced the idea of 'Euro-English' as a possible model in which 'the actual words and [...] the conventions are shared, but maybe other things like pronunciation [...] are not'. Such a situation, she felt, echoing Widdowson (1994, 1997), would reflect the reality that English was not only the 'property of a few countries' but 'something that we all use'.

Idiomatic spoken English

The third issue raised by the material was the extent to which idiomatic spoken British English should be taught. This was mentioned by two Spanish informants who addressed it at great length in the light of their own experience as language learners, and as language teaching professionals who were familiar with debates in the field. Having said that she would teach the forms in the *Cutting Edge* exercise for both recognition and production, Montse added that there were other features of 'native speaker' language which she saw as more problematic and of possible limited usefulness. She gave an account of a talk by a well-known British applied linguist who, she said, had made the case for teaching 'First class stamp, please' as a more realistic request to produce in a post-office than 'I would like to buy a first class stamp, please' – which, more typically, might be found in a coursebook. Montse disagreed, saying that while it was true that 'native speakers' did use the first type of request, they also knew how to make the second type and for a teacher not to teach the longer form would be to short-change the students. To shift from the second type of request to the first was easier than the other way around, she argued, and confirmed by her own experience as a language learner on trips to the UK.

Her second point was that because she was not in contact with spoken British English on a regular basis, she was unable to teach it. Her view was that teaching should be based on 'giving them the full structure' and 'showing them how the language works' and that students themselves could acquire more idiomatic forms in their own time, if they were in a situation where such language was being used and if they were interested. Such a position resonates with Catherine Wallace's (2002: 105) case for teaching 'literate English' as an elaborated 'supranational global' variety – which, Montse implies, can be customized subsequently by speakers themselves if the need and inclination arise.

A similar point was made by Eulàlia, who also gave an account of a talk, this time by another British academic, in which he compared a recording of two L2 English speakers and two 'native speakers' from the CANCODE corpus. The academic's point, she explained, had been that there was nothing more 'real' about the English in the culturally specific 'native speaker' exchange. She described how the talk enabled her to think of herself as a user of a global language in which the 'native/non-native speaker' distinction did not imply different ownership rights. The important thing she said was 'to make it ours'. In reply to my question about how she could do this, she replied,

> not feeling so much that there is a model, yeah that we, in measuring our capabilities and abilities in using the language according to that model of like native speakers [...] but seeing it, or looking at all these other people yeah, who also speak English, who are not native speakers and who can communicate in it and use it yes, and, and as well choose yeah, decide 'What do I want from the language? What kind of areas am I interested in? What kind of things do I want to do with it?'

Thus Eulàlia suggests a contrast between 'measuring' her English against the 'native speaker' model and looking instead to other L2 speakers with a view to choosing and deciding for herself the identifications she wishes to make. Many of the views articulated by the teachers in Activity 3 resonate with those expressed by Widdowson (1997: 140), who argued that the global spread of English must be seen as the spread of a set of latent or virtual possibilities, rather than the distribution of a 'stabilized and standardized code leased out on a global scale'. Clearly this suggests a tension between what we have seen is on offer in coursebooks and what many practitioners in this setting seem to want.

Activity 4: True/false statements

By the time we reached this stage of the interview many informants had been talking for nearly an hour. The final activity in which they responded to the statements on card took less time than the previous activities and in some cases responses took the form of short comments in which previously made points were reiterated or further nuanced.

Statement 1

'Teaching language is teaching culture.' (Kramsch 1993)

For half the teachers the response to this statement was of the 'it depends' type. All agreed that culture and language were linked but that the nature of the link could be interpreted differently depending on the context of instruction, and the interests and needs of the students. The four teachers who gave a categorical 'no' also recognized that language and culture were linked. Thus Jennifer, for example, affirmed that 'language is a reflection of culture' and Josep stated that 'culture is somehow embedded' in language. Their disagreement with the statement came from the belief that they did not 'teach' culture, in the same way that they taught language. In disagreeing with the statement, these teachers also rejected a view of English language teaching in which it was assumed there was a necessary link with aspects of life in Britain. Thus Robert said,

> You can learn a language without going into a great deal of culture [...] you've got to teach them sociolinguistic appropriacy but that doesn't mean to say they have to necessarily know that some people in Britain have porridge for breakfast.

Paradoxically, the teachers who answered 'yes' did not necessarily disagree with Robert. Thus Marta, who agreed with the statement, saw rules for sociolinguistic appropriacy as implying the teaching of culture, but added that 'you can talk about Paris, about the Nile, about many things in English, not necessarily of the British culture.' This would suggest that while informants were in general agreement about thematic content being seen as cultural – and necessarily variable, given the increasingly international nature of English – not all saw sociolinguistic appropriacy as cultural in the same way. Other teachers interpreted the statement very differently. Thus Caroline stated,

> when I teach language I draw a lot on the culture of the country I'm in, so I'm not actually teaching them about their own culture, I'm just using it to make the situation seem more real.

This focus on the culture of the students was also made by Jaime, Max and Janet – in Janet's words the students' own cultural background is the 'stepping stone' for any focus on culture , adding, 'my concept of teaching altogether is the fact that you work from what they've got, not from what you've got.' These teachers took the view that all cultural work should be cross-cultural in nature with the students being given opportunities to reflect on the similarities and differences between themselves and other groups.

Statement 2

> 'In teaching English we can impart to learners not only the present perfect, but also the power of knowing and caring about the world they live in.' (Prodromou 1992)

Teachers were also divided over this statement. Janet's response may be said to sum up the views of the seven teachers who agreed with Prodromou's view:

> knowing and caring about the world means being open to other cultures and other traditions, not being enclosed in your own, so that to me is the most important thing, that there's an opportunity and that they see that whoever is teaching them [...] gives them the opportunity to sometimes discuss other issues rather than the present perfect.

However, for the remainder, who saw language teaching as their main aim, this aspect was only tangentially relevant to their professional practice. The views of Max – 'my role is to get talk going' – and Rob – 'you choose whatever motivates them to talk' – were more representative of the group as whole, but all felt that educational themes were appropriate for those groups who wished to explore them. That said, a smaller number of teachers were critical of the statement. Judy saw it as 'very dangerous', and stated 'it's not our position as English teachers to educate the world.' Gary and Jennifer were also sceptical, with the latter warning that 'you have to be very careful not to impose your ideologies on students' which was what she saw coursebooks as doing. This perspective was echoed by Eulàlia, who pointed out that

> many times knowing and caring about the world we live in is transmitting the dominant culture [...] so we want to be careful about what we mean by this.

These comments resonate with several earlier comments made mainly by 'native speaker' teachers that 'preaching' to students was to be avoided because of the cultural superiority it implied (e.g. Gary, Janet and Judy). However, another element was that raised by Pere:

> If I tried to educate my forty-three year old general manager of a multinational company whose turnover is twenty thousand million pesetas, I'd probably get the sack (laughing).

The point being made here, yet again, is that ELT provision is essentially a service industry in many settings and that concerns of the type raised by the Prodromou quotation may be contextually inappropriate. When asked if they felt they were involved in education, only seven of the teachers said they were, although often indirectly and then only to an extent, with many citing learner training as the way in which this was manifested.

Statement 3

> The kind of English contained in coursebooks can be called 'cosmopolitan English' because it 'assumes a materialistic set of values in which international travel, not being bored, positively being entertained, having leisure, and above all, spending money casually and without consideration of the sum involved in the pursuit of these ends, are the norm'. (Brown 1990)

Only one teacher disagreed with this. At the same time, although the remainder took the view that coursebooks represented the world in materialistic terms, not all teachers judged this in quite the same way. Thus Jaime, agreeing completely:

> All the situations are perfect, everyone has money, credit cards, they take planes, they all leave on time and arrive on time, there's always a taxi waiting for them at the door, and nobody bothers about how much the hotel is going to cost [...] I think it's an ideal world [...] which to me seems a bit shallow.

Similar evaluations were made by Max and Edward. However, most informants made the point that coursebooks were aimed at middle-class students with certain expectations – rather than at working-class students – and that it was therefore unsurprising to see such expectations reflected in materials. 'In actual fact', Jennifer said, 'the whole of society assumes a very similar set of values here', a point echoed by Josep, Rosa, Clare, Robert and Melissa. In Josep's view, the young Catalans he taught in a private language school saw themselves reflected in the lifestyles represented in coursebooks – and in Judy's opinion successful business people were motivated by representations of success. Such material often 'worked', at least in these settings, and in Bob's view it was about 'trying to sugar-coat a little bit of the hard work [...] so that it's more palatable and enjoyable'.

However, informants also made the point that although travel and leisure were important features of many people's lives (and for that reason should be included in coursebooks), there was also a need to balance such content with a wider range of topics. But, as Montse explained, coursebooks were written to be used in the maximum number of settings:

> The writer of the book publishes a text and he doesn't know where this text is going to be read so he's extra careful about it [...] because they cannot risk someone somewhere in the world refusing to use that book because of that opinion stated there, because [...] that means losing money. And that's, that's the thing.

Many teachers expressed such views about the way in which the limitations of materials were linked to publishers' commercial imperatives. Because of this, local or more controversial topics which some teachers felt might be used to counterbalance the preponderance of the type of content identified by Brown had to be supplied by teachers themselves.

Statement 4

'In ELT coursebooks students are positioned at the receiving end of a one way flow of information'. (Alptekin and Alptekin 1984)

Several informants felt the need to clarify their understanding of the statement before responding. I explained that the authors were of the opinion that the absence of a cross-cultural dimension in a coursebook meant that students did not always have the opportunity to explore content from their own cultural perspective. All informants said that this was essentially true, although, as some pointed out, coursebooks did vary in this respect. Most argued that it was up to the teacher to present content in such a way that students had opportunities to respond, and there was general consensus that engagement occurred when materials raised issues which were controversial or which elicited a personal or locally based response from students. However, a small number of teachers (Karen, Janet and Eulàlia) saw the way in which personalization was approached in some coursebooks as problematic. In Eulàlia's words,

> sometimes I mean they just don't know how to draw a line, because sometimes you have things like 'What's the worst experience in your life?' [...] sometimes I think they go [...] too deep into personal things [...] 'Have you ever had an accident?', I mean I don't think this is something to talk about in a class [...] or 'What's your deepest regret?' I mean you get questions like this.

This criticism resonates with Kullman's charge (2003) that coursebooks have been colonized by a discourse of psychotherapy in which students are encouraged to talk in ways which are limiting and possibly inappropriate in many educational contexts. For Pere, the problem with much coursebook material was the absence of the *local*. He explained how he often supplemented the coursebook by downloading material on the local area from the Internet or by using texts on Barcelona which had been written for an English-speaking audience. By providing his students with the opportunity to see their local world represented in English, he suggested there was a possibility of greater depth of engagement overall and a resultant higher level of response. This view was similar to that expressed by those teachers who argued that the student's own culture was often the best starting place for any kind of focus on culture. On further prompting about the kind of content he thought useful in this respect, Pere said he would like to see coursebooks with

> more local topics and how those topics might relate to the Anglo-Saxon world, or the English speaking world [...] so for example 'Why do British tourists enjoy holidays in Salou? [A town on the coast] You know, this is an account of Tom and his wife Julie who spent a fortnight in a hotel in Salou, this is what they liked, this is what they disliked.

When asked why students might engage with the topic of British holidaymakers in Spain, he answered,

> Because it's a kind of bridge isn't it? it's not quite talking about us, it's not quite talking about them, it's talking about how they relate to us and we relate to them, it's closer to home.

In the context of the fourth statement, this metaphor connecting the local with the world of English appears to offer the possibility of a two-way traffic in which students are no longer positioned on the receiving end of a one-way flow of information but are encouraged to respond from their own locally based cultural perspective.

Discussion

What then are we to make to these views? Given my aim of exploring the views of practising teachers hold about the nature of cultural content and their understanding of the relationship between culture and ELT more generally, we can say that teachers tend to disapprove of content in which there are unmarked stereotypical representations of nationality and gender. They do so because they feel there is the potential for such stereotypes to be reinforced through their inclusion in a coursebook and the possible perception that they are also being endorsed by the individual teacher. Secondly, they tend to disapprove of content which is irrelevant to the context of instruction, preferring instead to use material which is related to students' professional needs, their leisure and travel pursuits, and in terms of their age and the topics they may be said to identify with. The context of instruction is therefore seen as an important factor in evaluating the relevance of any piece of material. At the same time, teachers are aware that content can serve to construct English in ways which are problematic – examples provided are the continuing adherence to English of discourses of colonialism (whether simply by association with overtly British content, or by direct reference to the consequences of colonialism) and the uncritical celebration of the 'dominant culture' in which individualism, wealth and celebrity are central. However, challenging such content in the classroom is seen as potentially problematic by some teachers, as students may be seen as customers and the teacher's own role can be understood as a neutral facilitator of language learning. Pennycook (1994) suggests that the increasing commercialization of ELT means that, in many contexts, teachers come to see themselves as technicists, trained solely to develop language skills – something which is reflected here.

In terms of content which met with approval, apart from that which was stereotype-breaking and seen as relevant to particular groups of students, the majority of teachers produced material which, although dealing with aspects of international culture or culture of the background studies type, was discussed largely in terms of its interactive and language-generating potential, rather than in terms of the content itself. Such a focus suggests that cultural content, when it is not seen as problematic, is viewed positively, *as a topic*, on account of its potential to generate talk – clearly one of the main aims of language teaching for the teachers in the study.

One of the key issues to emerge is that most informants view English as an international language and see their students as requiring it frequently for use with other L2 speakers. On this view, as has been mentioned elsewhere (e.g. Widdowson 1994; Cook 1999; Modiano 2001; McKay 2002; Alptekin 2002 *inter alia*), English is seen as no longer exclusively linked to any one country or the cultural life of any one group of people. At the same time, there is an awareness that in an increasingly globalized world there is a considerable degree of cultural convergence and that the differences which might have existed between Spain and other (mainly western) countries some years ago are now fewer in number. The view that English is no longer necessarily linked to any one country or groups of speakers has a number of implications for these teachers. Firstly, that cultural content in the aesthetic and the sociological senses can vary considerably, depending on the context of instruction, and the interests and needs of the students. Incidentally, the teachers tended not to use the vocabulary provided by the Adaskou *et al.* (1990) framework – perhaps on account of their view of English as being learnt largely as an international language in their context, or perhaps because such a vocabulary was relatively unfamiliar to them. However, the implications with regard to *language* are seen as more problematic, and here there is evidence of less consensus throughout the group. The data suggest that in the context of English being taught primarily as an international language the norm-providing role of British 'native speakers' is rendered somewhat problematic. There was widespread agreement on the need to expose students to a greater range of accents on the tapes used in class, but in terms of a model of pronunciation, if any, for students to aim for, there was less certainty. Pilar was alone in making a case for RP, while most 'native speaker' teachers were happy to see their own accent as the model for students to approximate. On the other hand, Eulàlia and Pere foresaw the emergence of new European or international models. This uncertainty is hardly surprising given the relatively recent emergence of data on such new uses of English (Jenkins 2000; Seidlhofer 2004). With regard to the language of politeness and the expression of pragmatic meaning more generally, teachers seemed to favour the rejection of overtly marked 'native speaker' features (at least for production) in favour of more neutral forms, although they were often constrained to teach these because of examinations. Doubts were also raised about the value of teaching a variety of English in which the idiomaticity of 'native speakers', particularly with regard to spoken English, played an important role. Finally, it was the culture of the students themselves which most teachers agreed on as being central to ELT – whether as the basis of the culture of the classroom, or as a 'stepping stone' for cross-cultural comparisons, or simply because of its potential to stimulate language practice.

In the final chapter I consider what light the 'circuit of culture' may be said to have shed on the global coursebook.

8
Future Directions

Introduction

The origin of this cultural study, as I explained at the outset, lay in the initial desire to understand ELT coursebooks as embodiments of 'particular constructions of reality' (Apple and Christian-Smith 1991: 3). The adoption of a cultural studies approach allowed for the identification of the representational repertoires in the coursebooks analyzed and suggested a high level of continuity in the representation of language – namely, a focus on standard British English, a privileging of the RP cluster of accents and relatively little representation of outer/expanding circle varieties of English. At the same time, the pervasive sexism of the first coursebook from the 1970s was shown to have been superseded by an equally pervasive and evolving discourse of feminism which was accompanied by the increasing deployment of a discourse of liberal multiculturalism, and a progressive globalizing of content. In terms of identity, the application of the descriptive framework suggests that students are positioned overall to respond to content as language learners for whom a limited range of responses are required. At the same time they are positioned as consumers, largely through the artwork, to identify with an imagined community of English speakers who are characterized by success, gender equality and an increasing cosmopolitanism.

The turn to the publishers as the site of production and regulation proved revealing. The guidelines on inclusivity may be said to have provided a blueprint for the construction of the representational repertoires with regard to gender, while those on inappropriacy shed light on systematic omissions. However, the interviews with the publishers served to expose some of the tensions within ELT publishing, particularly with regard to the representational practices associated with sexuality, race and disability. These interviews also served to draw attention to two things: firstly, the extreme market-sensitivity of ELT publishing, and secondly, the assumption that 'aspirational' content which is exclusively lifestyle-oriented is motivating and is what motivates students in most settings. The literatures on visual communication, consumerism and promotional culture shed further light on these representational practices allowing us to see the coursebook as first and foremost a promotional commodity which is constructed along lines similar to those of other consumer items. When it comes to the production of ELT coursebooks, commercial considerations – rather than ethical or educational concerns – are seen to be paramount.

However, as we have seen in Chapter 7, not all the meanings which are constructed in the coursebook resonate with those of the primary consumers. The interviews with the teachers revealed broad approval for the representational practices associated with the deployment of the discourses of feminism and multiculturalism – although in some cases it was felt that coursebooks did not go far enough in recognizing lesbian and gay identities. Teachers were also critical of content which was seen as irrelevant to the context of instruction and in some cases this critique extended to content which was seen as celebratory of consumerism. That said, it is particularly telling that Eulàlia, one of the most critical voices among the interviewees, made the point that such materials very often 'worked' despite the flaws she perceived. As shown in Chapter 7, material which produced talk was generally evaluated positively – even when the thematic content had been previously evaluated negatively by the same teachers. This suggests a view of language teaching as largely concerned with skill acquisition for these teachers, and as having little in the way of any broader educational remit. Dissenting voices were also raised with regard to the representation of language. The teachers' view of their own practice as largely concerned with the teaching of English as an international language meant that the 'native speakerism' of such materials was seen as problematic and not always relevant to students' needs. In what follows I will suggest that this application of the 'circuit of culture' offers us food for thought in at least three areas – teacher education; the teaching of English as an international language; and the question of the continuing viability of the global coursebook.

Teacher education

In Chapter 1 I cited Edge and Richards (1998), who argued that the interstitial location of ELT commits researchers and practitioners to inter-disciplinary boundary work. And although others have made a similar case, Kullman (2003: 74) concludes that ELT remains typified by a state of 'discourse paralysis', whereby 'the core discourse of ELT has arguably failed to incorporate perspectives from other related fields.' It is a view I largely share, particularly so in the light of this study. Two areas which stand out as being of direct relevance to teacher education are the usefulness of social semiotics as a means of analyzing the visual component of coursebooks and the value of a cultural studies perspective on culture.

Berger's (1972: 129) assertion that in 'no other form of society in history has there been such a concentration of images, such a density of visual messages' is one which bears repeating here. Even the most cursory look at ELT coursebooks produced in the early 1970s (and before) and those being produced today demonstrates clearly that the mode of address to the student has undergone a significant change. As I write this, I have on my desk two examples from coursebooks which underline this point dramatically.[1] The first is from *English in Situations* (O'Neill 1970), which was produced as the boom in commercial ELT was just getting started. An explanation of the present perfect on the left hand side of page 91 is accompanied by black-and-white artwork on the right hand side in which the past and the present are represented by two differently shaded circles. In a second diagram the two circles are linked together by the addition of a third (corresponding to the present perfect), thereby drawing the student's attention to the way in which the present perfect links the past with the present. The second piece of material is from *New Headway Pre-Intermediate* (Soars and Soars 2000b), which was produced 30 years later, by which time British ELT publishing had become an industry catering to a global market. Pages 58–59 take the form of a double page spread from the fictional *Hi! Magazine* profiling a fictional pop star Donna Flynn and the equally fictional footballer Terry Wiseman – both of whom bear more than a passing resemblance to real-life celebrities David and Victoria Beckham. The artwork consists of four colour photographs, in which the young attractive couple are shown in different parts of their luxurious house, smiling or staring openly at the imagined viewer/student. In contrast, the written text (which tells of their joint annual income of £20 million and their mutual love) occupies considerably less space on the page.

There are a number of things to say about these examples. In the case of the first it is worth noting that it is one of only two pieces of artwork in the entire coursebook and that the coding orientation of the visual modality is what Kress and van Leeuwen (1996) refer to as 'abstract', that is, it takes the form of a diagram. The second is taken from a coursebook in which each page in each unit has colour photographic artwork in which the coding orientation is predominately 'naturalistic' and 'sensory'. More significant however is the relation between the signifier and the signified in both visuals. As Kress *et al.* (2001: 5) state,

> In social semiotics [...] the assumption is that the relation between form and meaning, signifier and signified, is never arbitrary, but that it is always motivated by the interests of the maker of the sign to find the best possible, the most plausible form for the expression of the meaning that (s)he wishes to express.

While the first example may be said to have the aim of clarifying the grammar point, and is entirely congruent with the case made by Corder (1966) for the explanatory potential of artwork, the second is altogether more complex and less evidently related to language acquisition. The deliberate intertextual reference to *Hello! Magazine* and the type of celebrities who people its pages is an indication of the way in which contemporary coursebooks construct not only English, but also the students who are learning it. As Kress and van Leeuwen (1996: 30) suggest, students are increasingly addressed in pedagogic materials as 'people whose interests need to be solicited and *won*, who need to be entertained, humoured' – a mode of address which parallels contemporary developments in other genres in consumer society, such as advertising texts or those found in lifestyle magazines. In the case of the second piece of artwork, students are literally welcomed into a world of luxury through a set of deliberately constructed visual signs, all of which serve to index spectacular professional success. In this volume I have argued that the increasing use of such artwork forms a crucial element in constructing the promotional promise of English – represented as the language of a largely cosmopolitan elite whose lifestyles may be said to celebrate a benign version of globalization. It could be argued that teachers, as primary consumers of coursebooks, would benefit from training in the use of the tools of social semiotics – to enable them to design appropriate materials, and to select and evaluate published materials more effectively. However, despite the role accorded to materials design and evaluation on many kinds of initial teacher training and teacher education programmes (e.g. Cambridge certificate and diploma courses), there is little evidence that artwork is seriously addressed. Current versions of Cambridge certificate and diploma syllabuses make no mention of artwork as part of any materials-related competence to be developed. Furthermore, books which are aimed at Master's level students do not address the issue in any depth (e.g. Tomlinson 1998, 2003; McGrath 2002). The index to McGrath's (2002) otherwise excellent volume lists 'visual design' as a sub-heading under 'design of materials' and directs the reader to a single paragraph in which it is suggested that pedagogic considerations need to be balanced with the use of artwork. Brian Tomlinson's (2003) volume *does* include a chapter by David Hill on the visual element – although the focus is not on what such artwork implies, but on how its potential for language practice is under-exploited. Interestingly, Hill describes artwork which students do not have to use or refer to directly as part of a task as 'decoration' (ibid.: 176). My point in this book has been to argue that such artwork is a fundamental aspect of the imaging of English and is far from being purely decorative in purpose.

This leads to my second implication, which is that by incorporating a cultural studies perspective on culture into teacher education, issues of the type I have just raised can most usefully be explored. Although culture ebbs and flows as a subject of interest in the ELT literature, the cultural studies perspective as described here is rarely, if at all, addressed. That said, Kramsch (1993) and John Corbett (2003), both of whom may be said to subscribe to the Humboldtian view of language teaching outlined in Chapter 2, argue the value of using L2 advertising texts and other texts of popular culture in the language classroom as a means of enabling students to begin to understand how cultural meanings are created and as a means of developing intercultural communicative competence. Corbett usefully explains how the tools of social semiotics could be applied in the classroom and in doing so shows how language teaching could move beyond the 'edutainment' approach of so much contemporary material – although he does not suggest that such tools could be turned on the coursebook itself.

Another reason for incorporating a cultural studies perspective is that it offers a non-essentialist view of culture – something I believe to be an important corrective for a profession which has been bedevilled by an essentializing tendency to construct students as culturally problematic. Although this tendency has been contested (e.g. Pennycook 1998; Holliday 1999; Kubota 1999; Littlewood 1999; Kumaravadivelu 2008), it will be recalled from Chapter 2 that some handbooks for teachers continue to operate on the basis of a kind of cultural profiling whereby all classroom behaviours can be explained in terms of students' national culture. Coursebooks too, as I pointed out in Chapter 5, continue this essentializing through the stereotypical representations of 'good manners' from around the world and the reproduction of lists of cultural 'dos' and 'don'ts' which are presented to students as rules.

Furthermore, a cultural studies perspective allows teachers to interrogate coursebooks in terms of the identities such materials posit for students. When looked at in this way, teachers can begin to adapt materials to allow for different kinds of responses. Holliday (2005) argues that as education has become increasingly commodified and learning constructed in terms of measurable outcomes, the *student* has been recast as the *learner*. The latter, he explains,

> refers to only certain attributes of the person of the student as they are constructed in the classroom by teacher-designed events. 'Student', on the other hand, has always referred to a role in society which is occupied by the whole person. (ibid.: 68)

In fact, as we have seen above, students are increasingly constructed as consumers in coursebooks, particularly through the artwork. Thus trainee teachers, in particular, could be sensitized to this aspect of materials design and could learn to adapt activities so that students may give voice to more 'whole person' responses should they wish to. Canagarajah (1999: 189) provides useful examples of how comprehension questions can be rewritten to allow for localized responses which call into play identities not anticipated by the material or foreclosed by the activities students are asked to do. And finally, the concept of a representational repertoire allows for the exploration of the discourses on which coursebooks draw (and those which they ignore) in the construction of English. The issue of how English is textually constructed can be seen as a matter of concern, particularly at the present time – which Edge (2004, 2006) describes as a new age of empire. The quotation from Document 5 in Chapter 6 on the need for caution in portraying the US in a negative light is a reminder of the regulatory power of at least one ELT publisher in determining the way in which global powers can now be represented in coursebooks. Edge (2004) urges teachers to look again at the materials they use and to consider the worldviews they represent. Failure to do so, he suggests, constitutes a refusal to recognize the ways in which ELT is imbricated in wider global networks. Such issues need to be addressed on teacher education programmes if Kullman's (2003) charge of discourse paralysis is to be redressed.

In this regard it is interesting to compare the way in which another global language such as Spanish is imaged in Spanish-produced materials aimed at the global market. *Nuevo Español 2000* Nivel Superior

(Sánchez Lobato and García Fernández 2007) is altogether different from the coursebooks surveyed in this study. A cursory look indicates that the flavour of this course is noticeably more serious. The introduction explains that the book has been designed to allow students to access the Spanish language and 'its plural culture' ('su cultura plural') (ibid.: 5). What this appears to entail is exposure to a wide range of literary material and journalistic texts from quality newspapers by or about well-known, predominantly male, writers from across the Spanish-speaking world – for example, Octavio Paz, Ernesto Sábato, Miguel Delibes, Manuel Vicent, Rosa Chacel and Carlos Fuentes. Thus students read a newspaper article on the awarding of the 1989 Nobel prize for literature to Camilo José Cela and the latter's acceptance speech to the Swedish Academy. Elsewhere Mario Benedetti writes about the end of the dictatorship in Argentina in a piece which also includes an attack on the monetarist polices of Milton Friedman and the ways in which South American dictatorships offered him whole swathes of the region as 'the cheapest experimental laboratory' ('su más barato laboratorio experimental') (ibid.: 91) for his economic theories. In contrast, it is difficult to imagine Harold Pinter's 2005 Nobel acceptance speech in which he was overtly critical of British and North American foreign policy being reproduced in an ELT global coursebook.

Aula Internacional 3 (Corpas *et al.* 2006), another widely used coursebook, is more like the ELT materials surveyed in this study in that the overall flavour is lighter, and topics such as global travel for professional and leisure purposes are a noticeable feature. That said, in addition to readings on fashion, design and UFOs, there are reading texts on the history of Nicaragua (in which the interfering role of the US is made clear) and the possibility of greater regional integration in Latin America, alongside extracts from contemporary writers such as Eduardo Mendoza, Juan José Millás and Ernesto Cardenal. The kinds of tasks students are asked to complete are interesting too in terms of the identities they posit. For example, a unit entitled '¡Basta Ya!' (which could be translated as 'That's enough!') is introduced with a full colour close-up of a child holding an anti-war placard and prepares the students for a writing exercise in which they are asked to imagine themselves as members of a collective committed to achieving full equality for men and women – in the workplace, at school, in politics, at home and so on. The task is to write a political manifesto for their collective and to produce a placard for a demonstration on International Women's Day. The same unit ends with a text outlining key moments in the recent history of democratic Spain. This begins with the death of Franco in 1975 and concludes with the introduction of gay marriage in 2005. The text is superimposed on a colour photograph of a young black male anti-war demonstrator. The placard he is carrying indicates he is from a cross-union anti-war group in Valencia – the image thereby simultaneously indexing the multiethnic nature of modern democratic Spain. Clearly there is a need for more detailed comparative work, but it would appear that Spanish materials differ in significant ways from those ELT materials surveyed here.

That said, it must be recognized that pleas for better teacher education, particularly with regard to materials analysis, are in severe tension with the dependence of commercial ELT on minimally trained teachers who form part of a largely casualized labour force in many parts of the world.[2] This industry (unlike the state school and higher education sectors) does not require a workforce with more than a few weeks of training – and as Pennycook (1994) has pointed out, it may even view with suspicion the prospect of employing more educated teachers. It is therefore unlikely that what I am proposing here will be seen as relevant by those engaged in managing this industry. As an ex-CELTA (Certificate in English Language Teaching to Adults) trainer, I am sceptical of the potential of short courses to achieve more than they currently do in 4 or 5 weeks – namely, the transmission of a set of largely fixed and stable methodological practices with necessarily limited opportunities for reflection (Morton and Gray 2010). However, ELT takes place in a multiplicity of settings and many teachers who begin their careers in poorly paid insecure jobs do go on to engage in professional development and move into areas where greater education is required. Furthermore, English language teachers from other parts of the world frequently undertake longer training/education programmes in which it is possible to address such issues. I shall return again to some of these points in my concluding remarks on the future of global coursebook. I now turn to the contentious issue of teaching English as an international language.

Teaching English as an international language

One of the outcomes from the interviews with the Barcelona teachers is that they see themselves largely as involved in the teaching of EIL. They referred repeatedly to 'English as an international language', 'world hybrid English', 'world English', 'international English' and 'Euro English' as they discussed their views on culture and ELT coursebooks.

Although these terms were not necessarily defined or were seen as difficult to pin down, they can be seen as indicative of an awareness on the part of many that English has become increasingly plural and that this may have implications for the classroom. Just what these implications might be is a matter of some speculation – although there are some suggestions emerging from the data presented in Chapter 7 which, I will suggest below, are worthy of serious consideration.

One view in the field has coalesced around the work of Jennifer Jenkins (1998, 2000, 2006) and Barbara Seidlhofer (2001, 2004, 2005) and can be referred to as the 'English as a lingua franca' (ELF) position. Given the amount of debate ELF has generated it is worth reminding ourselves just what this position entails. Jenkins's (2000) early work made the case for not wasting valuable classroom time teaching aspects of pronunciation which she considered to be irrelevant for intelligibility – and certainly many ELT materials made heavy work of teaching such elements as intrusive sounds and the production of weak forms in connected speech. Why not, Jenkins asked, focus on a lingua franca core of elements which were essential to guarantee intelligibility? The lingua franca core included such items as the required aspiration of /p/, /t/ and /k/ and the acceptance of a range of substitutions for /θ/ and /ð/. The concept of a phonological core for ELF represented a move away from the imitative model of pronunciation contained in so many ELT materials and was predicated on the idea of the student assuming a language-speaking identity which was not seen as an attempted reidentification with a specific kind of 'native speaker' norm, but as a norm in its own right – appropriate for a different kind of speaker who does not wish be constructed as an ersatz 'native speaker'. In the years since it was first proposed such an approach has proved attractive to some scholars (e.g. Risager 2006), and much less so to others (e.g. Kuo 2006).

The ELF project has developed considerably in scope since its phonological beginnings, and the compilation of the Vienna-Oxford International Corpus of English (VOICE) is one such example. The VOICE website (www.univie.ac.at/voice) explains that it seeks to balance the extensive corpus-based descriptions of English as a native language (ENL) by providing a corpus of English 'as it is spoken by [the] non-native speaking majority of users in different contexts'. The corpus comprises over a million words of naturally occurring, non-scripted face-to-face interactions from professional, educational and leisure domains featuring mainly European L2 speakers of English. The emerging data suggest that a number of features which would generally be categorized as errors in a language classroom do not lead to communication breakdown in settings where English is being used as a lingua franca. These include:

- Dropping the third person present tense *–s*
- Confusing the relative pronouns *who* and *which*
- Omitting definite and indefinite articles where they are obligatory in ENL, and inserting them where they do not occur in ENL
- Failing to use correct forms in question tags (e.g. *isn't it?* or *no?* instead of *shouldn't they?*)
- Inserting redundant prepositions, as in *We have to study about ...*
- Overusing certain verbs of high semantic generality, such as *do, have, make, put, take*
- Replacing infinitive-constructions with *that*-clauses, as in *I want that*
- Overdoing explicitness (e.g. *black color* rather than just *black*). (Seidlhofer 2004: 220)

Furthermore, Seidlhofer (ibid.: 220) points out that the VOICE data show that 'unilateral idiomaticity', that is, the use of idiomatic 'native speaker' language by one interlocutor in interactions where English is being used as a lingua franca, can lead to communication breakdown. While such data are inherently interesting, there are certain problems with the ELF project in my view, the first of which is its pursuit of codification. As Canagarajah (2007: 925) points out, the language used in lingua franca exchanges

> is intersubjectively constructed in each specific context of interaction. The form of this English is negotiated by each set of speakers for their purposes. The speakers are able to monitor each other's language proficiency to determine mutually the appropriate grammar, phonology, lexical range, and pragmatic conventions that would ensure intelligibility. Therefore *it is difficult to describe this language a priori.* (emphasis added)

Such a perspective does not deny that English is increasingly used as a global lingua franca; rather it suggests that what those working in the ELF paradigm seek to describe is inherently plural and may not lend itself readily to description. Even if one took the view that lingua franca uses of English could be codified, the descriptions emerging from the analysis of the VOICE corpus would necessarily be limited by the nature of the predominantly European data on which it draws. A second problem arises from the implications of Bourdieu's (1991) view of language as a form of symbolic capital within the wider economy of linguistic exchanges – as outlined in Chapter 1. If we take the view that English is profoundly imbricated in globalization with all the injustices this means for so many who are not members of cosmopolitan elites, then access to socially legitimated varieties of English becomes important – particularly if those injustices are to be challenged on the world stage where prestige varieties of English hold sway. There is a danger, as Luke Prodromou (2007) points out, that those working within an ELF paradigm fail to recognize the importance of this when they imply that anything an L2 speaker produces in a lingua franca setting that does not cause communication breakdown is unproblematically acceptable. Of course it may well be in certain contexts, but, as Jan Blommaert (2005: 72) reminds us, not all varieties of language are accorded equal status in all settings:

> The fact is that functions performed by particular resources in one place can be altered in another place, and that in such instances the 'value' of these linguistic tools or skills is changed, often in unpredictable ways. The English acquired by many urban Africans may offer them considerable prestige and access to middle-class identities in African towns. It may be an 'expensive' extremely valuable resource to them. But the same English, when spoken in London by the same Africans, may become an object of stigmatisation and may qualify them as members of a lower strata of society. What is very 'expensive' in Lusaka or Nairobi may be very 'cheap' in London or New York.

To which we might add any number of domains in expanding circle settings. What 'works' linguistically in collaborative social settings which may be typified by a high degree of accommodation may fail in another where the stakes are altogether higher – even where all the speakers are using English as a lingua franca. That said, Canagarajah (2005: xxv) is surely right when he argues that to continue to focus our teaching on a single dialect of English 'fails to equip our students for real-world needs'. Such needs may be said to imply exposure to a repertoire of grammars and ways of speaking which take into consideration the varieties of language students are likely to encounter or which they themselves may feel the need to deploy in particular contexts. In my own case I recall colleagues at Queen's University Belfast teaching international students standard English for academic purposes (so that they could succeed in the academy) and seeing the same colleagues adapt and re-record textbook dialogues in Belfast English for use with the same students (so they could survive on the street). If students are to be prepared adequately for real-world needs then the English they are exposed to in the classroom needs to be pluralized.

With regard to the data presented in Chapter 7 there is a clearly expressed need to represent a wider range of accents in the listening materials. If students are to be prepared for interactions with speakers who do not use RP/modified RP and those who are not 'native speakers', it is surely necessary that listening materials include a wider range of non-RP accents and L2 speakers' accents than those identified in the analyses presented earlier. Finding other L2 speakers intelligible will be partly the result of familiarity with the accents and the variable grammars students are likely to encounter. At the productive level things are much more complex as this entails a consideration of what students are to be taught to produce and what is to be corrected.

It will be recalled from Chapter 3 that Kramsch (1993) suggests that learning another language involves the struggle to find a voice that can carry the weight of the student's own cultural experience. Too often the voice, when it is heard – particularly in the classroom – is compared with the idealized standard of the 'native speaker' and automatically judged to be in error. But as Leung (2005: 130) has argued, 'there isn't a universal model of native speakers' use of language' and as part of his case for re-orienting the concept of communicative competence, following Celia Roberts *et al.* (2001), he makes the case for epistemological relativity, reflexivity and critical consciousness. For ELT, the first of these 'means that one accepts that there are infinite ways of using language and that differences do not automatically call for judgemental evaluation' (Leung 2005: 138). Reflexivity consists in the willingness to question the basis for one's views on language use, while critical consciousness refers to an awareness of the ways in which English-speaking countries describe and analyze language and language pedagogy. In the light of this, with regard to classroom practice he advocates attention to standard and local Englishes while adding that it is important 'to tune into both established and emergent forms and norms of use' (ibid.: 139). This is an important point in my view as it entails an acknowledgement of the continued importance of standard English (idealized and problematic though the concept is), alongside an acceptance of the right of L2 speakers to use language in a plurality of ways.

However, this should not be understood as making the case for native speakerism – and here I think the VOICE corpus tells us something important about ENL idiomaticity which resonates with views expressed by many of the Barcelona teachers. Concerns about the usefulness of inner circle 'native speaker' idiomaticity were discussed at length, particularly by Eulàlia and Montse, and were outlined in Chapter 7. There we saw that idiomatic spoken British English was considered to be something not all students necessarily needed to be able to produce. Montse's case was for 'giving them the full form' and 'showing them how language works' but without the idiomatic accretions found in the speech of British 'native speakers'. These, she argued, could be added later by students themselves when, and if, the need arose. Similarly, with regard to the language of politeness and the expression of pragmatic meaning more generally, many of the Barcelona teachers favoured the rejection of overtly marked 'native speaker' features in favour of more neutral forms, seen as being appropriate for an international language. Such an approach represents what Prodromou (2007: 10) refers to as a 'third space' in which the teaching of English as an international language entails the rejection of both the kind of ENL idiomaticity increasingly found in coursebooks (utterances such as 'These trainers cost ninety quid!' quoted in Chapter 5) and what he refers to as the 'ELF grammatical common core'. Such a perspective implies the acceptance that language can be used in a plurality of ways, that native speakerism may be irrelevant in many settings *and* that standard English shorn of its 'native speaker' idiomaticity may be what serves many students best. I now turn to the implications of the study for the future of the global coursebook.

The future of the global coursebook

One of the themes to emerge from the interview data is that the context of use is an important factor in teachers' overall evaluation of a piece of material. Thus, material which 'worked' or was appropriate in one setting was judged to be unsuccessful or inappropriate in another. However, the global coursebook is predicated on the claim that it is suitable for all contexts and, as several of the Barcelona teachers pointed out, this tends to guarantee a certain kind of extremely 'safe' content, but at the same time it does not ensure that material necessarily 'works'. The point is surely that different contexts require different kinds of content – but this is a point publishers are often reluctant to accept. Take for example the issue of gay invisibility referred to in Chapter 1. Ben Goldstein's (2003) coursebook *Framework Pre-intermediate*, written initially for the southern European market, was innovative in its straightforward treatment of gayness and appeared to indicate a change in the representational practices associated with sexual orientation. One unit featured a gap-fill exercise in which a character named Ricardo explained how he met his boyfriend Simon. Both men were also featured in an accompanying colour photograph. However, in the new edition published in 2008 the couple have been removed – precisely because of the success of the earlier edition. Goldstein points out that the publishers 'saw the gay content as acceptable for Spain, Italy, UK, and Latin America' but adds,

> as soon as they opened it up to others (e.g. Turkey, Poland, etc.) the problems began and they forced the change. As there would only be one edition, they had to make that change for all markets. They also changed the gay content to straight for the American edition. (personal communication, 2009)

This shows how inclusive representational practices can be redesignated when the market expands and demonstrates the way in which the inappropriacy strand of publishers' guidelines trumps the inclusivity strand. It could be argued that this is not without consequences for lesbian and gay students. As Anthony Liddicoat (2009) shows, the relentlessly heteronormative framing of identity in ELT classrooms in which the personal world of the student is repeatedly foregrounded by materials (cf. Kullman 2003) means that lesbian and gay students are either silenced or forced into challenging the ways in which they are positioned. The point I wish to make is that by insisting on one edition only, the publishers ensure that material which had the potential to include lesbians and gays in a range of settings where such representations were possible now excludes them in all settings.

What then are the solutions to the problems posed by such materials? A number of alternatives have been suggested. Ingrid Freebairn (2000: 5), co-author of the *Strategies* series, has suggested the possibility of a 'skeleton coursebook' available on CD-ROM which 'is supplemented by up-to-the-minute topical material, local mother-tongue supplements, and alternative activities for mixed-level classes' which could be downloaded from the Internet, and a kind of DIY online coursebook which students and teachers could assemble together, depending on level and interests. Elsewhere I have suggested that 'editionizing' might represent a way forward – whereby publishers produce more tailor-made versions of coursebooks for smaller groups of consumers (Gray 2002). Kumaravadivelu (2006b) has argued that such a practice, while it might provide for greater diversity of subject matter, does nothing to challenge the structural relationship between publishers and those who consume their products. The charge is justified, and difficult to address. Thornbury (2000b) has made the case for a pedagogy based on the 'dogme' principles associated with the work of the Danish film collective by the same name. Its preference for hand-held cameras and a rejection of artificial lighting is paralleled by Thornbury's rejection of published materials in favour of a pared-down pedagogy based on scaffolded talk. However, such an approach may not be suitable for all contexts – particularly those in which groups are large.

Perhaps the best solution is that proposed by Pulverness (2003), who suggests that more regionally based publishing projects involving teachers themselves (and students, I would add) may offer a way around the 'one size fits all' principle on which the global coursebook is based. However, in the absence of many such initiatives, Canagarajah (1999) points out that, in many developing world countries in particular, teachers have to make do with whatever materials are available. In such settings the development of critical reading skills becomes paramount. A similar situation may be said to obtain in inner and expanding circle classrooms as well. While publishers are unlikely to encourage critical reading of the texts they produce, it must fall to teacher education courses to make the case for this approach to adapting materials. Additional questions of the type suggested by Wallace (1992: 123, citing Kress 1985: 7) to those posed in the coursebook indicate a possible way of contesting the one-way flow of information in the classroom – '1. Why is this topic being written about? 2. How is this topic being written about? 3. What other ways of writing about this topic are there?' Whatever the solution, it is clear from the Barcelona interviews that ELT coursebooks are seen to fall short in many respects of the requirements of materials for use in an EIL setting – at least in the opinion of this group of primary consumers.

But what form might cultural content take in a coursebook for the teaching of English as an international language? The answer, it seems to me, is best determined locally. Throughout this volume I have argued that cultural content has the function of making English 'mean' in particular ways. However, Hall's (1986) concept of articulation reminds us that the meanings identified here are only some of many which are possible. In fact, in parts of the expanding circle, English is already being rearticulated with discourses which are very different from those identified in this study. Kumaravadivelu (2006b) has drawn attention to TESOL Islamia, an Abu Dhabi-based group which came together in the wake of the 2003 Iraq invasion. Their objectives, which are listed on their website (www.tesolislamia.org), include commitments to

> promoting and safeguarding Islamic precepts and values in the teaching of English as a second or foreign language in the Muslim world [...] to 'empowering' Muslim learners to use the English language in ways that serve the [...] interests of Muslim communities worldwide [...] to raise awareness of the socio-cultural, socio-political, and socio-economic implications of the growing expansion of English and English language teaching in the Muslim world.

The website provides a limited amount of downloadable material for use in the classroom, a wide range of articles by scholars based in Middle Eastern and western universities and an active discussion board for teachers. That said, the material on the website (so far) appears to be of dubious pedagogic value, and, as Block (2010) points out, it is also politically conservative – 'as opposed to challenging the current state of global capitalism or even taking on more specific issues in Muslim and non-Muslim countries, such as workers' rights and feminism'. However, it is indicative of one attempt being made to rearticulate English with a set of alternative discourses far removed from those found in British ELT global materials. Clearly the Barcelona teachers have different interests and provide no indication that they seek to make English 'mean' along these lines. The point I wish to make is that the form cultural content takes is best decided by locals for whom English may have a range of meanings other than those determined for them by British ELT publishers. TESOL Islamia, whatever its limitations, also serves to remind us of the potential power of the Internet as a means of challenging the hegemony of the global coursebook – at least in some settings. The success of the dogme discussion board (http://www.groups.yahoo.com/group/dogme) and the appearance of the Breaking News English site (http://www.breakingnewsenglish.com), its sister site listing discussion topics of the kind not found in global coursebooks (http://www.esldiscussions.com) and Jamie Keddie's YouTube lessons (http://www.teflclips.com) are all indicative of a profession's need for alternatives to what is currently on offer. There is also no reason why dissatisfied teachers cannot exploit further the potential of the Internet to share alternative activities and ways of reading against existing commercially produced materials[3] – given that coursebooks are not likely to disappear in the short term. In fact, the future of such materials seems secure – as Ramin Akbari (2008: 647) points out, for all the recent talk of moves towards postmethod pedagogy, 'the concept of method has not been replaced by the concept of postmethod but rather by an era of textbook-defined practice'. Hence the need, not only for alternatives, but for customized improvements on what already exists.

Conclusion

In Chapter 1 I referred to teachers as the primary consumers of ELT coursebooks. Even in educational contexts where coursebooks are chosen by Ministries of Education, teachers retain considerable power in deciding how they are used in the classroom. For this reason, and given the scarcity of research on teachers' thinking with regard to materials, I made the decision to focus on the moment of consumption as it related to teachers. However, as Hall (1992b) suggests, the outcomes of research are always partial – in the sense that interpretations are always situated, and in the sense that a complete picture is never arrived at. With this limitation in mind, I suggest firstly that there is a need for research into the ways in which language students make sense of ELT materials and the meanings which such artefacts have for them. It will be recalled that Snapshot 1 suggested that the meanings which teachers and students construct from materials can be very different. Prowse (1998: 141) suggests that it would be 'interesting to compare the reactions of learners from different cultures to today's highly designed full colour coursebooks'. However, little is known about students' thinking on the subject of materials generally, and in particular on the issue of cultural content. As Peter Donovan's (1998) insider account of an ELT publishing house's piloting of materials shows, the process is almost exclusively focused on teachers and there is a minimum of direct consultation with students themselves. Secondly, as Littlejohn (1998) points out, analyzing materials is a very different matter from analyzing materials-in-action. By the same token, talking to teachers about cultural content in coursebooks, and they ways in which they construe the relationship between culture and ELT, is very different from conducting research in which the focus is on the ways in which those teachers actually use such materials in the classroom. Therefore I would suggest there is also a need for more classroom-based research in which the focus is on cultural content and the ways in which it is (re)interpreted, deployed and contested in a variety of ELT settings. And finally, there is a need for more comparative studies in which the textual construction of other global languages is systematically addressed.

I stated earlier that this research was carried out in the spirit of critical-ity which has typified a strand of applied linguistics thinking since the late 1980s. It will be clear from much of what I have said, and in com-mon with many of the teachers interviewed, that I view the ELT global coursebook as a deeply problematic artefact. Following Linn Forhan and Mona Scheraga (2000), I would suggest that for change to occur and for coursebooks to become more useful to teachers and students alike, we have to become socio-politically active in making the case for alterna-tive articulations of English to those currently on offer. In the meantime we can also play the publishers at their own game – as Hertz (2001: 158) points out, corporations 'cannot afford not to keep their customers happy'. One of the ironies of consumer society is that when citizens (teachers and students) are repeatedly positioned as customers they can start to behave like customers. Teachers need to begin to see themselves as powerful and begin to make demands on publishers. At the same time, we also need to remember that we are more than customers and to that end we have to start exploring more thoroughly the ways in which insights from other disciplines have relevance for our field and the ways in which such insights can contribute to materials analysis and improved materials design. In this way, through interdisciplinary boundary work, we can also begin, not only to widen and deepen the scope of the ELT materials literature, but also to challenge the structures within which we operate.

Appendices

Appendix 1

- social identity and social groups
  (ethnic minorities, social class, regional identity, etc.)
- social interaction
  (conventions of behaviour at differing levels of familiarity, as outsider and insider)
- belief and behaviour
  (taken-for-granted actions within a social group, moral and religious beliefs, daily routines, etc.)
- social and political institutions
  (state institutions, health care, law and order, social security, local government, etc.)
- socialization and the life-cycle
  (families, schools, employment, rites of passage, divergent practices in different social groups, national auto-stereotypes of expectations, etc.)
- national history
  (historical and contemporary events which are significant in the constitution of the nation and its identity)
- national geography
  (geographical factors seen as being significant, national boundaries and changes to them)
- stereotypes and national identity
  (notions of what is typical, origins of these notions, symbols of national stereotypes, etc.)

Byram's (1993) minimum cultural content for coursebooks

Appendix 2

1. The micro level – phenomena of social and cultural anthropology:

   a. the social and geographical definition of characters
   b. material environment
   c. situations of interaction
   d. interaction and subjectivity of the characters: feelings, attitudes, values and perceived problems.

2. The macro level – social, political and historical matters:

    e. broad social facts about contemporary society (geographical, economic, political, etc.)

    f. broad socio-political problems (unemployment, pollution, etc.)

    g. historical background.

3. International and intercultural issues:

    h. comparisons between the foreign country and the pupil's own

    i. mutual representations, images, stereotypes, etc.

    j. mutual relations: cultural power and dominance, co-operation and conflict.

4. Point of view and style of the author(s).

Risager's (1991: 182–183) framework for describing cultural content

Appendix 3

		Representations
	Words and phrases	**Visual representations: Where appropriate, note demographics of individuals (e.g. socioeconomic status, gender, race, age, etc.), scene and location (e.g. geographical location, urban, rural, etc.) and so on.**
Topical content Personal life Family life The community Sports Health and welfare Travel Education The workplace Current events Religion Arts, humanities Political systems Environment Other		

Hall's (2002: 180) analytic framework for analysis of EFL texts

Appendix 4

Present simple: Habits and states

Presentation

Statistics. There is, of course, no such thing as the average British family, but statistical data can help us to understand a society and social trends.

Every year, official statistics based on questionnaires and surveys are published and these provide a lot of useful information on people's habits. This profile is based on one of their recent publications.

The average British family: A STEREOTYPE

The average British family lives in a semi-detached house with a garden in the south of England. They own their house, which is situated in the suburbs of a large town. The house has three bedrooms. On average they have two children and a pet. The family drives a two-year-old Ford Cortina.

He works in the office of an engineering company for 40 hours a week and earns £200 per week. He starts at 9.00 in the morning and finishes at 5.30 in the evening. He goes to work by car, which takes him 20 minutes. He doesn't particularly like his job, but there are chances of promotion.

She works in a service industry for three days a week and earns £95. She works locally and goes there by bus. She quite likes her job as it gets her out of the house, she meets people, and it is close to the children's school.

The children go to a state school which is a few miles from home. A special bus comes to pick them up everyday. They are at school from 9.00 to 3.30.

The most popular evening entertainment is watching television or video, which the average person does for two and a half hours a day. After that, the next most popular activity is visiting friends, going to the cinema or restaurant, or going to the pub. The most popular hobby is gardening and the most popular sports are fishing, football and tennis.

Soars, J. and L. Soars (1986: 1–2) *Headway Intermediate*. Oxford: OUP.

Appendix 5

Practice

1 The following short dialogues are not very polite. Re-write them to make them sound better. Then practice the polite dialogues in pairs.

For example:

A: I want to speak to Maria.
Can I speak to Maria please?

B: She's in the bath. Call back later.
I'm sorry she's in the bath. Can I take a message?

a A: I want to use your scissors.
B: Yes.

b A: Pass me my coat.
  B: Here you are.
c A: Lend me £5 until tomorrow.
  B: I haven't got any money with me.
d A: Bring me the bill.
  B: Yes.
e A: Give me a light.
  B: My lighter isn't working.
f A: If you're going into town, give me a lift to the bus stop.
  B: Yes.
g A: Tell me the way to the National Gallery.
  B: I don't know this area very well myself.
h A: Pick my suit up from the dry-cleaner's while you're at the shops.
  B: I don't think I'll be able to carry it – I'll have a lot of other things.

2 a) Think of six things to ask other students in the class politely, using the following verbs.

- lend or borrow
- pass (me)
- turn on/turn off
- open or close
- move
- help (me)

b) Take turns to make your requests to each other. If the other student agrees, he/she must really do it. If your partner refuses, he/she must give a reason. Make sure your requests and answers sound polite.
  Would you mind lending me your dictionary?
  I'm sorry, I need it myself.
  Sure... here you are.
  Cunningham, S. and P. Moor (1998) *Cutting Edge Intermediate*. Harlow: Pearson Longman.

Appendix 6

Name/Date of interview	Country of origin	Qualifications	Years of service	Type of institution
Caroline 17 June 1999	Ireland	BA; CTEFLA[1]	13	Private language school (part of worldwide network of schools)
Gary 07 May 1999	UK	CTEFLA; Dip. TEFLA[2]	9	As above
Janet 21 May 1999	UK	English language teaching certificate; Dip. TEFLA; Teacher training certificate	18	As above
Judy 18 June 1999	Australia	Diploma of Teaching; BEd; CTEFLA; Dip. TEFLA	9	As above
Karen 08 June 1999	UK	BA; CTEFLA	15	As above
Max 02 June 1999	Switzerland/ US	BA; CTEFLA; Dip. TEFLA	23	As above
Melissa 07 June 1999	UK	BA; CTEFLA; Dip. TEFLA	14	As above
Robert 17 May 1999	UK	Certificate of Teaching; CTEFLA; Dip. TEFLA; MA TEFL	20	As above
Bob 13 May 1999	US	BSc; Dip. TEFLA	14	University language centre
Edward 12 May 1999	UK	BA; CTEFLA; Dip. TEFLA	13	As above
Clare 21 May 1999	US	BA; MA TESOL	18	As above
Jennifer 16 June 1999	Australia	BA; Diploma of Education; CTEFLA; Dip. TEFLA	18	As above
Rosa 31 May 1999	Spain	Degree; Diploma of English Studies; CAP[3]; PhD	7	As above

Eulàlia 11 May 1999	Spain	Degree; Oposición[4]; CTFLA; MA in Spanish as a Foreign Language	15	State language school for adults
Isabel 03 June 1999	Spain	Degree; Oposición	7	As above
Marc 22 May 1999	Spain	Degree; Oposición; CAP	9	As above
Marta 06 May 1999	Spain	Degree; MA in Spanish as a Foreign Language; Oposición	22	As above
Montse June 1999	Spain	Degree; Oposición	10	As above
Pilar June 1999	Spain	Degree; Oposición	26	As above
Jaime May 1999	Peru	Degree; CAP; Diploma of English Studies	20	Private language school (local institution)
Josep April 1999	Spain	Degree; CTEFLA	10	As above
Pere May 1999	Spain	Degree; Dip. TEFLA	12	As above

[1] Cambridge Certificate in English Language Teaching to Adults.
[2] Cambridge Diploma in English language Teaching to Adults.
[3] The Catalan Certificat d'Aptitud Pedagogica is an educational skills certificate.
[4] Civil service examination granting a teacher a permanent place in a state educational institution.

Notes

1 Introduction

1. I am grateful to Marnie Holborow (personal communication, 2009) for commenting on this as follows: 'Language can of course be described, in a loose sense, as a commodity; it is a commodity in an everyday sense like skill is – something that is useful for the workings of capitalism.' However, she adds, 'But it is not a commodity in the sense that it can be detached from the person who uses language' – a point on which I concur. At the same time, as I argue throughout this volume, a language can also be packaged, imaged and sold *as if* it were a commodity like any other. It is in this sense too that I would suggest that we can speak of the commodification of language.

2 Culture and English Language Teaching

1. Following Holliday (2005) I use inverted commas to indicate that, although pervasive, the term 'native speaker' is highly contested in the literature.

3 Describing and Analyzing ELT Coursebooks

1. After categorizing the accents, my colleague Joanne Kenworthy, author of *Teaching English Pronunciation* (1987), listened to one unit from each coursebook analyzed and coded the accents using the same categories. There was a difference of coding of one accent (consisting of one utterance) and one accent. This inter-rater reliability check represents agreement on the coding of 56 out of 58 voices.

4 Representational Repertoires 1: *Streamline Connections* and *Building Strategies*

1. All statements about content are extrapolated from the databases included as appendices in the doctoral thesis on which this volume is based (Gray 2007).
2. It is highly unlikely that a student would get the 'joke' in the name of the fictional Secretary General of the UN – 'Dr Sowanso' (i.e. 'so-and so').
3. Given that not all the coursebooks referred to in Chapters 4 and 5 have page numbers, I refer instead to the unit or lesson (depending on the terminology) in my referencing.
4. Serious broadsheet newspapers in Britain continued to publish photographs in black-and-white long after popular tabloids began publishing colour photographs.
5. This is a view also discussed by Kullman (2003) in a stimulating study of the construction of student identity in ELT materials.

5   Representational Repertoires 2: *The New Cambridge English Course 2* and *The New Edition New Headway Intermediate*

1. Individual units in *Cambridge English 2* are referred to as lessons.
2. The use of texts about indigenous peoples to teach the present simple is also found in other ELT coursebooks, for example, *Language in Use/Intermediate* (Doff and Jones 1994).

6   Production and Regulation of Content

1. Some of the issues discussed here were originally raised in Gray (2002).
2. I follow Daniel Chandler (2002) in using the terms signifier and signified while referring to the work of Peirce – although these terms are associated with the work of Saussure (1974). The Saussurean sign is dyadic and is composed of the signifier (e.g. the sound /ka:/) and the signified (the concept of a four-wheeled vehicle). The Peircean (1955) model is triadic and consists of the representamen (a 'sign' which stands for somebody or something, similar to the Saussurean signifier), the interpretant (the sense made of the sign by the addressee) and the object (that to which the sign refers). In the work of Charles Ogden and I. A. Richards (1923), the object is also known as the referent.
3. This point is further reinforced by Sontag's suggestion that in the hypothetical situation of being offered a choice between a portrait of Shakespeare by a great master and a poor quality photograph (imagining such a thing could exist), most devotees of Shakespeare would choose the photograph.

7   Consumption of Content

1. The interview data were recorded in the spring and summer of 1999 and could thus be open to the charge of being out of date. However, I do not think this is the case. What a group of experienced practitioners had to say about cultural content and the relationship between culture and ELT at a particular historical moment remains valid. The study is historical and the coursebooks analyzed date from 1979 to 2003. The direction in which coursebooks are headed, as suggested by the changes to *The New Edition New Headway Intermediate* (Soars and Soars 2003), are all the more interesting in the light of teachers' thinking as revealed in the interviews.
2. This has been removed from the 2003 edition.
3. All texts she referred to have been removed form the 2003 edition.

8   Future Directions

1. After protracted communication with the publishers in which samples of this volume had to be submitted for inspection, I was not granted permission to reproduce the images described here.
2. I am grateful to Deborah Cameron for drawing my attention to this.
3. I would also like to Deborah Cameron for this subversive suggestion.

Bibliography

Aarup Jensen, A., K. Jaeger and A. Lorentsen (1995) *Intercultural Competence*. Aalborg: Aalborg University Press.

Abbs, B., A. Ayton and I. Freebairn (1975) *Strategies*. London: Longman.

Abbs, B. and I. Freebairn (1984a) *Building Strategies/Student's Book*. Harlow: Longman.

Abbs, B. and I. Freebairn (1984b) *Building Strategies/Teacher's Book*. Harlow: Longman.

Abbs, P. (1974) *Autobiography in Education: An Introduction to the Subjective Discipline of Autobiography and Its Central Place in the Education of Teachers*. London: Heinemann.

Acklam, R. and S. Mohammed (1992) *The Beginner's Choice*. London: Longman.

Adamowski, E. (1991) 'What does "teaching culture" mean?' In J. Sivell and L. Curtis (eds) *TESL '90: Reading into the Future* (pp. 64–75). Toronto: TESL Ontario.

Adaskou, K., D. Britten and B. Fahsi (1990) 'Design decisions on the cultural content of a secondary English course for Morocco'. *ELT Journal*, 44(1): 3–10.

Akbari, R. (2008) 'Postmethod discourse and practice'. *TESOL Quarterly*, 42(4): 641–652.

Alexander, L. G. (1973) *Mainline*. London: Longman.

Alptekin, C. and M. Alptekin (1984) 'The question of culture: EFL teaching in non-English speaking countries'. *ELT Journal*, 38(1): 14–20.

Alptekin, C. (2002) 'Towards intercultural communicative competence in ELT'. *ELT Journal*, 56(1): 57–64.

Althusser, L. (1971) *Lenin and Philosophy and other Essays*. London/New York: New Left Books, Monthly Review Press.

Anderson, C. (2002) *Deconstructing Teaching English to Speakers of Other Language: Problematising a Professional Discourse*. Unpublished PhD thesis, Canterbury Christ Church University College.

Ang, I. (1985) *Watching Dallas*. London: Methuen.

Apple, M. (1992) 'The text and cultural politics'. *Educational Researcher*, 21: 4–11.

Apple, M. W. and L. K. Christian-Smith (eds) (1991) *The Politics of the Textbook*. London: Routledge.

Ariew, R. (1989) 'The textbook as curriculum'. In T. Higgs (ed.) *Curriculum, Competence and the Foreign Language Teacher* (pp. 11–33). Illinois: National Textbook Company.

Barthes, R. (1972) *Mythologies*. London: Cape.

Barthes, R. (1984) *Camera Lucida*. London: Fontana.

Baudrillard, J. (1981) *For a Critique of the Political Economy of the Sign*. St. Louis: Telos Press.

Baudrillard, J. (1998) *The Consumer Society: Myth and Structures*. London: Sage.

Bauman, Z. (2007) *Consuming Life*. Cambridge: Polity Press.

Baumgratz, G. (1987) 'Esquisse d'une conception pédagogique de l'enseignement des langues étrangères visant la compétence de communication transnationale, les conséquences pour le role et la compétence du professeur et les perspectives de la formation continue'. In G. Baumgratz and R. Stephan (eds) *Fremdsprachenlernen als Beitrag zur internationalen Verständigung* (pp. 64–75). München: Iudicium.

Beck, U. (2000) *What Is Globalization?* Cambridge: Polity Press.

Bell, J. and R. Gower (1998) 'Writing course materials for the world: A great compromise'. In B. Tomlinson (ed.) *Materials Development in Language Teaching* (pp. 116–129). Cambridge: Cambridge University Press.

Benjamin, W. (1931/1979) *One Way Street and Other Writings*. London: New Left Books.

Benwell, B. (2005) '"Lucky this is anonymous". Ethnographies of reception in men's magazines: A "textual culture" approach'. *Discourse and Society*, 16(2): 147–172.

Benwell, B. and E. Stokoe (2006) *Discourse and Identity*. Edinburgh: Edinburgh University Press.

Berelson, B. (1952/1971) *Content Analysis in Communication Research*. New York: Hafner.

Berger, J. (1972) *Ways of Seeing*. London: BBC/Penguin.

Berger, J. (1998/99) 'Against the great defeat of the world'. *Race and Class*, 40(2/3): 1–4.

Berk, L. (1980) 'Education in lives: Biographic narrative in the study of educational outcomes'. *Journal of Curriculum Theorising*, 2(2): 88.

Bernstein, B. (1981) 'Codes, modalities and the process of cultural reproduction: A model'. *Language and Society*, 10: 327–363.

Block, D. (2006) *Multilingual Identities in a Global City*. London: Palgrave.

Block, D. (2007) *Second Language Identities*. London: Continuum.

Block, D. (2008) 'Language education and globalization'. In S. May and N. Hornberger (eds) *Encyclopedia of Language and Education*, 2nd ed., *Vol. 1: Language Policy and Political Issues in Education* (pp. 1–13). Berlin: Springer.

Block, D. (2010) 'Globalisation and language teaching'. In N. Coupland (ed.) *Handbook of Language and Globalisation* (pp. 287–304). Oxford: Blackwell.

Block, D. and D. Cameron (eds) (2002) 'Introduction'. *Globalization and Language Teaching* (pp. 1–10). London: Routledge.

Blommaert, J. (2005) *Discourse*. Cambridge: Cambridge University Press.

Bourdieu, P. (1991) *Language and Symbolic Power*. Cambridge: Polity Press.

Bourdieu, P. (1998) 'Utopia of endless exploitation: The essence of neoliberalism'. *Le Monde Diplomatique*. Available at http://mondediplo.com/1998/12/08bourdieu, accessed on 24 October 2009.

Brown, G. (1990) 'Cultural values: The interpretation of discourse'. *ELT Journal*, 44(1): 11–17.

Bucholtz, M. (2003) 'Sociolinguistic nostalgia and authentication of identity ', *Journal of Sociolinguistics*, 7(3): 398–416.

Burke, H. (2000) 'Cultural diversity: Managing same-sex orientation in the classroom'. Paper at TESOL Spain, Madrid, 26 March 2000. Available at http://www. developingteachers.com/articles_tchtraining/culturaldiversity_henny.htm, accessed on 1 June 2001.

Burn, A. and A. Parker (2003) *Analysing Media Texts*. London: Continuum.

Butler, J. (2009) *Frames of War: When Is Life Grievable?* London: Verso.

Byram, M. (1988) 'Foreign language education and cultural studies'. *Language, Culture and Curriculum,* 1(1): 15–31.

Byram, M. (1989) 'Politics and language teaching'. *Curriculum,* 10(1): 45–50.

Byram, M. (1990) 'Foreign language teaching and young people's perceptions of other cultures'. In B. Harrison (ed.) *Culture and the Language Classroom.* ELT Documents 132. London: Modem English Publications in association with the British Council.

Byram, M. (ed.) (1993) *Germany/Its Representation in Textbooks for Teaching German in Great Britain.* Frankfurt: Verlag Moritz Diesterweg.

Byram, M. (ed.) (1994) *Culture and Language Learning in Higher Education.* Clevedon: Multilingual Matters.

Byram, M. (1997) *Teaching and Assessing Intercultural Communicative Competence.* Clevedon: Multilingual Matters.

Byram, M. and M. Fleming (eds) (1998) *Language Learning in Intercultural Perspective.* Cambridge: Cambridge University Press.

Byram, M. and K. Risager (1999) *Language Teachers, Politics and Cultures.* Clevedon: Multilingual Matters.

Byram, M. and G. Zarate (1994) *Definitions, Objectives and Assessment of Socio-Cultural Objectives.* Strasbourg: Council of Europe.

Cameron, D. (1985) *Feminism and Linguistic Theory.* London: Macmillan.

Cameron, D. (1994) 'Problems of sexist and non-sexist language'. In J. Sunderland (ed.) *Exploring Gender: Questions and Implications for English Language Education* (pp. 26–33). Hemel Hempstead: Prentice Hall.

Cameron, D. (1995) *Verbal Hygiene.* London: Routledge.

Cameron, D. (2000) *Good to Talk?* London: Routledge.

Cameron, D. (2002) 'Globalization and the teaching of "communication skills"'. In D. Block and D. Cameron (eds) *Globalization and Language Teaching* (pp. 67–82). London: Routledge.

Canagarajah, S. (1999) *Resisting Linguistic Imperialism.* Oxford: Oxford University Press.

Canagarajah, S. (2005) 'Introduction'. In S. Canagarajah (ed.) *Reclaiming the Local in Language Policy and Practice.* Mahwah, NJ: Lawrence Erlbaum.

Canagarajah, S. (2007) 'Lingua franca English, multilingual communities, and language acquisition'. *The Modern Language Journal,* 91: 923–939.

Carter, R. (1997) *Investigating English Discourse.* London: Routledge.

Carter, R. (1998) 'Orders of reality: CANCODE, communication, and culture'. *ELT Journal,* 52(1): 43–56.

Castells, M. (2000) 'Materials for an exploratory theory of the network society'. *British Journal of Sociology,* 51(1): 5–24.

Chandler, D. (2002) *Semiotics.* London: Routledge.

Cogan, D. (1996) 'Classroom cultures: East meets west'. In G. van Troyer, S. Cornwell and H. Morikawa (eds) *Curriculum and Evaluation.* Proceedings of the JALT 1995 International Conference on Language Teaching/Learning (pp. 104–108). Tokyo: JALT.

Cook, G. (1997) 'Schemas'. *ELT Journal,* 51(1): 86.

Cook, G. (1998) 'The uses of reality: A reply to Ronald Carter'. *ELT Journal,* 52(1): 57–63.

Cook, G. (2005) 'Calm seas or troubled waters? Transitions, definitions and disagreements in applied linguistics'. *International Journal of Applied Linguistics*, 15(3): 282–301.

Cook, V. (1983) 'What should language teaching be about?' *ELT Journal*, 37(3): 229–234.

Cook, V. (1999) 'Going beyond the native speaker in language teaching'. *TESOL Quarterly*, 33(2): 185–209.

Corbett, J. (2003) *An Intercultural Approach to English Language Teaching*. Clevedon: Multilingual Matters.

Corder, S. P. (1966) *The Visual Element in Language Teaching*. Harlow: Longman.

Corpas, J., A. Garmendia and C. Soriano (2006) *Aula Internacional 3*. Barcelona: Difusión.

Cortazzi, M. and L. Jin (1999) 'Cultural mirrors/materials and methods in the EFL classroom'. In E. Hinkel (ed.) *Culture in Second Language Teaching and Learning* (pp. 196–219). Cambridge: Cambridge University Press.

Council of Europe (1996) *Common European Framework of Reference for Language Learning and Teaching*. Strasbourg: Council of Europe.

Crystal, D. (1995) *The Cambridge Encyclopedia of the English Language*. Cambridge: Cambridge University Press.

Cunningham, S. and P. Moor (1998) *Cutting Edge*. Harlow: Addison Wesley Longman.

Cunningham, S. and P. Moor (2005) *New Cutting Edge*. Harlow: Addison Wesley Longman.

Cunningsworth, A. (1984) *Evaluating and Selecting EFL Materials*. London: Heinemann.

Dendrinos, B. (1992) *The EFL Textbook and Ideology*. Athens: N. C. Grivas Publications.

Doff, A. and C. Jones (1994) *Language in Use/Intermediate*. Cambridge: Cambridge University Press.

Donovan, P. (1998) 'Piloting – a publisher's view'. In B. Tomlinson (ed.) *Materials Development in Language Teaching* (pp. 149–189). Cambridge: Cambridge University Press.

Du Gay, P. (1997) 'Introduction'. In P. du Gay *et al.* (eds) *Doing Cultural Studies: The Story of the Sony Walkman* (pp. 1–5). London: Sage/The Open University.

Du Gay, P., S. Hall, L. Janes, H. Mackay and K. Negus (1997) *Doing Cultural Studies: The Story of the Sony Walkman*. London: Sage/The Open University.

Eckersley, C. E. (1938) *Essential English for Foreign Students*. London: Longmans.

Edge, J. (2004) 'English in a new age of empire'. Available at http://education. guardian.co.uk/tefl/story/0,5500,1191122,00.html, accessed on 13 May 2004.

Edge, J. (2006) *(Re)locating TESOL in an Age of Empire*. London: Palgrave Macmillan.

Edge, J. and K. Richards (1998) 'May I see your warrant, please?: Justifying outcomes in qualitative research'. *Applied Linguistics*, 19(3): 334–356.

EL Gazette (2003) Issue 282: 7. London.

Elbaz, F. (1991) 'Research on teacher knowledge: The evolution of a discourse'. *Journal of Curriculum Studies*, 23(1): 1–19.

Ellis, G. (1996) 'How culturally appropriate is the communicative approach?' *ELT Journal*, 50(3): 213–218.

Fairclough, N. (1993) 'Critical discourse analysis and the marketization of public discourse'. *Discourse and Society*, 4(2): 133–159.

Fairclough, N. (2002) 'Language in new capitalism'. *Discourse and Society* 13(2): 163–166.

Fairclough, N. (2003) *Analysing Discourse*. London: Routledge.

Featherstone, M. (1991) *Consumer Culture and Postmodernism*. London: Sage.

Ferguson, N. (2003) *Empire*. London: Penguin.

Ferguson, R. (2004) *The Media in Question*. London: Arnold.

Florent, J., K. Fuller, J. Pugsly, C. Walter and A. Young (1994) 'Case study 1: Guidelines for the representation of women and men in English language teaching materials'. In *Exploring Gender: Questions and Implications for English Language Education* (pp. 112–120). Hemel Hempstead: Prentice Hall.

Forhan, L. E. and M. Scheraga (2000) 'Becoming sociopolitically active'. In J. K. Hall and W. E. Eggington (eds) *The Sociopolitics of English Language Teaching* (pp. 195–221). Clevedon: Multilingual Matters.

Fowler, R. (1986) *Linguistic Criticism*. Oxford: Oxford University Press.

Freebairn, I. (2000) 'The coursebook – future continuous or past?' *English Teaching Professional* 15: 3–5.

Freire, P. (1970/1996) *Pedagogy of the Oppressed*. New York: Continuum.

Gairns, R. and S. Redman (2002) *Natural English*. Oxford: Oxford University Press.

Gee, J. P., G. Hull and C. Lankshear (1996) *The New Work Order: Behind the Language of the New Capitalism*. Cambridge: Polity Press.

Giddens, A. (1991) *Modernity and Self-Identity: Self and Society on the Late Modern Age*. Cambridge: Polity Press.

Gillespie, M. (1995) *Television, Ethnicity and Cultural Change*. London: Routledge.

Gnutzmann, C. (2004) 'Lingua Franca'. In M. Byram (ed.) *Routledge Encyclopedia of Language Teaching and Learning* (pp. 356–359). London: Routledge.

Gnutzmann, C. and F. Intemann (eds) (2005) *The Globalisation of English and the English Language Classroom*. Tubingen: Gunter Narr Verlag.

Goffman, E. (1979) *Gender Advertisements*. London: Macmillan.

Goldman, R. (1992) *Reading Ads Socially*. London: Routledge.

Goldstein, B. (2003) *Framework/Level 2*. London: Richmond Publishing.

Goldstein, B. (2008) *New Framework/Level 2*. London: Richmond Publishing.

Gray, J. (2000) 'The ELT coursebook as cultural artefact: How teachers censor and adapt'. *ELT Journal*, 54(3): 274–283.

Gray, J. (2002) 'The global coursebook in English language teaching'. In D. Block and D. Cameron (eds) *Globalization and Language Teaching* (pp. 151–167). London: Routledge.

Gray, J. (2007) *A Study of Cultural Content in the British ELT Global Coursebook: A Cultural Studies Approach*. Unpublished PhD thesis, Institute of Education, University of London.

Gray, P. and S. Leather (1999) *Safety and Challenge*. Addlestone: Delta.

Guilherme, M. (2000) 'Intercultural competence'. In M. Byram (ed.) *Routledge Encyclopedia of Language Teaching and Learning* (pp. 297–300). London: Routledge.

Gumperz, J. J. and S. C. Levinson (1991) 'Rethinking linguistic relativity'. *Current Anthropology*, 32(5): 613–623.

Haines, D. (1994) 'Comment: An international EFL publisher's perspective'. In J. Sunderland (ed.) *Exploring Gender: Questions and Implications for English Language Education* (pp. 129–134). Hemel Hempstead: Prentice Hall.

Hall, J. K. (2002) *Teaching and Researching Language and Culture*. Harlow: Pearson.

Hall, S. (1980a) 'Cultural studies: Two paradigms'. *Media, Culture and Society*, 2: 57–72.

Hall, S. (1980b) 'Encoding/decoding'. In S. Hall (ed.) *Culture, Media, Language* (pp. 128–138). London: Hutchinson.

Hall, S. (1981) 'Notes on deconstructing "the popular"'. In J. Storey (ed.) *Cultural Theory and Popular Culture: A reader* (pp. 477–487). Harlow: Pearson Education Ltd.

Hall, S. (1982) 'The rediscovery of "ideology": Return of the repressed in media studies'. In M. B. Gurevitch, T. Curran and J. Woollacott (eds) *Culture, Society and the Media* (pp. 56–90). London: Methuen.

Hall, S. (1983) 'The narrative construction of reality: An interview with Stuart Hall'. Available at http://www.centreforbookculture.org/context/no10/hall.html, accessed on 2 July 2004.

Hall, S. (1986) 'On postmodernism and articulation'. In D. Morley and K-H. Chen (eds) *Stuart Hall: Critical Dialogues in Cultural Studies* (pp. 131–150). London: Routledge.

Hall, S. (1992a) 'The question of cultural identity'. In S. Hall, D. Held and T. McGrew (eds) *Modernity and Its Futures* (pp. 274–316). Cambridge: Polity Press/Blackwell/The Open University.

Hall, S. (1992b) 'Introduction'. In S. Hall and B. Gieben (eds) *Formations of Modernity* (pp. 1–16). Cambridge: Polity Press/ Blackwell/The Open University.

Hall, S. (1996) 'Introduction: Who needs "identity"?'. In S. Hall and P. du Gay (eds) *Questions of Cultural Identity* (pp. 1–17). London: Sage.

Hall, S. (1997a) 'The centrality of culture: Notes on the cultural revolutions of our time'. In K. Thompson (ed.) *Media and Cultural Regulation* (pp. 208–238). London: Sage.

Hall, S. (1997b) 'The spectacle of the "other"'. In S. Hall (ed.) *Representation: Cultural Representations and Signifying Practices* (pp. 225–279). London: Sage.

Halliday, M. A. K. (1978) *Language as Social Semiotic*. London: Edward Arnold.

Halliday, M. A. K. (1985) *An Introduction to Functional Grammar*. London: Arnold.

Hannerz, U. (1992) *Cultural Complexity*. New York: Columbia University Press.

Harmer, J. (2001) *The Practice of English Language Teaching*. Harlow: Longman.

Hartley, B. and P. Viney (1979) *Streamline English Connections*. Oxford: Oxford University Press.

Hartman, P. L. and E. L. Judd (1978) 'Sexism and TESOL materials'. *TESOL Quarterly*, 12(4): 383–393.

Harvey, D. (2005) *A Brief History of Neoliberalism*. Oxford: Oxford University Press.

Hedge, T. (2000) *Teaching and Learning in the Language Classroom*. Oxford: Oxford University Press.

Heller, M. (1999) *Linguistic Minorities and Modernity: A Sociolinguistic Ethnography*. London: Longman.

Heller, M. (2002) 'Globalization and the commodification of bilingualism in Canada'. In D. Block and D. Cameron (eds) *Globalization and Language Teaching* (pp. 47–63). London: Routledge.

Heller, M. (2003) 'Globalization, the new economy, and the commodification of language and identity'. *Journal of Sociolinguistics*, 7(4): 473–492.

Heller, M. (2005) 'Language, skill and authenticity in the globalized new economy'. Noves SL. Revista de Sociolingüística, http://gencat.cat/llengua/noves Winter 2005, accessed 20 November 2008.

Hertz, N. (2001) *The Silent Takeover: Global Capitalism and the Death of Democracy*. London: Arrow Books.

Hewings, M. (1991) 'The interpretation of illustrations in ELT materials'. *ELT Journal*, 45(3): 237–244.

Hill, D. A. (2003) 'The visual element in EFL coursebooks'. In B. Tomlinson (ed.) *Developing Materials for Language Teaching* (pp. 174–182). London: Continuum.

Hill, P. (1980) 'Women in the world of ELT textbooks'. *EFL Gazette*, June/July.

Hodge, R. and G. Kress (1988) *Social Semiotics*. Cambridge: Polity Press.

Hofstede, G. (1980) *Culture's Consequences: International Differences in Work-Related Values*. London: Sage.

Holborow, M. (1999) *The Politics of English*. London: Sage.

Holborow, M. (2007) 'Language, ideology and neoliberalism'. *Journal of Language and Politics*, 6(1): 51–73.

Holsti, O. R. (1969) *Content Analysis for the Social Sciences and Humanities*. Reading, MA: Addison-Wesley.

Holliday, A. (1994a) 'Student culture and English language education: An international perspective'. *Language, Culture and Curriculum*, 7(2): 125–143.

Holliday, A. (1994b) *Appropriate Methodology and Social Context*. Cambridge: Cambridge University Press.

Holliday, A. (1999) 'Small Cultures'. *Applied Linguistics*, 20(2): 237–264.

Holliday, A. (2005) *The Struggle to Teach English as an International Language*. Oxford: Oxford University Press.

Hopkins, A. (2001) 'The Council of Europe/What is it? And what does it do for us?' *Modern English Teacher*, 10(4): 44–48.

Hornby, A. S. (1954) *Oxford Progressive English for Adult Learners*. Oxford: Oxford University Press.

Howatt, A. P. R. (1984) *A History of English Language Teaching*. Oxford: Oxford University Press.

Hughes, R. (1993) *The Culture of Complaint*. Oxford: Oxford University Press.

Hutchinson, T. and E. Torres (1994) 'The textbook as agent of change'. *ELT Journal*, 48(4): 315–327.

Humboldt, W. von (1836/1971) *Linguistic Variability and Intellectual Development*. Florida: University of Miami Press.

Hüllen, W. (2000) 'Humboldt, Wilhelm von'. In M. Byram (ed.) *Routledge Encyclopedia of Language Teaching and Learning* (p. 287). London: Routledge.

Hyde, M. (1994) 'The teaching of English in Morocco: The place of culture'. *ELT Journal*, 48(4): 295–305.

Hymes, D. (1972) 'On communicative competence'. In J. B. Pride and J. Holmes (eds) *Sociolinguistics: Selected Readings* (pp. 269–293). Harmondsworth: Penguin Books.

Jameson, F. (1984) 'Postmodernism, or the cultural logic of late capitalism'. *New Left Review*, 146. Available at www.newleftreview.org/?view=726, accessed on 12 March 2010.

Jaworski, A. (1983) 'Sexism in textbooks'. *The British Journal of Language Teaching*, 21(2): 109–113.

Jenkins, J. (1998) 'Which pronunciation norms and models for English as an international language?' *ELT Journal*, 52(2): 119–126.

Jenkins, J. (2000) *The Phonology of English as an International Language*. Oxford: Oxford University Press.

Jenkins, J. (2003) *World Englishes*. London: Routledge.

Jenkins, J. (2006) 'Current perspectives on teaching World Englishes and English as a Lingua Franca'. *TESOL Quarterly*, 40(1): 157–181.

Jewitt, C. and R. Oyama (2001) 'Visual meaning: A social semiotic'. In T. van Leeuwen and C. Jewitt (eds) *Handbook of Visual Analysis* (pp. 134–156). London: Sage.

Johnson, K. E. and P. R. Golombek (eds) (2002) *Teachers' Narrative Inquiry as Professional Development*. Cambridge: Cambridge University Press.

Joseph, J. E. (2004) *Language and Identity*. Basingstoke: Palgrave Macmillan.

Kachru, B. (1985) 'Standards, codification and sociolinguistic realism: The English language in the outer circle'. In R. Quirk and H. G. Widdowson (eds) *English in the World: Teaching the Language and the Literatures* (pp. 11–30). Cambridge: Cambridge University Press/British Council.

Kay, S. and V. Jones (2000) *Inside Out*. Oxford: Macmillan.

Kenworthy, J. (1987) *Teaching English Pronunciation*. Harlow: Longman.

Kincheloe, J. L. and S. R. Steinberg (1997) *Changing Multiculturalism*. Buckingham: Open University Press.

Klein, N. (2000) *No Logo*. London: Flamingo.

Kramsch, C. (1993) *Context and Culture in Language Teaching*. Oxford: Oxford University Press.

Kramsch, C. (1995) 'The cultural component of language teaching'. *Language, Culture and Curriculum*, 8(2): 83–92.

Kramsch, C. (1998a) 'The privilege of the intercultural speaker'. In M. Byram and M. Fleming (eds). *Language Learning in Intercultural Perspective* (pp. 16–31). Cambridge: Cambridge University Press.

Kramsch, C. (1998b) 'Taking the shock out of teaching culture'. *EL Gazette*, (217): 12.

Kramsch, C. and P. Sullivan (1996) 'Appropriate pedagogy'. *ELT Journal*, 50(3): 199–212.

Kress, G. (1985) *Linguistic Processes in Sociocultural Practice*. Oxford: Oxford University Press.

Kress, G. and T. van Leeuwen (1996) *Reading Images: The Grammar of Visual Design*. London: Routledge.

Kress, G. and T. van Leeuwen (2001) *Multimodal Discourse*. Arnold: London.

Kress, G., C. Jewitt, J. Ogborn and C. Tsatsarelis (2001) *Multimodal Teaching and Learning*. London: Continuum.

Kroeber, A. L. (ed.) (1953) 'Introduction'. *Anthropology Today: An Encyclopedic Inventory* (pp. xiii–xv). Chicago: University of Chicago Press.

Kubota, R. (1999) 'Japanese culture constructed by discourses: Implications for applied linguistics research and ELT'. *Applied Linguistics*, 33(1): 9–36.

Kuhn, A. (1985) *The Power of the Image*. London: Routledge and Keegan Paul.

Kullman, J. (2003) *The Social Construction of Learner Identity in the U.K.-Published ELT Coursebook*. Unpublished PhD thesis, Canterbury Christ Church University College.

Kumaravadivelu, B. (2006a) 'TESOL methods: Changing tracks, challenging trends'. *TESOL Quarterly*, 40(1): 59–81.

Kumaravadivelu, B. (2006b) 'Dangerous liaison: Globalization, empire and TESOL'. In J. Edge (ed.) *(Re)locating TESOL in an Age of Empire* (pp. 1–26). London: Palgrave Macmillan.

Kumaravadivelu, B. (2008) *Cultural Globalization and Language Education*. New Haven: Yale University Press.

Kuo, I-Chun (Vicky) (2006) 'Addressing the issue of teaching English as a lingua franca'. *ELT Journal*, 60(3): 213–221.

Lado, R. (1957) *Linguistics Across Cultures/Applied Linguistics for Language Teachers*. Ann Arbor: University of Michigan Press.

Lado, R. (1964) *Language Teaching: A Scientific Approach*. New York: McGraw-Hill.

Laplanche, J. and J. Pontalis (1988) *The Language of Psychoanalysis*. London: Karnac Books.

Leiss, W. (1983) 'The icons of the marketplace'. *Theory, Culture & Society*, 1(3): 10–21.

Leiss, W., S. Kline and S. Jhally (1990) *Social Communication in Advertising*. London: Routledge.

Leith, D. (1997) *A Social History of English*. London: Routledge.

Lessard-Clouston, M. (1996) 'Chinese teachers' views of culture in their EFL learning and teaching'. *Language, Culture and Curriculum*, 9(3): 197–224.

Leung, C. (2005) 'Convivial communication: Recontextualizing communicative competence'. *International Journal of Applied Linguistics*, 15(2): 119–144.

Leung, C. and J. Lewkowicz (2006) 'Expanding horizons and unresolved conundrums: Language testing and assessment'. *TESOL Quarterly*, 40(1): 211–234.

Lévi-Strauss, C. (1963) *Structural Anthropology*. Harmondsworth: Penguin.

Lévi-Strauss, C. (1978) *Myth and Meaning*. London: Routledge and Kegan Paul.

Liddicoat, A. (2009) 'Sexual identity as linguistic failure: Trajectories of interaction in the heteronormative language classroom'. *Journal of Language, Identity, and Education*, 8: 191–202.

Liebes, T. and E. Katz (1990) *The Export of Meaning*. Oxford: Oxford University Press.

Littlejohn, A. (1992) *Why Are ELT Materials the Way They Are?* Unpublished PhD thesis, Lancaster University.

Littlejohn, A. (1998) 'The analysis of language teaching materials: Inside the Trojan horse'. In B. Tomlinson (ed.) *Materials Development in Language Teaching* (pp. 190–216). Cambridge: Cambridge University Press.

Littlewood, W. (1999) Defining and developing autonomy in East Asian contexts'. *Applied Linguistics*, 20(1): 71–94.

Luke, C., S. de Castell and A. Luke (1989) 'Beyond criticism: The authority of the school textbook'. In S. de Castell, A. Luke and C. Luke (eds) *Language, Authority and Criticism: Readings on the School Textbook* (pp. 245–260). London: Falmer Press.

Mackay, H. (1997) *Consumption and Everyday Life*. London: Sage.

Malinowski, B. (1944) *A Scientific Theory of Culture and Other Essays*. Chapel Hill: University of North Carolina Press.

Mannheim, C. (1994) 'The boss was called Mr Power: Learners' perspectives on sexism in EFL materials'. In J. Sunderland (ed.) *Exploring Gender: Questions and Implications for English Language Education* (pp. 83–91). Hemel Hempstead: Prentice Hall.

Marx, K. (1867/1967) *Capital: A Critique of Political Economy*, Vol. 1. New York: International Publishers.

Masuhara, H. (1998) 'What do teachers really want from coursebooks?' In B. Tomlinson (ed.) *Materials Development in Language Teaching* (pp. 239–260). Cambridge: Cambridge University Press.

Matsuda, A. (2006) 'Negotiating ELT assumptions in EIL classrooms'. In J. Edge (ed.) *(Re)locating TESOL in an Age of Empire* (pp. 158–170). London: Palgrave Macmillan.

McCallan, B. (1990) *English in Eastern Europe. Special Report No. 2057*. London: The Economist Intelligence Unit.

McDonough, J. and C. Shaw (2003) *Materials and Methods in ELT*. Oxford: Blackwell.

McGrath, I. (2002) *Materials Evaluation and Design for Language Teaching*. Edinburgh: University of Edinburgh Press.

McKay, S. L. (2002) *Teaching English as an International Language*. Oxford: Oxford University Press.

McKay, S. L. (2003) 'Toward an appropriate EIL pedagogy: Re-examining common ELT assumptions'. *International Journal of Applied Linguistics*, 13(1): 1–22.

Menzel, P., C. C. Mann and P. Kennedy (1995) *Material World: A Global Family Portrait*. San Francisco: Sierra Club Books.

Milroy, J. and L. Milroy (1999) *Authority in Language*. London: Routledge.

Modiano, M. (2001) 'Ideology and the ELT practitioner'. *International Journal of Applied Linguistics*, 11(2): 159–173.

Morton, T. and J. Gray (2010) 'Constructing personal practical knowledge and identity in lesson planning conferences in pre-service English language teacher education'. *Language Teaching Research*, 14(3): 1–21.

Odgen, C. K. and I. A. Richards (1923) *The Meaning of Meaning*. London: Routledge & Kegan Paul.

O'Halloran, K. (1997) 'Why Whorf has been misconstrued in stylistics and critical linguistics'. *Language and Literature*, 6(3): 163–180.

O'Neill, R. (1970) *English in Situations*. Oxford: Oxford University Press.

O'Neill, R. (1971) *Kernal Intermediate*. London: Eurocentre/Longman.

O'Neill, R. (1973) *Kernal Upper Intermediate*. London: Eurocentre/Longman.

O'Sullivan, T., J. Hartley, D. Saunders, M. Montgomery and J. Fiske (1994) *Key Concepts in Communication and Cultural Studies*. London: Routledge.

Parekh, B. (1997) 'National culture and multiculturalism'. In K. Thompson (ed.) *Media and Cultural Regulation* (pp. 163–194). London: Sage.

Pauwels, A. (1998) *Women Changing Language*. Harlow: Longman.

Peirce, C. S. (1955) 'Logic as semiotic'. In J. Buchler (ed.) *Philosophical Writings of Peirce* (pp. 98–119). New York: Dover.

Pennycook, A. (1989) 'The concept of method, interested knowledge, and the politics of language teaching'. *TESOL Quarterly*, 23(4): 589–618.

Pennycook, A. (1994) *The Cultural Politics of English as an International Language*. New York: Longman.

Pennycook, A. (1998) *English and the Discourses of Colonialism*. London: Routledge.

Perlmutter, H. V. (1991) 'On the rocky road to the first global civilization'. *Human Relations*, 44(9): 897–920.

Persaud, R. B. and C. Lusane (2000) 'The new economy, globalisation and the impact on African Americans'. *Race and Class*, 42(1): 21–34.

Phillipson, R. (1986) 'English rules: A study of language pedagogy and imperialism'. In R. Phillipson and T. Skutnabb-Kangas (eds) *Linguicism Rules in Education* (pp. 124–343). Roskilde: Roskilde University Centre.

Phillipson, R. (1992) *Linguistic Imperialism*. Oxford: Oxford University Press.

Phillipson, R. (2009) *Linguistic Imperialism Continued*. London: Routledge.

Pinker, S. (1994) *The Language Instinct*. London: Allen Lane.

Porreca, K. (1984) 'Sexism in current ESL textbooks'. *TESOL Quarterly*, 18(4): 705–724.

Pratt, M. (1992) *Imperial Eyes*. London: Routledge.

Preisler, B. (1999) 'Functions and forms of English in a European EFL country'. In T. Bex and R. J. Watts (eds) *Standard English: The Widening Debate* (pp. 239–267). London: Routledge.

Probyn, E. (1990) 'New traditionalism and post-feminism: TV does the home'. *Screen*, 31(2): 147–159.

Prodromou, L. (1992) 'What culture? Which culture? Cross-cultural factors in language learning'. *ELT Journal*, 46(1): 39–50.

Prodromou, L. (1997) 'Global English and its struggle against the octopus'. *IATEFL Newsletter*, February/March: 12–14.

Prodromou, L. (2007) 'ELF models and "linguistic capital"'. *IATEFL Voices*, 199: 9–10.

Prowse, P. (1998) 'How writers write'. In B. Tomlinson (ed.) *Materials Development in Language Teaching* (pp. 130–145). Cambridge: Cambridge University Press.

Pulverness, A. (1999) 'Context or pretext? Cultural content and the coursebook'. *Folio*, 5(2): 5–10.

Pulverness, A. (2003) 'Materials for cultural awareness'. In B. Tomlinson (ed.) *Developing Materials for Language Teaching* (pp. 426–438). London: Continuum.

Radway, J. (1984) *Reading the Romance: Women, Patriarchy, and Popular Literature*. Chapel Hill: University of North Carolina.

Rajagopalan, K. (2004) 'The concept of "World English" and its implications for ELT'. *ELT Journal*, 58(2): 111–117.

Rao, R. (1938) *Kathapura*. New York: New Directions.

Richards, J., J. Platt and H. Weber (1985) *Longman Dictionary of Applied Linguistics*. London: Longman.

Richardson, K. (1994) 'Interpreting breadline Britain'. In U. H. Meinhof and K. Richardson (eds) *Text, Discourse and Context: Representations of Poverty in Britain* (pp. 93–121). London: Longman.

Risager, K. (1991) 'Cultural references in European textbooks: An evaluation of recent tendencies'. In D. Buttjes and M. Byram (eds) *Mediating Languages and Cultures: Towards an Intercultural Theory of Foreign Language Education* (pp. 180–192). Clevedon: Multilingual Matters.

Risager, K. (2006) *Language and Culture: Global Flows and Local Complexity*. Clevedon: Multilingual Matters.

Ritzer, G. (1996) *The McDonaldization of Society*. London: Sage.

Ritzer, G. (1998) 'Introduction'. In J. Baudrillard, *The Consumer Society: Myths and Structures* (pp. 1–24). London: Sage.

Ritzer, G. (2007) *The Globalization of Nothing 2*. Thousand Oaks, CA: Pine Forge Press.

Rivers, W. (1981) *Teaching Foreign-Language Skills*. Chicago: University of Chicago Press.

Roberts, C., M. Byram, A. Barro, S. Jordan and B. Street (2001) *Language Learners as Ethnographers*. Clevedon: Multilingual Matters.

Ryan, P. (1994) *Foreign Language Teachers' Perceptions of Culture in the Classroom: A Case Study*. Unpublished PhD thesis, University of Utah, Salt Lake City.

Sánchez Lobato, J. and N. García Fernández (2007) *Nuevo Español 2000*. Madrid: SGEL Educación.

Sapir, E. (1949/1985) *Selected Writings in Language, Culture, and Personality*. Berkeley, LA: University of California Press.

Saussure, F. (1974) *Course in General Linguistics*. London: Fontana/Collins.

Scholte, J. A. (2000) *Globalization*. London: Macmillan.

Schroeder, J. E. (2002) *Visual Communication*. London: Routledge.

Seidlhofer, B. (2001) 'Closing a conceptual gap: The case for a description of English as a lingua franca'. *International Journal of Applied Linguistics*, 11(2): 133–158.

Seidlhofer, B. (2004) 'Research perspectives on teaching English as a lingua franca'. *Annual Review of Applied Linguistics*, 24: 209–239.

Seidlhofer, B. (2005) 'Standard future or half-baked quackery?' In C. Gnutzmann and F. Intemann (eds) *The Globalisation of English and the English Language Classroom* (pp. 159–173). Tubingen: Gunter Narr Verlag.

Sen, A. (2006) *Identity and Violence*. London: Penguin.

Sennett, R. (2006) *The Culture of the New Capitalism*. London: Yale University Press.

Sercu, L. (2000) *Acquiring Intercultural Communicative Competence from Textbooks*. Leuven: Leuven University Press.

Sheldon, L. E. (1988) 'Evaluating ELT textbooks and materials'. *ELT Journal*, 42(4): 237–246.

Silviera, J. (1980) 'Generic masculine words and thinking'. *Women's Studies International Quarterly*, 3: 165–178.

Simpson, P. (1993) *Language, Ideology and Point of View*. London: Routledge.

Skierso, A. (1991) 'Textbook selection and evaluation'. In M. Celce-Murcia (ed.) *Teaching English as a Second or Foreign Language* (pp. 432–453). Boston: Heinle and Heinle.

Soars, J. and L. Soars (1986) *Headway/Intermediate*. Oxford: Oxford University Press.

Soars, J. and L. Soars (1996) *New Headway/Intermediate*. Oxford: Oxford University Press.

Soars, J. and L. Soars (1998) *New Headway/Upper-Intermediate*. Oxford: Oxford University Press.

Soars, J. and L. Soars (2000a) Responses to 'Window-dressing vs Cross-dressing in the EFL Sub-Culture' at http://www.teflfarm.com/teachers/articles/0/response/dressing_response.htm, accessed on 2 February 2000.

Soars, J. and L. Soars (2000b) *New Headway/Pre-Intermediate*. Oxford: Oxford University Press.

Soars, J. and L. Soars (2003) *New Edition New Headway/Intermediate*. Oxford: Oxford University Press.

Sontag, S. (1973) *On Photography*. New York: Farrar, Strauss & Giroux.

Spender, D. (1980) *Man Made Language*. London: Routledge & Kegan Paul.

Steiner, G. (1975) *After Babel*. Oxford: Oxford University Press.

Stern, H. H. (1983) *Fundamental Concepts of Language Teaching*. Oxford: Oxford University Press.

Stieglitz, G. J. (1955) 'The Berlitz method'. *Modern Language Journal*, 39: 300–310.

Strevens, P. (1983) 'What is "standard English"?' In L. Smith (ed.) *Readings in English as an International Language* (pp. 87–93). Oxford: Pergamon Press.

Sunderland, J. (ed.) (1994) *Exploring Gender: Questions and Implications for English Language Education*. Hemel Hempstead: Prentice Hall.

Swan, M. and C. Walter (1990a) *The New Cambridge English Course 2*. Cambridge: Cambridge University Press.

Swan, M. and C. Walter (1990b) *The New Cambridge English Course 1*. Cambridge: Cambridge University Press.

Sweet, H. (1899) *The Practical Study of Languages: A Guide for Teachers and Learners*. London: Dent.

Tan, P. K. W. and R. Rubdy (2008) *Language as Commodity: Global Structures, Local Marketplaces*. London: Continuum.

Thomas, D. (ed.) (1995) *Teachers' Stories*. Buckingham: Open University Press.

Thomas, D. (1999) *Culture, Ideology and Educational Change: The Case of English Language Teachers in Slovakia*. Unpublished PhD thesis, Institute of Education, University of London.

Thompson, J. B. (1990) *Ideology and Modern Culture*. Stanford: Stanford University Press.

Thornbury, S. (1999) 'Window-dressing or cross-dressing in the EFL sub-culture'. *Folio*, 5(2): 15–17.

Thornbury, S. (2000a) 'Reading and writing as arithmetic'. *Modern English Teacher*, 9(4): 12–15.

Thornbury, S. (2000b) 'A dogma for EFL'. *IATEFL Issues*, 153: 2 (February–March).

Thornbury, S. (2005) *Beyond the Sentence*. Oxford: Macmillan.

Tinic, S. A. (1997) 'United colors and untied meanings: Benetton and the commodification of social issues'. *Journal of Communication*, 47(3): 3–25.

Tomlinson, B. (ed.) (1998) *Materials Development in Language Teaching*. Cambridge: Cambridge University Press.

Tomlinson, B. (ed.) (2003) *Developing Materials for Language Teaching*. London: Continuum.

Tomlinson, J. (1999) *Globalization and Culture*. Cambridge: Polity Press.

Trudgill, P. (1999) 'Standard English: What it isn't'. In T. Bex and R. J. Watts (eds) *Standard English: The Widening Debate* (pp. 117–128). London: Routledge.

Urry, J. (1990) *The Tourist Gaze: Leisure and Travel in Contemporary Societies*. London: Sage.

Urry, J. (2001) 'Globalizing the tourist gaze'. Paper. Available at www.lancs.ac.uk/fss/sociology/papers/urry-globalising-the-tourist-gaze.pdf, accessed on 25 March 2006.

Van Ek, J. A. (1975) *Systems Development in Adult Language Learning: The Threshold Level*. Strasbourg: Council of Europe.

Van Ek, J. A. (1976) *The Threshold Level for Modern Language Learning in Schools*. Strasbourg: Council of Europe Press.

Van Ek, J. A. and J. L. M. Trim (1991) *Threshold Level 1990*. Strasbourg: Council of Europe Press.

Van Leeuwen, T. and C. Jewitt (2001) *Handbook of Visual Analysis*. London: Sage.

Viney, P. (2004) Viney.uk.com articles. Available at http://www.viney.uk.com/original_articles/streamlineart/slhist.htm, accessed on 16 December 2009.

Wajnryb, R. (1996) 'Death, taxes, and jeopardy: Systematic omissions in EFL texts, or life was never meant to be an adjacency pair'. ELICOS plenary delivered in Sydney, Australia (sent as email attachment).

Wallace, C. (1992) 'Critical literacy awareness in the EFL classroom'. In N. Fairclough (ed.) *Critical Language Awareness*. London: Longman.

Wallace, C. (2002) 'Local literacies and global literacy'. In D. Block and D. Cameron (eds) *Globalization and Language Teaching* (pp. 101–114). London: Routledge.

Wernick, A. (1991) *Promotional Culture*. London: Sage.

Whorf, B. L. (1956) *Language, Thought, and Reality/ Selected Writings of Benjamin Lee Whorf* (edited by J. B. Carroll). Cambridge, MA: The M.I.T. Press.

Widdowson, H. G. (1990) *Aspects of Language Teaching*. Oxford: Oxford University Press.

Widdowson, H. G. (1994) 'The ownership of English'. *TESOL Quarterly*, 28(2): 377–389.

Widdowson, H. G. (1997) 'EIL, ESL, EFL: Global issues and local interests'. *World Englishes*, 16(1): 135–146.

Williams, R. (1976) *Keywords*. London: Fontana Press.

Woods, P. J. (1993) 'Managing marginality: Teacher development through grounded life history'. *British Educational Research Journal*, 19(5): 447–465.

Woodward, K. (1997) 'Motherhood: Identities, meanings and myths'. In K. Woodward (ed.) *Identity and Difference* (pp. 239–298). London: Sage.

World Bank (2000) *Poverty in an Age of Globalization*. Available at http://www1.worldbank.org/economicpolicy/globalization/.

Index

activity-based interviews, 139–43
Adaskou, Kheira, Donard Britten and
 Badia Fahsi, 34–5, 140, 141
advertising, 129, 131, 133–6
 Benetton advertisements, 93, 106,
  135
affluence, 3
age, 66–7, 75–6, 88, 103, 113, 136
Akbari, Ramin, 189
Althusser, Louis, 82
Anderson, Christopher, 70, 95, 96,
 111, 129
Anglobalization, 16, 17
Apple, Michael, 2, 3, 6, 7, 68
articulation, 24–5, 37, 188–9
artwork, 5, 19, 43–8, 110, 131–4,
 176–8
 in *Building Strategies*, 75
 in *Cambridge English 2*, 93, 94
 Corder on, 43, 177
 in *Headway Intermediate*, 102, 103–4
 in *Streamline Connections*, 55–9
 see also advertising; disability;
  guidelines for authors;
  photography; social semiotics
aspirational content, 126–7, 175
audience research, 139
 dominant-hegemonic, negotiated
  and oppositional positions,
  25–6

Barthes, Roland, 22–3, 132
Baudrillard, Jean, 128, 129
Bauman, Zygmunt, 14
Berger, John, 130, 133, 176
Bernstein, Basil, 46
Block, David, 16, 129, 189
Blommaert, Jan, 184
Bourdieu, Pierre, 2, 13, 14, 15, 183
British Council, 113, 130, 131
Brown, Gillian, 126

Building Strategies, 53, 70–82, 108
 fictional and non-fictional
  characters, 75–80
 representation of race, 80
 representation of spoken English, 71
 representation of women and men,
  75–8, 81–2
 treatment of functional English,
  70–1
Burke, Henny, 10
Butler, Judith, 131
Byram, Michael, 30–4, 49, 50, 141
 minimum content for textbooks,
  41, 42, 92, 148, 192

Cambridge English 2, 4, 53, 83–96, 108
 representation of race, 91–3
 representation of spoken English, 84
 representation of women and men,
  88–91
Cameron, Deborah, 10, 27–8, 113,
 114, 129
Canagarajah, Suresh, 7, 179, 183, 184,
 188
carrier content, 6
Carter, Ronald, 108
Castells, Manuel, 14
celebrity, 67–8, 88, 157, 176
choiceoisie, 103
Christian-Smith, Linda, 2, 3
circuit of culture, 19, 37–8, 110, 111
class, 23, 113, 136, 169
 classed biographies of students and
  teachers, 6, 68–9
commodity
 commodification of language, 14–7,
  48: culture, 129; non-material
  services, 128–9; social issues,
  134–6
 commodification and
  neoliberalism, 14
 commodity feminism, 134–5

218   *Index*

CPSIA information can be obtained
at www.ICGtesting.com
Printed in the USA
LVOW10s1843270317
528626LV00012B/1821/P